Fostering Resilience Before, During, and After Experiences of Trauma

This edited volume recognizes that resilience, and the most effective means of harnessing it, differ across individuals, contexts and time. Presenting chapters written by a range of scholars and clinicians, the book highlights effective evidence-based approaches to nurturing resilience, before, during and after a traumatic experience or event.

By identifying distinct therapeutic tools which can be used effectively to meet the particular needs and limitations associated with different age groups, clients and types of experience, the volume addresses specific challenges and benefits of nurturing resilience and informs best practice as well as self-care. Approaches explored in the volume include the use of group activities to teach resilience to children, the role of sense-making for victims of sex trafficking, and the ways in which identity and spirituality can be used to help young and older adults in the face of pain and bereavement. Chapters also draw on the lived experiences of those who have engaged in a personal or guided journey towards finding new meaning and achieving posttraumatic growth following experiences of trauma.

The rich variety of approaches offered here will be of interest to clinicians, counsellors, scholars and researchers involved in the practice and study of building resilience, as well as trauma studies, psychology and mental health more broadly. The personal and practice-based real-life stories in this volume will also resonate with individuals, family and community members facing adversity.

Buuma Maisha is an assistant professor of psychotherapy and counselling at Saint Paul University, Ottawa, Canada.

Stephanie Massicotte is a licensed psychotherapist with a master's degree in counselling and spirituality. She currently works as a crisis counsellor in Ottawa, Canada.

Melanie Morin holds a master's degree in counselling and spirituality. She currently works at the Public Service Commission of Canada.

Explorations in Mental Health

Pet Loss, Grief, and Therapeutic Interventions
Practitioners Navigating the Human-Animal Bond
Edited by Lori Kogan and Phyllis Erdman

Frantz Fanon's Psychotherapeutic Approaches to Clinical Work
Practicing Internationally with Marginalized Communities
Edited by Lou Turner and Helen A. Neville

Deinstitutionalizing Art of the Nomadic Museum
Practicing and Theorizing Critical Art Therapy with Adolescents
Eva Marxen

Applications of a Psychospiritual Model in the Helping Professions
Principles of InnerView Guidance
Cedric Speyer and John Yaphe

Effective Group Therapies for Young Adults Affected by Cancer
Using Support Groups in Clinical Settings in the United States
Sarah F. Kurker

Fostering Resilience Before, During, and After Experiences of Trauma
Insights to Inform Practice Across the Lifetime
Edited by Buuma Maisha, Stephanie Massicotte and Melanie Morin

Hip-Hop and Spoken Word Therapy in School Counseling
Developing Culturally Responsive Approaches
Ian Levy

For more information about this series, please visit www.routledge.com/Explorations-in-Mental-Health/book-series/EXMH

Fostering Resilience Before, During, and After Experiences of Trauma

Insights to Inform Practice Across the Lifetime

Edited by
Buuma Maisha, Stephanie Massicotte and Melanie Morin

Routledge
Taylor & Francis Group
NEW YORK AND LONDON

First published 2021
by Routledge
52 Vanderbilt Avenue, New York, NY 10017

and by Routledge
2 Park Square, Milton Park, Abingdon, Oxon OX14 4RN

Routledge is an imprint of the Taylor & Francis Group, an informa business

Library of Congress Cataloging-in-Publication Data
Names: Maisha, Buuma, editor. | Massicotte, Stephanie, editor. | Morin, Melanie, editor.
Title: Fostering resilience before, during, and after experiences of trauma : insights to inform practice across the lifetime / edited by Buuma Maisha, Stephanie Massicotte and Melanie Morin.
Description: New York, NY : Routledge, 2021. |
Series: Explorations in mental health | Includes bibliographical references and index.
Identifiers: LCCN 2020050969 (print) | LCCN 2020050970 (ebook) | ISBN 9780367702861 (hardback) | ISBN 9781003150855 (ebook)
Subjects: LCSH: Resilience (Personality trait) | Psychic trauma. | Adjustment (Psychology)
Classification: LCC BF698.35.R47 F67 2021 (print) | LCC BF698.35.R47 (ebook) | DDC 155.2/4--dc23
LC record available at https://lccn.loc.gov/2020050969
LC ebook record available at https://lccn.loc.gov/2020050970

ISBN: 978-0-367-70286-1 (hbk)
ISBN: 978-0-367-71434-5 (pbk)
ISBN: 978-1-003-15085-5 (ebk)

Typeset in Baskerville
by Taylor & Francis Books

Contents

Illustrations

Figures

Tables

Contributors

Laura Lynne Armstrong, PhD, is an associate professor, clinical psychologist and researcher in the School of Counselling, Psychotherapy, & Spirituality, Saint Paul University, Ottawa, Ontario, Canada. She also holds Diplomate Clinician certification in Logotherapy from the Viktor Frankl Institute of Logotherapy. She has developed a SSHRC-funded mental health promotion programme for school children called D.R.E.A.M. (Developing Resilience through Emotions, Attitudes, & Meaning).

Christian R. Bellehumeur, PhD, is a full professor in the Faculties of Human Sciences and Philosophy at Saint Paul University, Ottawa, Ontario, Canada. His main research interests focus on the applications of Gilbert Durand's theory of Anthopological Structures of Imaginary (ASI) in the contexts of human development, positive psychology, psychotherapy and, recently, eco-psychology.

Ghislaine Benmoussa is a doctoral candidate at Saint Paul University. She holds a master's degree in counselling and spirituality. She provides individual, couple and family psychotherapy services in the Ottawa region. Her master's thesis focused on young adult widowhood, attachment style and marital mourning. Her doctoral research explores relationship-centred-therapy with sexual offenders.

Hélène Campbell is a young woman from Ottawa, Ontario, who has raised great awareness for organ donation working with different organizations around the world. Hélène underwent a successful double lung transplant at the Toronto General Hospital. She is a motivational speaker and is passionate about sharing her experiences with anyone.

Laure-Marie Carignan, PhD, is a registered couple and family therapist (OTSTCFQ) and a registered psychotherapist (CRPO). She has maintained a clinical practice in community service settings as well as private practice for over 25 years. Her PhD thesis pertained to Durandian theory on the structure of the imaginary and the development of family resilience. Laure-Marie lectures in the Faculty of Human Sciences at Saint Paul University, Ottawa.

Nicolas Galton is a doctoral student in Counselling and Spirituality at the School of Counselling, Psychotherapy and Spirituality (Saint Paul University, Ottawa, Canada). He is interested in the therapeutic application of psychedelics.

Buuma Maisha, PhD, is an assistant professor of psychotherapy and counselling at Saint Paul University, Ottawa, Ontario, Canada. Dr Maisha's research interests are centred on child sexual abuse and war-related sexual violence. He mainly investigates the impact of sociocultural norms (social taboos) on survivors' self-image and image of other. He is working on developing a culturally and context informed therapeutic model for sexual trauma.

Judith Malette, PhD, is a clinical psychologist and full professor at the School of Counselling, Psychotherapy and Spirituality, Saint Paul University, Ottawa, Ontario, Canada. Her main research focus is on adaptation to ageing, and to the end of life, and on the use of Life Review and Spiritual reminiscence during these life periods. Other major research interests include sexual abuse, and altered state of consciousness.

Stephanie Massicotte is a licensed psychotherapist with a master's degree in clinical counselling. She currently works as a crisis counsellor in Ottawa, Canada, for a multinational company.

Melanie Morin holds a master's degree in counselling and spirituality. She works at the Public Service Commission of Canada where she helps emerging leaders in the government develop their skills and competencies at the senior executive level.

Shanna Ossé graduated from the University of Ottawa with a Honours Bachelors of Arts in Communications and with a minor in Digital Humanities. Shanna has dedicated her studies to representation studies and the discrimination of Black people in media.

Willem F. Scholte (MD PhD, psychiatrist and psychotherapist), **Linda M. Verhaak** (MSc, clinical psychologist and psychotherapist) and **Rina S. Ghafoerkhan** (MSc, psychologist) are experienced clinicians and trauma specialists. They collaborate in a treatment programme for victims of human trafficking at ARQ National Psychotrauma Centre in Amsterdam, Netherlands.

Winnie Pak Wan Yeung, PhD, teaches at Tyndale University. Her research focuses on the well-being of immigrants and their children, and the integration of counselling and spirituality. She is an experienced registered psychotherapist, marriage and family therapist and registered play therapist.

Hélène's Story

What Does Resilience Look Like? A Personal Testimony on My Journey

Hélène Campbell

"You're the most unselfish person I have ever met!" is a refrain I commonly hear. Putting others first has always been easy for me. I've always thought of myself as a very considerate person. But being too considerate, I've discovered, has drawbacks. I put others first because, often, it's the easy way out. It helps me cope, although not necessarily deal, with issues in my own life. If I focus on helping others, I figure, perhaps my troubles won't loom quite so large.

Those tired and overused clichés about how people should be more accepting of their flaws because that's what makes them beautiful? Well, it's true, especially where resilience is concerned. I carry my share of emotional and physical baggage with me, failings and foibles that make me who I am. But one so-called "defect," a genetic glitch that no one would ever choose to have, has made my life better: I had bad lungs.

I remember the day the physician gave me my diagnosis. "Your life will forever change" was really all I heard. I had returned home from Barcelona, where I'd gone to learn Spanish and had met people from all over the world, people who shared my passion for travel and adventure. At 20, my life, I thought, was just beginning. I had developed a cough while there, and an occasional shortness of breath, but also felt exhilarated, invincible, unstoppable.

I had been diagnosed with asthma at the age of 16, so it seemed reasonable when, upon returning to Canada, my family doctor prescribed an inhaler to deal with my arrested breathing.

When that failed to address the problem, I found myself in the hospital emergency department, a concerned doctor examining X-rays of my chest and explaining that both my lungs had collapsed. The X-ray images, he added, looked nothing like those of a 20-year-old. "It looks like you've been a chain smoker for years," he said. "There is a lot of irreversible damage here."

I didn't get a diagnosis right away; it was too complex a case. No one knew how or where it came from, and there were many unanswered medical questions. They had never seen this type of fibrosis in someone so young. These were the facts: I had an aggressive lung disease causing me to deteriorate quickly. I had lost 74 per cent of my lung capacity. The damage was irreversible; I needed oxygen, and a double lung transplant. It turns out I had something called pleuroparenchymal fibroelastosis, a form of "interstitial lung disease that causes fibrosis. It originates in the upper lung zones and typically progresses to involve the entire lung" (English, Mayo, Levy, Yee & Leslie, 2015).

I was suddenly facing the possibility that the life I thought was just beginning was coming to a close. I was a victim, powerless, and would need to put everything on hold, start using oxygen, move to Toronto to be close to the transplant hospital, choose a support person to come with me, find a place to live. So many things were about to change, and I felt both responsible and guilty about the changes my family would be required to make. I felt bad about the complete redirection our lives were about to take. I didn't want to ask anything of anyone.

I was not sad, angry, confused or bitter. Rather than despairingly ask "Why me?" I decided to ask "Why not me?" It helped me accept my new reality. I was glad that it was me going through it, rather than someone else – as if there were a finite number of cases to go around. Softening the blow was my belief that suffering was a normal part of our lives as humans. Besides, my attitude towards the diagnosis wasn't going to change the disease, its progressions, nor the time waiting for a transplant. I couldn't control what was happening to my lungs, but I could control the way I reacted to it. Choosing to accept my condition and make the best of it is what made all the difference.

My admission to a pulmonary rehabilitation programme helped give me some perspective. I needed to learn how to slow down and manage my energy efficiently. My body's resolve to compensate for the lack of oxygen was causing stress on other areas. If I didn't learn to slow down, pace myself and manage the energy, my heart, for example, would overwork, which could possibly lead to not just the need for a lung transplant, but a heart replacement as well.

The rehab programme introduced me to some truly inspiring people, all with heartbreaking stories of tragedies and accidents that brought them there. One woman woke up one morning completely paralyzed from the neck down. One man went into the hospital for a minor knee surgery and emerged from a coma two months later, without a leg. These were people who, like me, had their lives change in an instant. I listened to their stories, barely able to imagine what their lives were like. At least I had the possibility of getting my life back with a transplant. The new normal I was experiencing wouldn't be permanent. That perspective helped me realize that there are far worse situations out there than mine. With that in mind, I decided to be very focused about where I directed my attention, an optimistic, but realistic, outlook. Taking a step back to re-evaluate my situation allowed me to recognize that I was so fortunate to have far more positives than negatives in my life. I realized I was fortunate to have had a healthy and "normal" life for 20 years, and that many people my age spent their entire lives in and out of hospitals. I was grateful for the fact that for the last 15 years, I was able to start my day with a shower, then go to school and live a full day. I took that ability and that energy for granted.

While in rehabilitation, I was told I had to manage my energy. If I wanted to shower, for example, it would be the only thing I could do that day. The mundane quotidian tasks, such as brushing my teeth, combing my hair, getting dressed, tying my shoes, were suddenly overwhelming and wholly draining.

I had to stop doing so many things. When my siblings heard that I couldn't clean my room, they were jealous. But I wanted to clean my room; if I could do that, then it meant I could do fun things, too. My resulting focus on what I had, as opposed to what I didn't, made an enormous difference. As US professor emeritus of medicine Jon Kabat-Zinn wrote, "As long as you are breathing, there is more right with you than there is wrong, no matter how ill or how hopeless you feel" (Kabat-Zinn, n.d.).

Humour carried me far. My family called me YouTube. I started a band called Air Supply. I called myself L'il Wheezy. I enjoyed coming up with as many lung puns as possible; a way for me to feel I had some control over the unmanageable.

The loss of my independence was a greater blow than the uncertain future of a lung transplant. My reliance on others was a hard pill to swallow. I needed help getting dressed, and carrying my oxygen in and out of cars. Yet asking for help felt like a weakness. I imagined moving to Toronto by myself, maybe working as a barista while I waited for the operation, then getting my new lungs and moseying on back home. I remember telling my family, "No one has to know."

So I was disappointed when the lung team told me that to be listed for transplant, I needed a support person to stay with me. I didn't want to ask anyone for help. I hated that someone's life was going to be adversely affected because of my bad luck. In the end, my mother, a nurse, took a leave of absence to accompany me, while the rest of my family continued with their lives in Ottawa.

Needing help indicated a loss of control. I wanted to be the helper, not the one needing help. The church our family attended started a prayer chain, and so news of my condition spread. People began reaching out. Someone proposed staging a fundraiser, a difficult offer for me to accept, but I recognized that there would be a huge financial strain on my family, and this would help. Suddenly, my idea of going through this anonymously was thrown out of the window.

Around the same time, the Bucknell family offered to make a website for our family. Unrelated to my story, their church pastor had given each member of the congregation $100 with the notion of paying it forward. Taber Bucknell, the father, told some of his work colleagues about his website idea, and one of his coworkers donated $180. Their planned website would serve two purposes: a blog to provide updates, and a platform for fundraising. When they first approached me about the idea, I declined their offer. My parents, however, convinced me that it would be helpful, that it wasn't all about me, and that accepting the offer would actually get me a step closer to independence. And so the website, A Lung Story, was born. When the site went live, people everywhere began sharing it. The friends I had made in Barcelona sent it to their friends and families, and $20 donations started to pour in from all over the world.

A journalist interviewed me. I remember him asking my mom how she felt about her daughter going through this, not only as a mother but as a nurse. I'll never forget her answer. "It is hard," she said, "but we hope that through Helene's story, people will recognize the need for organ donation." That was the first time I realized that my story could have meaning, that I could use it to raise awareness. Austrian neurologist and Holocaust survivor Viktor Frankl said "When we find meaning in suffering, suffering ceases to exist" (Frankl, 2006). And true enough, I felt empowered. I had given my health issues a purpose, allowing me to feel some measure of control. I went from "The Girl with Bad Lungs" to "Helene, who happens to have bad lungs." My bad blowers didn't define who I was; the way I reacted did. Being positive about my situation created a supportive environment. When people saw my reaction, it inspired them to try and change their perspective, and when I heard of their new-found perspectives, I was inspired. It wasn't always easy, but I told myself everything would be great after my transplant operation.

Yet I struggled following my transplant, far more than I expected, and more even than while I awaited surgery. In the weeks and months leading up to the operation, all I could think about was how good my life would be after the transplant. People see transplants as a cure; once you have one, they think, you're set. People believed that a transplant would be my happy ending. I believed it, too, telling myself that my problems would disappear once I had better lungs. With the benefit of hindsight, I now realize how ridiculous that was, but that's how I coped.

I was rudely awakened after surgery, when the pressures and expectations that I had brought to the operating table didn't materialize as I'd anticipated. My post-operative mood was nothing like I had imagined it would be. I was not overjoyed. In fact, I felt guilty – I should never have had this surgery, I told myself. Someone died so that I could live. I felt regretful, undeserving.

What I failed to appreciate was that no one died so that I, specifically, could live. Yes, someone died, and in that tragedy, their loved ones made a decision that allowed me to live; they chose to donate organs and tissue that could save other lives. They saved my life.

But I also didn't immediately understand the distinction between happiness and gratitude. You can be extremely grateful without always being happy. Yet when, at times, I felt discouraged or disappointed, I worried that that indicated a lack of thankfulness on my part, which in turn made me feel undeserving.

I'd had this idea that if I could make it through a lung transplant, any other challenge would be a walk in the park. I created a script for myself after the transplant in which I wouldn't suffer again. I didn't allow space for challenges and uncomfortable things in my life, because if I did, it would feel to me as though I was wasting my second chance. In so doing, I created more problems, and kept myself from learning valuable lessons. I should have been acknowledging hardships, talking about my issues and allowing myself to feel the wide range of emotions, especially the negative ones. I had a lung transplant; I didn't receive a new central processing unit. These thoughts were repeated when my body eventually rejected my new lungs and I was told I would need another transplant. I refused to let myself despair about my situation, lest that suggest I wasn't thankful, and that I wasn't deserving. I felt I had to keep up an appearance of strength, of gratitude.

I never grieved my loss or cursed my bad genes. I never said that I was angry at or frustrated by my lot in life. I always said I was fortunate to be alive, which is true, but I also should have said how terrible it sometimes was. How could it not be? But rather than talk openly about it, I remained in denial. I only found my resilience once I gave voice to all my emotions.

For resilience is about engaging a problem, not running from it. It is not about doing anything extraordinary; but slowly building emotional strength. It's through difficult times that we grow and evolve. Life is a path with bumps, potholes and unpredictable twists and turns. We can only see so far ahead – not even around the next corner. Resilience doesn't provide answers or solutions; resilience adds the shock absorbers that make the bumps in the road at least endurable. Like a muscle, work needs to be put in to build resilience. There aren't any steroids or drugs to make you immune to the challenges, stresses and pain in life. Everyone reacts to life events in different ways. Some people allow themselves to become overwhelmed by mundane tasks. And it feels like there are others who react far more positively to some challenging experiences.

I have had times where facing adversity is what helped me thrive, and I developed an ability to bounce back because of it. I do know that I have some personality traits that would add to that perspective, with a mindset of positivity, and trying to focus on what I have as opposed to what I don't. But I also think it is circumstance. I have been able to develop some resilience because of the issues I faced with my health challenges. But I learnt that just because someone reacts positively to adversity in one situation doesn't mean that they will always react the same way in other moments. The resilience a person has will change if the situation is altered, and will vary depending on the event.

It's easy to get caught up in life's negatives, to feel powerless and overwhelmed by the challenges we face each day. But those can be overcome by focusing on your abilities, on what you can do, and not on what you've lost. Yes, happy moments can exist without resilience, but a happy life is only possible with it.

References

English, J.C., Mayo, J.R., Levy, R., Yee, J., & Leslie, K.O. (2015). Pleuroparenchymal fibroelastosis: A rare interstitial lung disease. *Respirology Case Reports*, 3(2), 82–84.

Frankl, V.E. (2006). *Man's search for meaning*. Boston: Beacon Press.

Kabat-Zinn, J. (n.d.). www.goodreads.com/work/quotes/16181-mindfulness-for-beginners, retrieved on September 15, 2020.

1 Introduction

Resilience: When, Where, Why and for Whom Is It Relevant?

Buuma Maisha, Melanie Morin and Stephanie Massicotte

Over recent decades, the concept of resilience has grown in popularity; it has been explored in many different spheres of research, from individual, community and institutional levels. Today, resilience seems to be omnipresent in the world of psychology. In its early stages, before it was considered a research topic, neurologist and psychiatrist Viktor Frankl experienced first-hand the power individuals could have over their lives by focusing on a sense of meaning and purpose despite uncontrollable external factors while in the Auschwitz concentration camp. In his classic work, *Man's Search for Meaning*, Frankl's observations of human behaviour in the face of trauma and adversity describes man's ability to either overcome these difficulties or give in to defeat. Frankl (1984) stated:

> most men in a concentration camp believed that the real opportunities in life had passed. Yet, in reality, there was an opportunity and a challenge. One could make a victory of those experiences, turning life into an inner triumph, or one could ignore the challenge and simply vegetate.
>
> (p. 93)

In this same work, Frankl observed and also personally experienced a sense of meaning and a sense of purpose that were powerful enough to provide men with the capacity to survive in the face of adversity. Based on his experience and observations, Frankl's therapeutic approach, logotherapy, focuses on the future and on finding a sense of meaning for each client. His conceptualization of an individual's strength and determination, which was central in his search for meaning and purpose in the face of adversity and challenges, highlights the preliminary steps of resilience as a concept.

The beginning stages of the conceptual framework of resilience can be traced back to research that focused on children and youth with schizophrenic parents in the 1960s and 1970s (Masten, 2007). The results echoed Frankl's work by showing that, in spite of difficulties and adversities, some children had found opportunities in the challenges they faced and had actually experienced victory and inner triumph. During the 1980s, the concept of resilience was further developed, and important publications helped refine and clarify the concept. For example, Garmezy, Masten and Tellegen's (1984) study explored the importance of competence among children who experienced life stressors.

As research on this subject progressed, it became evident that resilient adaptations did not only derive from internal factors, but also from external ones. In fact, there were three sets of factors that were commonly seen in the development of resilience: attributes of children themselves; aspects of their families; and characteristics of their social environment (Masten, 2007).

Resilience implies hardship, regardless whether it has already been experienced, is ongoing or is yet to happen. As for hardship, it is part of human experience at any age. It comes in different forms such as an illness, relational conflict and violence, loss, natural disaster, etc. It is experienced to varying degrees in every part of the world and concerns any individual or social group. This makes resilience a universal concept, which has been studied from many angles; including individual (Hegney et al., 2007), relational (Slezackova & Sobotkova, 2017; Sanford, Backer-Fulghum & Carson, 2016; Patterson, 2002) and institutional (De Stefano et al., 2012; Carthey, De Leval & Reason, 2001). Also, a number of studies have focused on resilience prior to being exposed to traumatic events with the goal of preparing individuals and groups for the effects of such events (Finkelstein et al., 2005; Poulsen, 1993). Other studies have sought to understand resilience during the occurrence of adversity, hence looking into factors that facilitate building resilience during difficult life experiences (Abakoumkin, Stroebe & Stroebe, 2010). Furthermore, studies look into resilience as a contributing factor to personal growth following a traumatic event (Nehra et al., 2019). While literature often presents resilience in reference to how one can respond to a traumatic situation, this book offers a broader playfield for resilience as a therapeutic tool prior to, during and after a challenging situation. In fact, the present collection presents scholarly chapters on resilience covering all three time periods; a rarity in the topic. Resilience prepares us for adversity, supports us during such events and times, and provides a reliable stepping stone towards posttraumatic growth. As the world deals with the COVID-19 pandemic and events like the antiracism marches, reminding us of a traumatic history for humanity, this multidisciplinary volume on resilience is timely. It explores and explains individual and context-specific factors in building, recognizing and nurturing resilience in a variety of adversities at different stages of life.

Outline of the book

Presenting chapters written by a range of mental health experts, this book explores resilience as a tool which differs in nature across individuals, contexts and within an individual's lifetime. The book invites clinicians to build on individual's experiences and potential for resilience in their work with clients prior to, during and after a challenging situation. Recognizing that resilience does not have a "one size fits all" formula, therefore, the book responds to the fact that resilience can be challenging to recognize, foster and develop. Based variably on empirical research, theory and practice, the book chapters identify distinct therapeutic tools which can be used effectively to harness the potential, and meet the particular needs and limitations associated with different age groups, clients and traumatic experiences. These tools range from interactive and engaging activities for children, to utilizing the senior population's rich life experiences in order to build resilience.

This book comprises three parts studying resilience. Each part includes chapters that discuss a variety of adversities that individuals have been able to, or can, overcome with the help of resilience. The first part includes chapters which emphasize the importance of building resilience prior to traumatic events; the second part highlights how individuals might harness traumatic experiences to nurture resilience during the lived hardship; the third part focuses on the concept of posttraumatic growth and how retrospective consideration of traumatic experiences can help nurture individuals' resilience going forward. These adversities range from experiencing chronic pain or illness, the unique hardships of surviving violence including human trafficking and sexual violence, challenges immigrant families must overcome to better adjust to a new culture, as well as systemic racism and violence endured by black communities. The book will draw on personal and collective experiences of resilience analysed from a rich variety of therapeutic approaches (attachment and relationship based, logotherapy, biopsychosocial, narrative and spirituality integrated), age groups (child, young adult and senior) and cultural and geographical contexts (Africa, Asia, Europe and North America).

In Part I, readers will learn about resilience as a tool for preparedness to facing mental health challenges and facing potential traumatic events. Authors share knowledge on teaching children mood management skills, equipping social media users with strategies to avoid its potential impact on mental health (low self-esteem, relationship issues and anxiety), fostering resilience to ageing and end of life, and exploring developmental resilience factors among adults being trafficked for sexual exploitation. The authors' work builds on case analysis from a variety of clinical approaches; mainly attachment, logotherapy and narrative.

In Part II, authors discuss identity and resilience during adversities. The discussions explore how individuals' identities are impacted during traumatic events (Hutchison, 2010; Tummala-Narra, 2001) and consider reactions to a range of traumatic events such as chronic pain, hate crime, sudden onset of chronic illness and acculturation stress due to immigration. Reflecting on a number of clinical cases, authors conceptualize resilience from attachment and anthropological perspectives, with an interest in the role of spirituality in building and accessing resilience.

Finally, in Part III, authors discuss factors and benefits of resilience in supporting growth following traumatic events such as the loss of a loved one, rape and historical events of racial discrimination. The authors' contribution draws from attachment- and relationship-based therapeutic approaches, including an emerging approach from a qualitative-grounded theory research programme.

Authors analyse the contributions of resilience to posttraumatic growth; the role of spirituality in building and accessing resilience is also explored.

Resilience may look different for various persons and groups of individuals and at different moments. This is the message Hélène Campbell, a double lung transplant survivor, shares in her testimony above; a message also echoed in many other personal and professional testimonials shared by the authors throughout the book. Whether you are anticipating hardship, going through it, or recovering from it, this book attempts to provide you with the support you need. While the authors have shared personal and professional stories of resilience throughout the book, you are invited to reflect on your own. This might be more effective with the guidance of a mental health professional as you journey with us through the different chapters of this collection and make sense of your story.

References

Abakoumkin, G., Stroebe, W., & Stroebe, M. (2010). Does relationship quality moderate the impact of marital bereavement on depressive symptoms? *Journal of Social and Clinical Psychology*, 25(5), 510–526.

Carthey, J., De Leval, M.R., & Reason, J.T. (2001). Institutional resilience in health-care systems. *Quality in Health Care*, 10, 29–32.

De Stefano, L., Duncan, J., Dinar, S., Stahl, K., Strzepek, K.M., & Wolf, A.T. (2012). Climate change and the institutional resilience of international river basins. *Journal of Peace Research*, 49(1), 193–209.

Finkelstein, N., Rechberger, E., Russel, L.A., VanDemark, N.R., Noether, C.D., O'Keefer, M., Gould, K., Mockus, S., & Rael, M.V. (2005). Building resilience in children of mothers who have co-occurring disorders and histories of violence. *Journal of Behavioral Health Services & Research*, 32, 141–154.

Frankl, V.E. (1984). *Man's search for meaning*. Boston: Beacon Press.

Garmezy, N., Masten, A.S., & Tellegen, A. (1984). The study of stress and competence in children: A building block for developmental psychopathology. *Child Development*, 55, 97–111.

Hegney, D.G., Buikstra, E., Baker, P., Rogers-Clark, C., Pearce, S., Ross, H., King, C., & Watson-Luke, A. (2007). Individual resilience in rural people: A Queensland study, Australia. *Rural and Remote Health*, 7, 620.

Hutchison, E. (2010). Trauma and the politics of emotions: Constituting identity, security and community after the Bali bombing. *International Relations*, 24(1), 65–86.

Masten, A. (2007). Resilience in developing systems: Progress and promise as the fourth wave rises. *Development and Psychopathology*, 19, 921–930.

Nehra, D., Herrera-Escobar, J., Al Rafai, S., Havens, J., Askari, R., Nitzschke, S., Velmachos, G., Kasotakis, G., Brasel, K., Levy-Carrick, N., Salim, A., & Haider, A. (2019). Resilience and long-term outcomes after trauma: An opportunity for early intervention? *Trauma Acute Care Surgery*, 87(4), 782–788.

Patterson, J.M. (2002). Understanding family resilience. *Journal of Clinical Psychology*, 58(3), 233–246.

Poulsen, M.K. (1993). Strategies for building resilience in infants and young children at risk. *Infants & Young Children*, 6(2), 29–40.

Sanford, K., Backer-Fulghum, L.M., & Carson, C. (2016). Couple resilience inventory: Two dimensions of naturally occurring relationship behavior during stressful life events. *Psychological Assessment*, 28(10), 1243–1254.
Slezackova, A., & Sobotkova, I. (2017). Family resilience: Positive psychology approach to healthy family functioning. In U. Kumar (Ed.), *The Routledge international handbook of psychosocial resilience* (pp. 379–390). New York: Routledge.
Tummala-Narra, P. (2001). Asian trauma survivors: Immigration, identity, loss, and recovery. *Journal of Applied Psychoanalytic Studies*, 3, 243–258.

Part I

Developing Resilience Prior to Facing Mental Health Challenges and Adversity

2 An Experiential Learning Tool for Teaching About the Promotion of Child Resilience to Mental Health Concerns

Moods Managed

Laura Lynne Armstrong

The Canadian Code of Ethics for Psychologists has "Responsibility to Society" as a core principle for practice (Canadian Psychological Association (CPA), 2017). Specifically, in teaching research, or clinical work, psychologists have "responsibilities to the societies in which they live or work and to the welfare of all human beings in those societies" (CPA, 2017, p. 33). One of the stated values in the Code of Ethics is that psychologists must use their "time and talents in helping to meet these collective responsibilities" (CPA, 2017, p. 33). One key contemporary societal concern is that only one in six children and youth requiring psychotherapy or other mental health services ever receives services (Szatmari, 2018). Therefore, to practice ethically and be responsible to society, it is important to teach university student trainees both how to treat clients presenting for services as well as how they can contribute to the developmental resilience of the five in six young people who will not access treatment. Health-care is moving towards value-based care and population health and, as a result, experiential learning tools are recommended to teach students about important societal issues related to their work beyond one-on-one client treatment (Hsieh & Coates, 2018). Experiential pedagogical strategies are beneficial in creating heightened confidence and commitment to societal change (Dailey, Washington & Havig, 2016; Edgington & Pimlott, 2009). In addition to enhancing students' civic commitment, experiential learning also helps students to better connect theory to practice (Ratsoy, 2016). The following is a description of an experiential learning exercise in which master's and baccalaureate psychopathology class students collaborated in the creation of a board game to learn about building resilience in children through a mental health promotion activity.

Board Games and Mental Health Promotion

Disturbingly, 20 per cent of Canadian children and adolescents experience mental illness (Canadian Mental Health Association (CMHA), 2014). Given the low access to treatment services among this population, there is a critical role for prevention programming in the promotion of resilience to mental health concerns (World Health Organization, 2004). Approximately half of mental health concerns begin by the mid-teenage years (Kessler, Amminger, Aguilar-Gaxiola, Alonso, Lee & Ustun, 2007). Prevention of mental illness before symptoms arise has been estimated to result in a lifetime savings of $280,000 per child, as prevention reduces the potential for negative academic, social or developmental outcomes (Smith & Smith, 2010). Therefore, there is an increasing emphasis on the importance of developing prevention approaches, particularly in group-based settings with families or in schools (Mental Health Commission of Canada (MHCC), 2012; Streng, 2009). One potential group-based means of mental illness prevention includes the enhancement of mental health knowledge and positive coping strategies through the use of a board game (Wiener, Battles, Mamalian & Zadeh, 2011).

Play is the language of young people (Gil, 1994) and board games are a powerful means of learning about coping skills, self-care, family relationships, mood, stress, peer relationships and self-esteem (Klingemann, 1995; Wiener et al., 2011). There is a growing awareness of the usefulness of board games to promote well-being, including mental health (Wiener et al., 2011). In general, research suggests that a hands-on, experiential learning approach can be helpful for children and families (Malchiodi, 2005). Conveying information through play engages the whole person, affects the brain, and leads to better memory for concepts, self-discovery and change (Malchiodi, 2005).

In addition to being a medium for conveying information, play, such as that experienced while engaged in a game, is a key ingredient in family or peer attachment-building (Creed & Kendall, 2005; Gil, 1994; Walter & Petr, 2006). Play provides opportunities for "mutual attunement," which is central to the development or re-establishment of positive, secure attachments (Malchiodi & Crenshaw, 2014). Further, through play, children's thoughts and feelings are expressed in a hands-on, multisensory manner (Gil, 1994; Lowenstein & Sprunk, 2010). While engaged in a multisensory manner in playing a game, children and adolescents can learn new behaviours, become better problem-solvers, and gain insight into challenges (Streng, 2009; Wiener et al., 2011). Communication about important issues can also emerge, as play activities move participants from the intellectual, cognitive world of adults to the world of imagination familiar to young people (Bailey & Sori, 2000). Games further provide opportunities and safety to address scenarios and feelings that might otherwise be difficult to discuss (Streng, 2009; Wiener et al., 2011).

Board games specifically have been found to inspire family and peer communication about positive coping strategies, consequences of difficult situations, and shared decision-making (Kennedy et al., 2017; Wiener et al., 2011). Concerning follow-on action, children were more likely to try out new ways of thinking and acting as a result of learning from a board game than if an adult were to offer suggestions (Streng, 2009). Specifically, through family or peer social processes as a function of board game play, children can be supported in learning about and engaging in their own self-care and healthy decision-making (Kennedy et al., 2017). For example, when classrooms of children between the ages of 7 and 11 engaged in learning about healthy eating from repeated exposure to a board game, these children had a significantly lower body mass index and engaged in more physical fitness than children assigned to a control group who received education as usual (Viggiano et al., 2018). Specifically, the board game promoted resilience to weight gain and unhealthy eating (Viggiano et al., 2018).

Given the apparent benefits of board game engagement, particularly in relation to the health or mental health and well-being of children and families, board game creation grounded in this research may be an ideal teaching tool concerning resilience-building.

Theoretical Framework in Game Development and Content

To provide the 51 university psychopathology class students (48 MA in psychotherapy students; 3 BA in human relations students) with skills necessary to develop approaches to address population health beyond one-on-one client care, students were briefly taught about programme development and evaluation theory, including the importance of a Needs Assessment and integrated Knowledge Translation (KT). A collection of KT definitions suggests that KT involves moving an approach from academic settings to people and organizations who can put it to practical use (Graham et al., 2006), while a Needs Assessment is used to inform development of an approach grounded in target population needs (Trochim, 2006). Target population needs for a Needs Assessment can be found in the research literature, as well as through engaging the target population in collaborative development or in describing their own experiences. Engaging the target population in the design of an approach is central to integrated KT (Armstrong, 2017): Involving stakeholder engagement at all stages of development can ensure greater buy-in and use of the prevention approach, as well as a better fit for the population that the approach serves (Amsden & VanWynsberghe, 2005; Armstrong, 2017; Commissioner for Children and Young People, 2016). Thus, a KT integrated approach is beneficial in moving approaches beyond academic settings, as those who would use the product or programme are engaged in the whole process of design and implementation.

Students learned that they themselves are stakeholder groups relevant to promoting child mental health, as they are:

1 family members with child relatives;
2 parents or grandparents;
3 adults who experience typical daily stressors;
4 graduate psychotherapy trainees with knowledge of evidence-based therapy or educational tools to enhance well-being in children; or
5 undergraduates with knowledge of psychology, resilience-based approaches, child development, and the human condition.

The students suggested that other relevant stakeholder groups would include children themselves and diverse families from different socioeconomic backgrounds (e.g. non-university educated), sexual or gender orientations, or cultural groups beyond the profile of the students in the classroom.

The graduate psychopathology class students had a solid awareness of the importance of using a theoretical framework to conceptualize one-on-one therapy approaches and treatment planning. Therefore, the students were provided with a theoretical framework with which to conceptualize board game content in the promotion of child resilience to mental health concerns. Students learned about R.E.A.L. therapy (Armstrong, 2016, 2017).

R.E.A.L. (Rational Emotive, Attachment, Logotherapy; Armstrong, 2016, 2017) is a Second Wave Positive Psychology (PP2.0) theoretical framework. PP2.0 is concerned with "the good life" and the importance of the "dialectics" between the positive and negative aspects of life as fundamental to optimal functioning (Lomas & Ivtzan, 2016). Specifically, well-being is viewed in PP2.0 as the right balance between positives and negatives: optimism versus pessimism; self-esteem versus humility; freedom versus restriction; forgiveness versus anger; and happiness versus sadness (Lomas & Ivtzan, 2016). As a PP2.0 approach, R.E.A.L. emphasizes the importance of all emotions, both lighter and darker, in the journey towards meaning and well-being (Armstrong, 2016). Transforming difficult personal experiences into something meaningful is also underscored in R.E.A.L. as a PP2.0 approach (Armstrong, 2017), as concepts such as posttraumatic growth and finding meaning in challenges are central to PP2.0 (Lomas & Ivtzan, 2016). In R.E.A.L., darker and lighter experiences, failures, frustrations and challenging emotions are viewed as an opportunity to create meaningful attitudinal change, action, gratitude or mindful attunement to good moments (Armstrong, 2017). In comparison to a control group, a R.E.A.L. approach has been found to promote resilience to mental health concerns in children through significantly enhancing meaning, self-esteem, openness to learning, feelings and other new experiences, and hope for the future (Armstrong, 2017). R.E.A.L. explores well-being from attitudinal, behavioural, attachment and meaning-centred angles (Armstrong, 2017).

Rational-Emotive theory and practice. Rational Emotive [Behaviour] Therapy (REBT) is an evidence-based cognitive-behavioural approach developed by Albert Ellis (Dobson, 2010; Ellis, 2004) to tackle unhelpful thinking, behaviour and feelings. In REBT it is believed that irrational thoughts mask pain and pleasure, which can lead to problematic or chronic anger, sadness and fear (Ellis, 2004). Building on this, in R.E.A.L., emotions are seen as "alarm bells" or opportunities for helpful action and attitudinal change (i.e. orientation towards meaning or healthy thinking). REBT also includes behavioural coping strategies, such as relaxation and behavioural activation (Ellis, 2004). These REBT skills aid in self-regulation, enabling one to get along better with others, a skill that is important for resilience to mental illness (DeWall, Baumeister & Vohs, 2009).

Attachment theory and practice. Enhancing perspective taking and social problem-solving, such as through game play with others, can enhance empathy and building connections with others (Schonert-Reichl et al., 2015). Shared, creative play activities also help to build connections with peers and family members (Malchiodi & Crenshaw, 2014). Attachment to the community through engagement or volunteerism can lead to a sense of belonging, enhanced motivation and well-being (Billig, 2000; Kids Matter, 2017). In R.E.A.L., secure attachment with others is viewed as a key pathway to experience meaning and well-being (Armstrong, 2017).

Logotherapy theory and practice. Logotherapy is an existential, meaning-based theory developed by Viktor Frankl (Frankl, 1986). A key tenet of logotherapy is that life has meaning under all circumstances, and that each person must discover the meaning potential of each situation (Frankl, 1986). Logotherapy's pathways to meaning include:

1 doing a deed for others or creating something;
2 by experiencing something or developing secure connections with others; and
3 choosing our attitudes (healthy thinking).

Meaning is significant predictor of child, youth and adult mental health (St. John, 2017; Frankl, 1986). Through the pathways to meaning, young people can gain enhanced self-esteem, an awareness and openness to new possible experiences, and hope for the future (Erikson, 1964; Markstrom & Kalmanir, 2001; Search Institute, 2009; VanderVen, 2008). All of these factors are associated with resilience to mental health concerns (e.g. Centres for Disease Control and Prevention, 2016; Frankl, 1986; St. John, 2017).

With the above lens, students carried out the experiential learning activity to understand how to build child resilience through a mental health promotion approach: game development and play.

Experiential Learning Activity

Students were invited to consider their own experience as parents, grandparents or relatives of children and write down three common everyday situations that might trigger anger, fear or sadness in children. If they had regular access to these children, then they could also ask the children themselves about everyday situations that are difficult for children their age. The students also wrote down helpful coping tools that they or their relatives use or could use in the common situations, fitting into the R.E.A.L. framework. Specifically, the coping strategies fit into the categories of healthy thinking or behaviour; peer, family or community connection-building activities; or strategies that fit into one of Frankl's pathways to meaning. Students also wrote down everyday hassles, stressors or challenges that could trigger difficult feelings for adults, and strategies to address these, as the game is meant for children and adults to play together, unless played within a classroom setting. Students who had no connections in their lives to children only wrote down the adult scenarios and coping tools. To supplement student-provided scenarios, and collaborate with the additional stakeholders whom the students suggested were important to include, I posted a notice on Facebook that I was creating a family board game for a psychopathology class to teach students about building child resilience to mental health concerns. I asked for parents and children who were willing to provide scenarios of common challenges that trigger sadness, anger or fear, as well as things they do that are helpful in these situations. I noted that all of these scenarios would be converted to "fairy tales" for the purpose of the game. Within 24 hours, over 30 children and parents from diverse cultural, socio-economic, sexual and gender orientation, and family type groups provided scenarios. The over 250 scenarios presented by psychopathology students, children and families were transformed into fairy tales. Students agreed that fairy tales would create a space to safely discuss everyday feelings and challenges, as well as to make the game fun and child-friendly.

The undergraduate psychopathology class students carried out this game with multiple families, with children between the ages of 6 and 12, and groups with three or more individuals. They were then assigned to write reflection papers on the use of the game to promote resilience in children and families. Specifically, students were asked to explore or address:

1 whether the game players learned skills that they could use in their everyday life and, if so, what skills they learned;
2 what they learned about resilience in a real-world setting and to connect this to the research literature on resilience;
3 what game players liked about the game; and
4 suggestions for improvement or further development of the game.

Student Reflections

Students suggested that, collectively, the game participants reported healthy thinking, behavioural, spiritual, attachment-based and meaning-centred strategies that they learned while playing the game that individuals and families would like to incorporate into their own lives. Game players perceived these strategies to be helpful in managing everyday situations that lead to sadness, anger or fear. Connecting to the research literature that games can be a positive bonding tool to build attachment, which is a protective factor for mental health concerns (Hickey, Fitzgerald, & Dooley, 2017), students indicated that the game players perceived the game to be a positive bonding activity. Further, when parents have a greater awareness of, and model positive strategies to cope with stressors, children and adolescents are better able to cope and manage challenging feelings, whereas negative parental coping strategies intensify child emotional responses and behavioural challenges (Fabes, Leonard, Kupanoff & Martin, 2001; Landau, 2010; Sherman, Grusec & Almas, 2017). Grounded in this literature, students suggested that the game provided parents with positive coping tools to model good coping and to help their children manage everyday challenges and, therefore, would likely promote resilience to emotional or behavioural concerns. To discuss feelings, research suggests that children are not often comfortable communicating their feelings directly, but that therapeutic play invites more open feeling discussion (Streng, 2009). Students noted that game players were able to openly discuss feelings in relation to the presented scenarios and even make connections to their own lives. They suggested that the game also sparked insightful discussions in which players debated the merits of each coping method, thus enhancing healthy problem-solving. Healthy problem-solving is important for resilience (Armstrong, 2017).

Students noted that they particularly appreciated that, even though the game was devised as a fairy tale, the main characters deviated from traditional gender stereotypes (e.g. the knight character was a female, the unicorn was a male). They thought that this design of the game would be a fit for both cisgender and transgender children and families. Students stated that the game rules were clear and easy to follow and that the use of a game was an engaging method for teaching skills for resilience. Regarding improvement, game players suggested the game board should have a gloss finish so that the pieces could slide more easily. Further, they suggested including a list of emotional synonyms that fit under anger, sadness or fear (e.g. worry, stress, nervousness, etc. for fear) to further enhance emotional literacy.

One year after the MA and BA students were given the experiential exercise to develop scenarios and coping methods, I asked the students what, if anything, they gained from participating in this exercise. They mentioned that, not only did it help them learn about building resilience in children and families, but it helped them to build resilience in their own lives. Some students stated that they incorporated the strategies generated by themselves and by their classmates into their everyday lives and that they are still using these strategies today. They also stated that developing the game helped them to see how they could contribute to societal well-being beyond one-on-one client interactions. They reported that this exercise has made them interested in engaging in resilience-building through community mental health promotion or public presentations on strategies to build resilience in children and families. The MA students noted that, as a result of this exercise, they were inspired to incorporate creativity into their work, such as creating games to teach families tools in the therapy office.

Conclusion

Purposeful experiential learning appeared to enhance student awareness of community-based resilience-building and the value of creativity or the use of games with children and families. Students were also able to link their experiential observations to the existing resilience research literature. They maintained and built upon learned skills both in their own lives and in their therapeutic approach with children and families. Given the apparent value of incorporating experiential learning, professors should consider including such exercises with psychotherapy trainees to teach about strategies, and about collaborating with key stakeholders, to develop approaches that contribute to society beyond the one-on-one therapy setting. As for "Moods Managed," this game can further contribute to student learning as a potential future research study for an MA thesis student. The student would hopefully be able to experientially and quantitatively demonstrate the resilience-building power of a board game to positively enhance resilience to child or family mental health concerns.

References

Amsden, J., & VanWynsberghe, R. (2005). Community mapping as a research tool with youth. *Action Research*, 3: 353–377.

Armstrong, L.L. (2016). R.E.A.L. therapy: Rational-emotive attachment-based logotherapy for families. *The Family Journal*, 24: 164–173. doi:10.1177/1066480716628626.

Armstrong, L.L. (2017). The D.R.E.A.M. program: Developing resilience through emotions, attitudes and meaning – program development and evaluation through a knowledge translation-integrated approach. *Counselling and Spirituality*, 36: 93–120. doi:10.2143/CS.36.1.0000000.

Bailey, C.E., & Sori, C.E.F. (2000). Involving parents in children's therapy. In C.E. Bailey (Ed.), *Children in therapy: Using the family as a resource* (pp. 475–502). New York: W.W. Norton.

Billig, S. (2000). *Profiles of success: Engaging young people's hearts and minds through service-learning*. Berkeley, CA: Grantmaker Forum on Community & National Service.

Canadian Mental Health Association (CMHA) (2014). Mental illness in Canada: Statistics on the prevalence of mental disorders and related suicides in Canada. Retrieved from www.cmha.ca.

Canadian Psychological Association (CPA) (2017). *Canadian code of ethics for psychologists*, 4th edn. Ottawa: Author.

Centres for Disease Control and Prevention (2016). Health related quality of life. Retrieved from www.cdc.gov.

Commissioner for Children and Young People (2016). *Involving children and young people: Participation guidelines*. Western Australia: Author.

Creed, T.A., & Kendall, P.C. (2005). Therapist alliance-building behavior within a cognitive-behavioral treatment for anxiety in youth. *Journal of Consulting and Clinical Psychology*, 73, 498–505.

Dailey, A.L., Washington, K.T., & Havig, K. (2016). Brown lettuce and rodent traps, granola and trees: A qualitative study of an experiential teaching tool to promote socially just practice. *The Journal of Social Work Values and Ethics*, 13, 47–55.

DeWall, C.N., Baumeister, R.F., & Vohs, K.D. (2009). Satiated with belongingness? *Journal of Personality & Social Psychology*, 95, 1367–1382.

Dobson, K.S. (2010). *Handbook of cognitive-behavioral therapies*, 3rd edn. New York: Gilford Press.

Edgington, E.M., & Pimlott, J.F.L. (2009). An experiential learning model for teaching social advocacy education. *Journal of Dental Hygiene*, 83, 231-232

Ellis, A. (2004). *Rational emotive behavior therapy: It works for me, it can work for you*. New York: Albert Ellis Institute.

Erikson, E.H. (1964). *Insight and Responsibility*. New York: Norton.

Fabes, R.A., Leonard, S.A., Kupanoff, K., & Martin, C.L. (2001). Parental coping with children's negative emotions: Relations with children's emotional and social responding. *Child Development*, 72, 907–920. doi:10.1111/1467-8625.000323.

Frankl, V. (1986). *Man's search for meaning*. New York: Simon & Schuster.

Gil, E. (1994). *Play in family therapy*. New York: Guilford.

Graham, I.D., Logan, J., Harrison, M.B., Straus, S.E., Tetroe, J., Caswell, W., & Robinson, N. (2006). Lost in knowledge translation: Time for a map? *Journal of Continuing Education Health in the Health Professions*, 26, 13–24. doi:10.1002/chp.47.

Hickey, E., Fitzgerald, A., & Dooley, B. (2017). The relationship between perceived family support and depressive symptoms in adolescence: What is the moderating role of coping strategies and gender? *Community Mental Health Journal*, 53, 474–481. doi:10.1007/s10597-017-0087.

Hsieh, D.T., & Coates, W.C. (2018). Poverty simulation: An experiential learning tool for teaching social determinants of health. *AEM Education and Training*, 2, 51–54. doi:10.1002/aet2.10076.

Kennedy, A., Semple, L., Alderson, L., Bouskill, V., Karasevich, J., Riske, B., & van Gunst, S. (2017). Don't push your luck! Educational family board (not bored) game for school-age children living with chronic conditions. *Journal of Pediatric Nursing*, 35, 57–64. doi:10.1016/j.pedn.2017.02.032.

Kessler, R.C., Amminger, G.P., Aguilar-Gaxiola, S., Alonso, J., Lee, S., & Ustun, T.B. (2007). Age of onset of mental disorders: A review of recent literature. *Current Opinion in Psychiatry*, 20, 359–364.

Kids Matter (2017). *Belonging at school makes a difference*. Melbourne: Government of Australia.

Klingemann, H. (1995). Board game players survive or crash (drug prevention game developed in Switzerland). *The Journal of the Addiction Research Foundation*, 24, 11, 1-3.

Landau, J. (2010). Communities that care for families: The LINC model for enhancing individual, family, and community resilience. *American Journal of Orthopsychiatry*, 80, 516–524. doi:10.1111/j.1939-0025.2010.01054.x.

Lomas, T., & Ivtzan, I. (2016). Second wave positive psychology: Exploring the positive–negative dialectics of wellbeing. *Journal of Happiness Studies*, 17, 1753–1768. doi:10.1007/s10902-015-9668-y.

Lowenstein, L., & Sprunk, T.P. (2010). Creative family therapy techniques: Play and art-based activities to assess and treat families. Retrieved from www.lianalowenstein.com.

Malchiodi, C.A. (2005). The impact of culture on art therapy with children. In E. Gil & A. Drewes (Eds.), *Cultural issues in play therapy* (pp. 99–111). New York: Guilford Press.

Malchiodi, C.A., & Crenshaw, D. (2014). *Creative arts and play therapy with attachment problems*. New York: Guilford Press.

Markstrom, C.A., & Kalmanir, H.M. (2001). Linkages between the psychosocial stages of identity and intimacy and the ego strengths of fidelity and love. *Identity: An International Journal of Theory and Research*, 1, 179–196.

Mental Health Commission of Canada (MHCC) (2012). *Changing directions, changing lives: The mental health strategy for Canada*. Calgary: Author.

Ratsoy, G.R. (2016). The role of faculty in connecting Canadian undergraduate arts and humanities students to scholarly inquiries into teaching: A case for purposeful experiential learning. *The Canadian Journal for the Scholarship of Teaching and Learning*, 7, 1–13. doi:10.5206/cjsotl-rcacea.2016.1.2.

Schonert-Reichl, K.A., Oberle, E., Lawlor, M.S., Abbott, D., Thomson, K., Oberlander, T.F., & Diamond, A. (2015). Enhancing cognitive and social-emotional development through a simple-to-administer mindfulness-based school program for elementary school children: A randomized control trial. *Developmental Psychology*, 51, 52–66. doi:10.1037/a0038454.

Search Institute (2009). *40 developmental assets for children grades K-3.* Minneapolis, MN: Author.

Sherman, A., Grusec, J.E., & Almas, A.N. (2017). Mothers' knowledge of what reduces distress in their adolescents: Impact on the development of adolescent approach coping. *Parenting: Science and Practice*, 17, 187–199. doi:10.1080/15295192.2017.1333789.

Smith, J.P., & Smith, G.C. (2010). Long-term economic costs of psychological problems during childhood. *Social Science & Medicine*, 71, 110–115.

St. John, E. (2017). Meaning as an early determinant of childhood mental health: Potential influence of religious attendance (Master's thesis). Retrieved from University of Ottawa database. http://dx.doi.org/10.20381/ruor-20307.

Streng, I. (2009). Using therapeutic board games to promote child mental health. *Journal of Public Mental Health*, 7, 4–16. doi:10.1108/17465729200800024.

Szatmari, P. (2018). Children's Mental Health Week: Feeling hopeful for the future of mental health care for children and youth. SickKids Centre for Community Mental Health. Retrieved from www.sickkidscmh.ca/News-Information/Children%E2%80%99s-Mental-Health-Week-Feeling-hopeful-for.aspx.

Trochim, R. (2006). *The research methods knowledge base.* Cincinnati, OH: Atomic Dog Publishing.

VanderVen, K. (2008). *Promoting positive development in early childhood: Building blocks for a successful start.* Pittsburg, CA: Springer.

Viggiano, E., Viggiano, A., & Amaro, S. (2018). Healthy lifestyle promotion in primary schools through the board game Kaledo: A pilot cluster randomized trial. *European Journal of Pediatrics*, 177, 1371–1437. doi:0.1007/s00431-018-3091-4

Walter, U.M., & Petr, K. (2006). *Therapeutic alliance with children and families: A review of the national literature.* Lawrence: State of Kansas Department of Social and Rehabilitation Services:.

Wiener, L., Battles, H., Mamalian, C., & Zadeh, S. (2011). ShopTalk: A pilot study of the feasibility and utility of a therapeutic board game for youth living with cancer. *Support Care Cancer*, 19, 1049–1054. doi:10.1007/s00520-011-1130-z.

World Health Organization (2004). *Prevention of mental disorders: Effective interventions and policy options.* Geneva: Author.

3 Social Media and Resilience

Stephanie Massicotte and Melanie Morin

Whether it be Facebook, Twitter, Instagram, Tumblr, WhatsApp, Snapchat or YouTube, Millennials love social media. They allow us to stay linked to our friends and family around the world with minimal actions needed on our part to maintain connections. The creation of these virtual communities and networks allows for the sharing of ideas, information and self-expression on a level that has never been seen before. In addition to offering people a chance to be seen, heard and validated, it can also help fulfil our essential need for connection. One of the main reasons why social networking sites are so popular and difficult to dismiss is our innate need to connect with other human beings (Hess & Pickett, 2010). Although we may use social media to celebrate life events, special moments and show off our lifestyle with loved ones and acquaintances, what occurs on the other side of the screen may be a very different story. According to studies, two of the main factors motivating people to log onto such sites are loneliness and boredom (Tomczyka & Selmanagic-Lizde, 2018). With this inconsistency in mind, it is important that users be aware of the impact and potential risks social media may present to our mental health. Over the years, since their introduction to the world, there have been a number of studies about the impact of social media on individuals' mental health. The results, however, have been contradictory, with some indicating a negative impact and others showing a positive one, "stressing its potential for human development" (Benvenuti, Mazzoni & Piobbico, 2017). In fact, technology has often been considered a double-edged sword. The famous physicist Albert Einstein expressed this point of view during a speech he gave in 1948 at the Peace Congress of Intellectuals at Wroclaw in Poland:

> Penetrating research and keen scientific work have often had tragic implications for mankind, producing, on the one hand, inventions which liberated man from exhausting physical labor, making his life easier and richer; but on the other hand, introducing a grave restlessness into his life, making him a slave to his technological environment, and – most catastrophic of all – creating the means for his own mass destruction. This, indeed is a tragedy of overwhelming poignancy!
>
> (Einstein, 1954)

Albert Einstein expressed his views about the risks and rewards that technology provides humankind long before the internet and social media were even possible. Although his statement was made over 70 years ago, it somehow resonates today in a world where technology and innovation are at the forefront of human evolution.

Although researchers are starting to shy away more and more from labelling internet use as "good" or "bad," some have categorized social media consumption into two polarized options: a "functional internet use" and a "problematic internet use," which makes the distinction between an empowering experience and a trapping one (Benvenuti et al., 2017). Terms such as "problematic" versus "functional" are particularly suitable for issues such as internet addiction (Benvenuti et al., 2017), but can the habits of an average social media user be so easily categorized? An article produced by BBC in 2017 provides an interesting example of the murky waters that is our relationship with social media – especially among young people. The article chronicles the experience of nine high school students in England who accepted the challenge of cutting out social media altogether for a week. However easy it seemed to them at first glance, in the end, only three of the nine succeeded (BBC News School Project Report, 2017). In fact, studies demonstrate that "quitting social media" is harder than it looks; one in four fail to do so (Tomczyka & Selmanagic-Lizde, 2018). One of the students who did not succeed in the challenge explains that social media is not a "need" for him and it does not negatively impact his life, nor do his relationships nor his responsibilities suffer because of his social media use. However, he adds that he failed the challenge because he was too bored and could no longer resist social media, and since the majority of his peers failed as well, he suggests that his social media use could not be categorized as problematic (BBC News School Project Report, 2017). Since social media is considered to be a "popular leisure activity" in modern societies worldwide (Andreassen, Pallesen & Griffiths, 2017) and since our consumption is steadily increasing, exploring how we might enhance the quality of our experience and find a healthy balance might be the question of the day. Unfortunately, in spite of social media's popularity, a growing amount of findings discouragingly connect it to negative consequences such as depression, anxiety, stress, isolation and social pressure (Moningka, 2017). As disconcerting as this may be, social media in and of itself is generally not considered the true culprit (Benvenuti et al., 2017). Surprising? Let us explain. When we understand social media to be simply a leisure activity, or a tool per se, it becomes easier to shift the focus from the tool to the user. Just like the skills, or hand-eye coordination, of the person wielding a hammer is brought into question rather than the hammer's integrity of being good or bad. In this chapter, we will attempt to explore some common challenges and bad habits with which many of us struggle and ask ourselves how we might address these and overcome some of our social media pitfalls. We will also explore the possibility of adopting resilience in our regular social media use.

The Struggle Is Real

Although social media facilitates an age of easy interactions and allows us to remain connected with others, there are some considerable drawbacks to these advantages. Fortunately, studies demonstrate that only a small percentage of the population may be categorized as "problematic users" (Andreassen et al., 2017). But without necessarily struggling with a diagnosable internet addiction, there exist common social media related struggles and pitfalls worth examining which may resonate with some of us. To ignore such drawbacks and pitfalls would certainly render our media consumption less than healthy. Thus, developing a resilient outlook on our social media usage can help not only safeguard us from the consequences and vicious cycles produced by those pitfalls, but it can also help us recover a healthy relationship with social media. In an attempt to promote insight and awareness, which are crucial instruments in the process of resilience, we shall explore potential obstacles, temptations and pitfalls which pose as common struggles for the modern-day user on the other side of the screen.

Is Social Media Anxiety-Producing for You?

Identity and Social Media

Is self-representation on social media making you second-guess yourself? Although social media is a relatively new concept, famous thinkers and philosophers of old have pondered and speculated for many years on the topic of "the authentic self" (Woolever, 2013). Trying to define and understand what is an "authentic self" was already in vogue during philosopher Kierkegaard's life in the 1800s and it continues to perplex us today in the twenty-first century, especially within the context of social media.

Since social media is increasingly becoming a part of modern society, some suggest that it plays a progressive role in self-development. One of the ways it does this is by enabling users to narrate or "story" their lives as well as present an image of themselves (McLean & Breen, 2016). The uniqueness of social media is the ability to reveal what we want to reveal about ourselves. In fact, social media allows us not only to selectively show the best aspects of our lives, but some argue that with a little creativity it also grants the freedom to access the "development of unlimited self-identity" (Moningka, 2017). Researchers such as Smith (2008) suggest that there is no such thing as a "fake" identity in cyberspace since it remains an extension or representation of who the users are. This implies a different way of validating an identity and suggests that the criterion to determine if the identity is "functional" is whether or not the identity is accepted by an online community (Smith, 2008). This certainly grants the social media users a great deal of freedom in the way they represent themselves online. And yet, this vast freedom seems to delight only for a moment or two before new struggles emerge. Suddenly the lines between online identity and offline identity start to blur. Although there might not be a "real" or "fake" identity online, the relationship between the online identity and the offline identity certainly does fall in the category of "real" or "fake" (Smith, 2008). According to renowned psychologist Carl Rogers, every person has a "real self" as well as an "ideal self" they strive and aspire to become which motivates the person to evolve (Ismail & Tekke, 2015). Unfortunately, the larger the gap between the ideal self and the real, or current self, the more anxiety the person experiences due to the inconsistency they perceive in themselves (Ismail & Tekke, 2015). A large gap between the two selves also damages the person's sense of self-worth and triggers more defensive responses (Ismail & Tekke, 2015). Therefore, if we represent our ideal selves on social media and we recognize a significant inconsistency between our ideal online representation and our "real" offline identity, we may experience anxiety, insecurities and dissatisfaction with ourselves and our lives. Although social media is supposed to provide a limited glimpse of ourselves, we may be at risk of reversing the process and allowing social media to dictate who we should be and what our lives should look like instead of reflecting what they are. Any solutions? Well, according to Rogers, we would need to find a way to reduce the gap between our ideal online representation so it can be closer to our real offline selves and the two selves can be more congruent or "authentic."

Self-Comparison

Self-comparison is another potential anxiety-producing culprit. By easily connecting with others through social media, we also have more opportunities to see glimpses of other people's lives. With that beautiful opportunity, we also encounter a potential pitfall of living in community: comparing ourselves with others. Because we are social creatures, self-comparison in small doses is normal and even useful since it helps us adjust our behaviour by being aware of cultural behavioural norms which improves our chances to belong and be accepted by others (Hess & Pickett, 2010). We often do this without even realizing it. But in spite of being socially beneficial in small doses, self-comparison can lead to rather damaging ends if left unchecked. In fact, the previously mentioned notion that cyberspace enables a limitless development of identity (Moningka, 2017) offers a frightening new perspective of self-comparison in the age of social media. Indeed, if the users' online self-representation is limitless, then we may find ourselves comparing our "real" lives with idealized virtual representations that are not necessarily rooted in the non-virtual reality. In this way, self-comparison would be like measuring ourselves by using an optical illusion as a measuring stick. In fact, according to a study, "frequent Facebook users believed that other users were happier and more successful than themselves [because] people compared their realistic self with the idealized online selves of others" (Moningka, 2017). This comparison game can become a very slippery slope, especially since it can be difficult to tell how truly idealized other people's online representations are. Unfortunately, the psychological consequences of self-comparing such as stress, anxiety and depression can be significant (Moningka, 2017). As previously mentioned, renowned theorist Carl Rogers stipulated that everyone strives to reduce the gap between their ideal and their real version of self which increases our well-being and enables us to be well balanced "self-actualized" people (Ismail & Tekke, 2015). But the struggle of comparing our current real self with the ideal self we aspire to be can be quite discouraging and psychologically troubling if the gap is considerably large. If we add self-comparison on social media to this equation, a new struggle appears on the horizon. Suddenly, users not only struggle to bridge the gap between their ideal and real selves, but they also struggle to keep up with everyone else's ideal self as represented online. All of a sudden, an overwhelming tidal wave of idealistic gaps must be filled instead of one. Although the consequences of self-comparison on social media can be numerous, for the purposes of this chapter, we will divide self-comparison into harmful by-products: pride and competition, as well as low self-esteem.

Pride

As previously mentioned, the psychological consequences of self-comparison can take quite a toll. Therefore, with such risks to our mental health, why do we find it difficult to stop comparing ourselves on social media? Some of us might even describe this as a compulsive habit. But what might be at the root, driving this desire or habit? What is it that prompts us to measure ourselves against another? Self-comparison, as a psychological phenomenon, can be defined as "the act of comparing oneself to others in order to gain personal worth" (Moningka, 2017). In other words, self-comparison can be described as a quest seeking self-validation. The reasons why we undertake that quest might differ from one person to another, after all everyone is different. But a potential consequence of measuring ourselves against others is developing a mentality of competition which unfortunately transforms the people around us into competitors. Another way of understanding this competition of self-worth is pride. "There are two kinds of pride, both good and bad. 'Good pride' represents our dignity and self-respect. 'Bad pride' is the deadly sin of superiority that reeks of conceit and arrogance" (Maxwell, n.d.).

Scholars often disagree with each other on the topic of pride, although many argue that there are different versions of pride ranging from the good, the bad and the ugly (Carter & Gordon, 2017). The type of pride we are exploring in this context is essentially the competitive nature striving to establish superiority over our fellow human beings. C.S. Lewis, a renowned British thinker, illustrated this phenomenon with the explanation that if someone takes pride in their intelligence, they do not in fact take satisfaction in their intelligence itself, but rather in having more of it than the next person. Indeed, if everyone suddenly became equally as brilliant overnight, that person would simply stop taking pride in their intellect (1952). The same can be said about taking pride in our accomplishments, good looks or popularity, if it suddenly became average and commonplace, there would be no "bragging rights." Therefore, pride is by its very nature competitive because it strives to "one up" everyone else. It is "the comparison that makes you proud: the pleasure of being above the rest. Once the element of competition has gone, pride has gone" (Lewis, 1952). Alas, this is part of our human nature and no one can entirely escape the siren call of pride. After all, wanting to be seen and validated is only a natural longing. But pride goes beyond this longing by identifying itself according to its ego or "self-importance" (Carter & Gordon, 2017). Self-importance tends to convince us there is no better way of validating ourselves than proving that we stand above the masses of commoners. Perhaps showing off our superiority might seem like an efficient way of gaining approval, validation and ultimately the relationships and affection every human being wants. But pride has a way of backfiring. Indeed, everyone's pride, or ego, is in constant competition with everyone else's pride (Lewis, 1952). C.S. Lewis suggested that the easiest way of determining how prideful we are, for indeed we all are to some degree, is to ask ourselves how deeply offensive other people's pride is to us. The more offended we are at someone else's self-importance and prideful disposition, the more prideful we are likely to be because pride is "one vice of which no [one] in the world is free; which everyone in the world loathes when he sees it in someone else; and of which hardly any people … ever imagine that they are guilty themselves … And the more we have it ourselves, the more we dislike it in others" (Lewis, 1952, p. 121).

Fortunately, many of us are not overly afflicted by pride and self-importance. But then again, to say that others are more prideful than we are, is a terribly prideful comparison in itself. Clearly, pride is a slippery slope with many twists and turns. But within the context of social media, one of the damaging consequences has to be relational. After all, who among us enjoy the company of someone constantly seeking to promote themselves above everyone else's interests? Who would look forward to being told that in the great competition of humanity, you rank after them? Logically, you would conclude that this person's self-interest outranks their interest in you, which makes their company less trustworthy, let alone enjoyable. After all, pride is typically considered a "self-oriented emotion" (Carter & Gordon, 2017). Since it is part of our human nature to want to belong and connect with other people, it seems as though pride is doing the opposite. Instead of bridges, pride creates barriers. Within the world of social media, pride's competitive nature and airs of superiority would logically facilitate isolation instead of the relationships and genuine community for which we all long. But can we reverse the effects of pride in our relationships? Can we keep our pride in check and reign in our ego? Fortunately, yes. These questions will be explored later in this chapter in the section on "Positive Mediators."

Low Self-Esteem

Low self-esteem is one of the unfortunate by-products of self-comparison. The concept of self-esteem is essentially the subjective process of evaluating ourselves in our different roles to determine our self-worth (McLean & Breen, 2016). In other words, we try to determine if we're good friends, partners, workers, and if we have desirable characteristics in general which people around us find valuable. This self-evaluation can become more complex when we start using other people as standards by which to measure our own value. Self-comparison can leave social media users feeling pressured to measure up to what they perceive to be other people's average, and failing to do so may create a painful sense of inferiority. As previously mentioned, Facebook users often believed that others seem happier and more successful (Moningka, 2017). Low self-esteem can be the unfortunate consequence of self-comparison when we arrive to the subjective conclusion that we do not measure up to our own ideal (Ismail & Tekke, 2015), let alone when compared to everyone else's ideals.

But self-comparison isn't all bad, as previously mentioned, it can come in handy in order to adjust our behaviour according to the norm. A quick comparison might inform a child that picking your nose in public is frowned upon and anti-social. As human beings, we all have a "fundamental need to belong" and thus we strive to be accepted in order to avoid the pain of rejection (Hess & Pickett, 2010). This is normal. It is also normal to aspire to make a good impression in social circumstances and want to put your "best foot forward" so to speak. After all, who would not cringe at the thought of making a fool of oneself in public? We've all been there – and no one wants to go back.

An amusing example of this is a test conducted as part of the Asch Conformity Experiments which took place in the 1950s with a group of strangers in an elevator. The goal of this famous experiment was to determine if a person riding the elevator would conform to the majority, who were paid actors, and face the back of the elevator for no apparent reason. After a quick glance around, each of the unsuspecting candidates of this psychological experiment realized that they were the only ones facing the front and decided to conform with the rest of the group by turning their back to the door. Asch's experiments showed that the desire to conform to a group is a normal part of being a social creature. However, he also demonstrated the depth to which social pressure can influence individuals to do nonsensical things they normally wouldn't do (Asch, 1955). The experiments found that individuals who conformed the most believed that the difference between them and the majority suggested a flaw or deficiency which needed to be hidden and thus "they desperately tried to merge with the majority, not realizing the longer-range consequences to themselves" (Asch, 1955). In this regard, self-comparison can awaken insecurities and motivate the self-conscious person to hide by conforming to the majority. This can easily become a vicious cycle of low self-esteem: we use self-comparison as a way to seek reassurance, but the self-comparison reveals differences which strengthen the desire or belief that conformity is necessary. In this case, if we believe that everyone else is better off than us, then the practice of self-comparison becomes nothing more than a practice of self-criticism, reminding ourselves of all the ways we fall short. This type of self-preoccupation is nothing short of a heavy and painful burden which seeks liberation from the self. Although every human being without exception has unconditional value, worth and intrinsic dignity (Woolever, 2013), self-comparison can easily sneak in and silently sow seeds of doubts and insecurities. In an attempt to remedy this and increase our self-esteem, or self-evaluation, some of us may be tempted to turn to social media for validation. However, social media might also produce more anxiety if the "cure" to self-esteem is believed to be an ever-growing "harvest of 'likes'" (Andreassen et al., 2017). This can lead to detrimental disappointments when the person does not receive as many "likes" or positive comments as first expected or sought after. This may lead to a vicious cycle of feeding a need to please and a fear of rejection online, especially for those of us who perceive social media as an extension of self (Moningka, 2017). Being mindful of the need driving our social media consumption can prove enlightening and help us avoid pitfalls such as believing that the degree to which we please others on social media is a reflection of our self-worth and merit.

Positive Mediators: the Building Blocks of Resilience

Although this is not an extensive list of potential struggles modern-day users encounter on social media, self-comparison, self-representation, pride/competition, low self-esteem and fear of rejection might possibly represent some of the most popular obstacles damaging our experience of social networking sites. And this begs the question – how can we cope with these struggles and recover a healthier way of approaching social media in an age where they reign uncontested? How can we improve our hand-eye coordination when using our hammer, so to speak? As we previously explored, social media can enable us to narrate our lives and present an image of self which becomes an extension of our identity to some degree. This helps explain why we feel so attached to what happens on social media and the depth of its impact on our lives. Because it has so much power to influence us and the way we see ourselves and others, it seems only logical that we would aspire to have as healthy a relationship with social media as possible. This is where resilience is key. However, resilience can be difficult to define properly because it looks so different from one person to another. Because everyone has their own unique baggage, weaknesses, insecurities, aspirations and obstacles to overcome, it stands to reason that no two struggles are identical; just like one person's social media habits might not work for another person. One person may be indifferent to self-comparison on social media while another person may suffer from the negative consequences of a compulsive habit of comparing themselves to others. But regardless of the individual struggles, the first step to resilience is acknowledging that something is not as it should be and therefore needs improvement.

Since virtually no research has explored resilience with social media to this day, here is a simple way of merging these two topics. Our understanding of having a resilient relationship with social media is not the absence of struggles, but rather the ability to be conscious of those struggles and yet seek a way to adapt more positively within that environment. The way in which people may "adapt positively" may change from one person to another, but the commonality is found in the desire to adopt a healthier, more balanced status quo where the positive factors are maximized and the negative ones minimized. So how can we incorporate resilience in our social media use? Here are some suggestions, considered "protective factors" (Benvenuti et al., 2017), to help us adapt positively to the world of social media and overcome these common pitfalls.

Humility

One of the main benefits of social media is the ability to connect with others, which offers the opportunity to satisfy our human need to thrive through relationships (Woolever, 2013). In fact, some researchers suggest that building genuine relationships online can help increase one's general satisfaction in life because positive interactions online lead to a more positive view of self in the non-virtual world (Moningka, 2017). In other words, healthy online relationships lead to a healthier offline life. But in order to establish healthy and genuine relationships online or offline, one has to step away from a competitive self-comparison outlook. As previously mentioned, the consequences of pride can create relational barriers instead of bridges. In order to distance ourselves from pride, we must explore its opposite. Humility can be defined, according to the Merriam-Webster dictionary, as "freedom from pride or arrogance," and thus is generally considered the opposite of pride (Carter & Gordon, 2017). C.S. Lewis, in his renowned BBC radio talk aired during the Second World War, interestingly referred to humility as the "getting rid of the false self" as though pride demanded games and masquerades aimed at winning praise from an audience (1952). He suggested that this "getting rid of the false self" was so refreshing that "to get even near [humility], even for a moment, is like a drink of cold water to a man in a desert" (1952). Indeed, to step away from these tiresome and endless games sponsored by our pride and acquire humility is considered a great relief which leads to self-contentment. In fact, empirical studies have found that "humility involves having an accurate view of self" and the ability to be honest about one's strengths and weaknesses without experiencing a need to impress others (Lavelock et al., 2014). However, humility must not be mistaken for low self-esteem or even self-abasement which is a common misconception. In fact, "humility is not thinking less of yourself, it's thinking of yourself less" (Lewis, 1952). Humility does not consist of belittling ourselves, but rather of "transcending ourselves" because it enables us to be more altruistic since it minimizes our ego and restrains "egotistic motives" (Lavelock et al., 2014). Even Albert Einstein has expressed the great merit of one who "has attained liberation from the self" (Einstein, 1954). Therefore, humility has been proven to be an important trait in facilitating high quality relationships because it liberates from self-preoccupation and enables "a worldview that expands beyond self-interest" (Lavelock et al., 2014). In the same BBC talk, C.S. Lewis described a humble person as someone who takes genuine interest in other people without necessarily drawing or requiring attention to themselves (1952). Therefore, humility transforms the other from a mere praise-dispensing audience to a real independent human being with his or her own strengths and weaknesses. Although humility is proven to be associated with many benefits such as physical health, higher academic and professional performance, adaptability during transitions and openness to new ideas (Lavelock et al., 2014), it is because it facilitates better relationships that humility is profitable within social media. An example of a practical application of humility on social media could be a change of perspective from seeking self-validation to deliberately giving back to others. This intentional decision may not come naturally, but it certainly is the best way to break our self-seeking habits. As the inspiring author and civil rights activist, Maya Angelou, famously said: "I've learned that people will forget what you said, people will forget what you did, but people will never forget how you made them feel." Generously validating others may be the most efficient way to remove the focus from ourselves and our self-comparison ways. And since humility represents a lack of competitive self-interest, relationships tend to flourish, which also facilitates a higher self-esteem (McLean & Breen, 2016).

Mindfulness

A change of perspective is certainly an important aspect of resilience. Indeed simply acknowledging that the status quo is not good enough and that something better is possible is already an enormous change of perspective and a fundamental change facilitating resilience. And as wonderful as humility can be, there are also other practices which can help us improve our relationship with social media. The popular practice of mindfulness comes highly recommended by experts to help us be more conscious and intentional in our daily practice – which includes our social media use (Benvenuti et al., 2017). Central to the practice of mindfulness is the cultivation of a non-judgemental attitude thus leading towards self-compassing which positively influences "one's interpretation of internal experiences" (Miron, 2012). Unlike self-esteem, which falters during periods of failures, self-compassion means extending kindness, caring and understanding towards ourselves, our shortcomings, flaws, imperfections and our pain. It is also considered to be "a significant predictor of happiness and positive [emotions], and may act as a buffer against negative emotions and experiences" (Miron, 2012). In fact, although mindfulness can help us be more self-compassionate, it is self-compassion itself which is considered the greater indicator of well-being and good mental health (Miron, 2012). Within our social media use, self-compassion can certainly help us remember that perfection is not attainable and therefore we should accept ourselves with "unconditional positive regard" (Woolever, 2013).

Gratitude

The timeless practice of gratitude also comes highly recommended. In fact, gratitude has been a practice universally encouraged across various ethnicities and every major religion (Emmons & McCullough, 2003). Similarly to humility changing our perspective from self-oriented to other-oriented, gratitude can change our perspective from focusing on what we lack to focusing on what we currently enjoy. It is considered an "adaptive psychological strategy" which increases our "ability to notice, appreciate, and savor" that which contributes to our well-being (Emmons & McCullough, 2003). In other words, gratitude can be a tool to help us adapt and respond more positively to our circumstances and enjoy aspects of our well-being.

Studies have found that gratitude cultivates benefits such as a higher level of well-being, more positive feelings, stronger prosocial behaviours, altruism, "broadened mindsets" and also "facilitates coping with stress and adversity" (Emmons & McCullough, 2003). Within the context of social media, gratitude can help us gain a new perspective by realizing that our lives are fuller than we might have expected. By appreciating the fullness of our lives and our ability to enjoy "the experience of living into [our] unique potential" (Woolever, 2013), we might be better at remembering that life is vastly greater than a profile picture or the amount of comments sought after. Indeed, since social media can only show a limited glimpse of who we are, the depth of a full life cannot be adequately captured and represented on social media.

Conclusion

For many of us, our relationship with social media can bring up mixed emotions as we journey through its many shades of grey. It is not surprising that it can be rather easy and even unintentional to fall into an unhealthy pattern when using social media sites and applications. If you think about it, there are no manuals or seminars on how to properly use social media outlets. Although there is a plethora of studies that examine the impact social media can have on our mental health or social connections, there are limited resources available for users that provide information on how to use social media in a positive and constructive way.

If we think back to the example of the hammer, some of us may have been taught by others how to properly use this tool; we may have even learned a lesson after accidentally hammering our thumb rather than the nail. Most of us will learn to intentionally change our actions and our behaviours in order to avoid this pain again. Naturally we become more attentive the next time we use the hammer, we may pay more attention to our grip and take slower, more calculated swings that are aimed at the nail rather than our thumb or fingers. In the end we become more aware of our actions and intentions. Hopefully this chapter has achieved its goal and encourages its readers to be more self-aware in the world of social media. By identifying some of the pitfalls of our social media use we hope that novice and experienced users become more attentive and conscious of the way they are using various outlets. By further questioning our intentions and needs when it comes to social media, we have more power in affecting change for ourselves and others. By utilizing humility we learn to think of others rather than ourselves, and when implementing mindfulness and self-compassion we practice being kind to ourselves and others even in light of our shortcomings and differences. Gratitude brings us to the present, giving us the opportunity to truly be thankful for what we have in our lives and for who we are, rather than being fixated on what we lack, what we don't have, or what we wish we were. Although self-awareness can be painful at times, it is a deeply rewarding endeavour which promotes a healthier and more balanced lifestyle – and hopefully a healthier and more balanced relationship with social media as well.

References

Andreassen, C., Pallesen, S., & Griffiths, M. (2017). The relationship between addictive use of social media, narcissism, and self-esteem: Findings from a large national survey. *Addictive Behaviors*, 64(1), 287–293.

Asch, S.E. (1955). Opinions and social pressure. *Scientific American*, 193(5), 31–35.

BBC News School Project Report (2017, 1 March). FOMO: How the fear of missing out drives social media "addiction". BBC News.

Benvenuti, M., Mazzoni, E., & Piobbico, G. (2017). Being online in emerging adulthood: Between problematic or functional use of the internet. In Michelle F. Wright (Ed.), *Identity, sexuality, and relationships among emerging adults in the digital age* (pp. 226–246). United States: IGI Global.

Carter, J.A., & Gordon, E.C. (2017). *The moral psychology of pride*. New York: Rowman & Littlefield.

Einstein, Albert (1954). *Ideas and opinions*. New York: Crown Publishers.

Emmons, R.A., & McCullough, M.E. (2003). Counting blessings versus burdens: An experimental investigation of gratitude and subjective well-being in daily life. *Journal of Personality and Social Psychology*, 84, 377–389. doi:10.1037/0022-3514.84.2.377.

Hess, Yanine D., & Pickett, Cynthia L. (2010). Social rejection and self- versus other-awareness. *Journal of Experimental Social Psychology*, 46(2), 453–456.

Ismail, N.A.H., & Tekke, M. (2015). Rediscovering Rogers's self theory and personality. *Journal of Education, Health and Community Psychology*, 4(3), 2088–3129.

Lavelock, C.R., Worthington, E.L., Davis, D.E., Griffin, B.J., Reid, C.A., Hook, J.N., & Tongeren, D.R. (2014) The quiet virtue speaks: An intervention to promote humility. *Journal of Psychology and Theology*, 42(1), 99–110.

Lewis, C.S. (1952). *Mere Christianity*. New York: HarperCollins.

McLean, K., & Breen, A. (2016). Selves in a world of stories during emerging adulthood. In J.J. Arnett (Ed.), *The Oxford handbook of emerging adulthood* (part 8, pp. 1–31). Oxford: Oxford University Press.

Maxwell, John C. (n.d.). BrainyQuote.com. Retrieved December 27, 2020, from www.brainyquote.com/quotes/john_c_maxwell_600899.

Miron, L. (2012). A comparison of self-compassion and mindfulness in predicting psychological distress, health status, and well-being. ProQuest Dissertations Publishing.

Moningka, C. (2017). Self-comparison: The self in digital world. In Michelle F. Wright (Ed.), *Identity, sexuality, and relationships among emerging adults in the digital age* (pp. 18–26). United States: IGI Global.

Smith, Aaron P. (2008). Real vs. fake: Identity creation in cyberspace. ProQuest Dissertations Publishing.

Tomczyka, Łukasz, & Selmanagic-Lizde, Elma (2018). Fear of missing out (FOMO) among youth in Bosnia and Herzegovina: Scale and selected mechanisms. *Children and Youth Services Review*, 88, 541–549.

Woolever, Susan (2013). The process of self-becoming in the thought of Søren Kierkegaard and Carl Rogers. ProQuest Dissertations Publishing.

4 Resilience in the Older Adult

Judith Malette and Nicolas Galton

The Story of Ava

Ava is 75 years old. Twenty-five years ago, she divorced from her husband of 30 years, went back to school, obtained a degree in nursing. She states being proud to have worked in the field until she retired at 65. She has been living with her daughter, Helena, for a few years. Both women describe a secure attachment which contrasts with what they experienced with Ava's husband, Helena's father, whom they describe as a violent man. Ava has been diagnosed with kidney failure and she undergoes hemodialysis three times a week. The treatment is demanding, and Ava feels exhausted afterwards. It also leaves her little time to visit friends, whom she misses very much. Steps have also been taken to promote autonomy and a sense of competence in Ava. For instance, Helena helped her mother to befriend the idea of using a walker, and she now goes for short walks, by herself. Also, Helena once took the taxi with Ava to show her how to get to the Dialysis Centre. This learning experience taught Ava how to get to the Centre by herself, i.e. without having to wait for Helena to drive her back and forth. Ava was concerned about her walker and wondered if the taxi driver would allow her to bring it with her in the car; she identified this as a stressor. When he arrived at their house, she addressed the issue with him. He readily accepted to put the walker in the trunk of the car. Ava was pleased, and relieved, and asked him if she could reserve his services three times a week to which he agreed. Ever since, Ava has called him her "chauffeur" and considers him a friend as she has gotten to know him over the years. Also, with her social worker, Elisa, Ava explored how she could still keep in touch with her friends, e.g. meeting with them on Zoom with the initial assistance from Helena. Finally, Ava took part in Life Review (LR) with Elisa. LR, a narrative technique described later in the chapter, promotes resilience and facilitates adaptation to the ageing process. Through LR, Ava identified the importance of relationships with her daughter, friends, chauffeur and social worker (quality of attachments), God (spiritual beliefs) and the importance of taking care of one's body (by doing chair yoga, and taking walks) as the pillars of her life.

Introduction

The industrialized world has witnessed an unprecedented surge in longevity over the last century, with Canadian women's life expectancy increasing by 20.5 years, and men's by 23 years from 1920 to 2011 (Statistics Canada,

2018a). It is expected that the Canadian older adult population will represent approximately 25 per cent of the total population by 2036 (Statistics Canada, 2018b). Despite this significant increase, some countries like the United States, and the United Kingdom, have been experiencing a decline in life expectancy, especially in individuals younger than 65 years of age, mainly due to the ongoing opioid epidemic (Ho & Hendi, 2018). Canada is not foreign to this tragic reality as "(L)ife expectancy … has stopped increasing for the first time in more than four decades, due largely to soaring overdose deaths in the Western provinces" (Woo, 2019). Since people do die younger than the average life expectancy, for a number of other reasons as well, e.g. cancer, cardiovascular disease, chronic vascular disease, accidents (Statistics Canada, 2019), might getting older be a privilege rather than a burden, as it is often depicted through negative stereotypes of older adults described as either ill or disabled (Palmore, 1999)? Indeed, the process of ageing spans further than the losses commonly associated with this stage of life. In this chapter, we will explore the role of resilience in the experience of ageing. First, we will define what the term "older adults" refers to from a chronological lens. Then, general characteristics associated with older adults and ageing will be presented and will hopefully demystify this life period. In the second section of the chapter, resilience in older adults, and its determinants (personal characteristics, quality of attachments, beliefs and temporality) will be described. Then, resilience will be differentiated from successful ageing. Finally, we will describe how a narrative therapy technique, namely Life Review (LR, hereafter), can foster resilience in the elderly.

Older Adults: A Definition

Chronological Age

In the general population, as well as in research and policy-making, one will often hear the terms senior population or older adult population, which typically refer to individuals aged 65 years and older (American Psychological Association, 2014). However, sociologists Little and McGivern (2014) refer to three phases of ageing: the young-old (65–74 years old), the middle-old (ages 75 to 84) and the old-old (over age 85). In comparison, psychologists and psychiatrists Reynolds, Pietrzak, El-Gabalawy, Mackenzie and Sareen (2015) divide the elderly population into four groups: the young-old (55–64 years old), the middle-old (65–74 years old), the old-old (75–84 years old), and the oldest-old (85 years and older). According to Del Corno and Plotkin (2017a), Little and McGivern (2014) and Reynolds et al. (2015), ageing is not a monolithic experience, and it can vary across generations. For instance, Little and McGivern (2014) mention that the young-old age group reports being happier, healthier and wealthier than the previous generation. Also, an increasing number of individuals live beyond 80 years of age, and even beyond 100 years: these two groups being expected to double and triple, respectively, by 2036 (Statistics Canada, 2018b). Therefore, being an older adult cannot be limited to a single experience, regrouping everyone aged 65 years and older. Let us now describe the general characteristics associated with ageing, beyond what is known as ageism, a multidimensional construct described by stereotypes (misconceptions about older adults), separation (distance between older adults), and affective attitudes (negative emotions towards older adults) (Rupp, Vodanovich, & Credé, 2005), and also beyond an idealized perception of ageing, positive ageism, where values such as wisdom, serenity, and thrift are projected onto the elderly population (Palmore, 1999).

General Characteristics

Ageing is both inevitable and normal. It takes place in every being: plants, animals and humans. Nature reminds us that nothing is permanent in life and that one is ever changing. However, in industrialized countries where progress in medicine can give one the illusion of eternal youth, or of slowing down the ageing process, addressing what old age entails can be associated with much anxiety (de Hennezel, 2009; Jacquemin, 2010; Rupp et al., 2005).

In humans, normal ageing is associated with an increase in cardiovascular diseases and sleep disturbances as well as some sensory impairment in sight and hearing (Palmore, 1999) along with touch, taste and smell becoming less precise and sensitive afterwards (United States National Library of Medicine, 2019). As senses play a significant role in one's social interactions, especially touch in interpersonal relationships (Rovers, Malette & Guirguis-Younger, 2018), sensory impairment can be restrictive, and thus increase isolation. Still, according to Del Corno and Plotkin (2017b, p. 763) "the capacity for relatedness[1] may be preserved or even increase" in ageing, and as such can potentiate resilience (Cyrulnik & Jorland, 2012) as will be seen in the section "Determinants of Resilience in Older Adults." These sensory changes can be attributed to the impact of ageing on the nervous system: with age, the brain and the spinal cord decrease in weight and volume, which leads to psychomotor retardation (a slowing in physical and affective reactions), and a slowing of memory and cognitive processing (United States National Library of Medicine, 2019). Cognitive decline though varies significantly from one person to the next with some being affected very lightly, while others suffer from dementia (Ploton & Cyrulnik, 2014; United States National Library of Medicine, 2019). This speaks to the heterogeneity of the experience of ageing: some individuals do not recognize their own family members whereas others are highly functional and still hold significant responsibilities at an advanced age. For instance, Ruth Bader Ginsburg was 87 years old, and a United States Supreme Court Justice, and Pope Francis is 83 years old, and is the head of the Catholic Church.

The changes described earlier take place in a normal ageing process and can yield to a gradual loss of independence, autonomy and even, possibly, agency (Del Corno & Plotkin, 2017b). Additionally, the loss of friends and family members to illness, death or separation due to the admission to a residential care facility can amplify the loneliness experienced following sensory impairment, and in some cases contribute to the development and/or maintenance of depression, anxiety and substance abuse (Reynolds et al., 2015). Yet, despite such losses, ageing has consistently been associated with emotional well-being, life satisfaction and a capacity to find meaning in one's life (Blazer, 2006; Butler, 1995; Cappeliez, 2018; Del Corno & Plotkin, 2017a; Kenyon, Bohlmeijer & Randall, 2011; MacKinlay, 2012). Reynolds et al. (2015) also indicate "a general pattern of decreasing rates of psychiatric disorders with increasing age" (p. 74). This does not mean that the prevention, diagnosis and treatment of mental health disorders should be undermined in older adults. However, it does suggest that subjective and psychological well-being[2] can be experienced in the later years. Indeed, Jest et al. (2013) and Thomas et al. (2016) conducted two independent Successful AGing Evaluation (SAGE) studies, with 1,006 participants aged 50–99 years, and 1,546 aged 21–100 years, respectively. Both studies found a linear improvement in mental health, i.e. mood, stress management and life satisfaction, over the adult lifespan despite the presence of physical and cognitive functioning declines, even after controlling for income, education and marital status. They also stressed the importance of taking into consideration psychosocial and biological variables, as described earlier, in order to improve the understanding of resilience in older age. Tkatch et al. (2017) reached a similar conclusion, emphasizing the roles of these two variables and their reciprocal interactions on resilience in older adults.

The above paradox on ageing has been explained in a number of ways. The first explanation relies on an increased awareness of one's mortality and of others', which engenders a shift in one's life goals where relationships and activities described as meaning-giving take precedence over performance and production (Carstensen, 2011; Jest et al., 2013; Malette & Oliver, 2006; Malette & Pencer, 2003). The second explanation emphasizes wisdom,[3] defined as "a multi-component personality traits that includes empathy, compassion, self-knowledge, openness to new ideas, decisiveness, emotional regulation, and doing things for others" (Jest, 2016, para. 12). The third explanation points towards an increased response of the amygdala[4] to positive images compared to negative/stressful images (Mather et al., 2004).

To our knowledge, no definitive conclusion has been reached to elucidate this "paradox." What if this was not a paradox and was actually part of "growing older," of learning and developing a new way of being as opposed to "getting older"? Indeed, despite its typical physical and variable cognitive limitations, research has shown that ageing can be a period of opportunity to learn new roles (retiree, grandparent, mentor), and new ways of doing and being (Del Corno & Plotkin, 2017b; Malette & Oliver, 2006; Malette & Pencer, 2003). In a qualitative study on the experience of retirees, Malette and Oliver (2006) found that adjusting to a new compensatory mode of being and doing promotes:

1 a more benevolent self-definition;
2 the possibility of learning; and that
3 changing at an advanced age is possible.

For instance, one may not be as productive as they used to be, but they remain fruitful, sharing their knowledge, passion and values with people who are meaningful to them, e.g. mentoree, friends, family members. This capacity to change and compensate for losses is reflected by research on the neuroplasticity of the brain which "retains a considerable functional plasticity" (Mora, 2013, p. 45), providing certain conditions are met, such as physical exercise and a reduction of chronic stress.

The general characteristics associated with ageing – normality, inevitability, heterogeneity, the said age paradox – and the possibility of change seem to speak to the importance of adaptation in one's experience of ageing. Furthermore, this possibility of change is not foreign to the development and maintenance of resilience.

Resilience in the Older Adult

Definition

The American Psychological Association (2020, para. 4) defines resilience as: the process of adapting well in the face of adversity, trauma, tragedy, threats or significant sources of stress – such as family and relationship problems, serious health problems, or workplace and financial stressors. As much as resilience involves "bouncing back" from these difficult experiences, it can also involve profound personal growth. Boris Cyrulnik, a leading figure in the study of resilience, also emphasizes the adaptive process when defining resilience as opposed to it being a personality trait:[5] "(it is) the capacity to succeed, to live, to develop, in spite of adversity" (Cyrulnik, 2002, back cover; free translation by the authors). He later included the concept of trauma in his definition: "(resilience is) the resumption of a new development after trauma" (Cyrulnik, 2012 as cited in Cyrulnik & Jorland, 2012, p. 192; free translation by the authors). Fricchione and Nejad's (2012) definition, which applies to any age period, closely resembles those of the APA and Cyrulnik's, with their focus on adaptation in the face of significant adversity:

> (Resilience) consists of: 1) experiencing reward and motivation; 2) circumscribing fear responsiveness so that one can continue to be effective through active coping strategies despite fear; 3) using adaptive social behaviors to secure support through bonding and teamwork, and to provide support through altruism; 4) using cognitive skills to reinterpret the meaning of negative stimuli in a more positive light; and 5) integrating a sense of purpose in life with a sense of moral compass, meaning, and spiritual connectedness.
> (Fricchione & Nejad, 2012, p. 367)

Lejeune and Ploton (2012) and Kagan and Pellerin (2014) echo the aforementioned authors and define resilience in older adults as a dynamic process, i.e. a process demanding a capacity to adapt to chronic adversity, e.g. a number of progressive losses or illnesses.

According to Cyrulnik (2014) and Lejeune and Ploton (2012), older adults who adapt best to losses, grief and sensory impairment are those who have developed a secure attachment and a capacity to mentalize, i.e. to use words corresponding to one's emotional and cognitive experience (Delage, 2014), prior to trauma, or the experienced adverse situation.

A qualitative study conducted by Deegan (2005) on resilience in people with psychiatric disabilities, aged 20 to 69, found that when clinicians showed more interest in the patients' resources than in their pathological symptoms, they developed more resilience. She calls this shift of focus "salutogenesis or the origin of health" (Deegan, 2005, p. 30), and noted its impact on the patients' development of a new sense of self that is no longer restricted to their pathology. This study is in the same vein as Tkatch et al.'s (2017), which showed that older adults are not limited to their losses, sensory impairment or chronic diseases, and that support from family and friends impact their perception of health. We shall see in the next section how the quality of attachments represents one of the psychological determinants in older adults' resilience.

Let us now go back to Ava. After 30 years of marriage, during which she experienced domestic violence, she made the decision to divorce. She then earned a degree in nursing and worked until retiring. Despite the trauma experienced, Ava continued to grow, professionally and personally, developing an identity she has been proud of. Such experience corresponds to resilience, as described earlier. Another resilient dimension of Ava's experience has been her adapting to a chronic medical condition, and learning new ways to remain autonomous, competent and connected with her friends.

Anti-Resilience Factors

Resilience can smoothen the ageing process. However, anti-resilience factors can hamper the latter. Such factors include sensory isolation, often associated with loneliness; denial of ageing; ageing-associated losses; ageism; lack of empathy from staff in residences; family secrets never addressed in therapy or otherwise, yielding to distress, shame and further self-isolation; meaninglessness; and the possibility of losing one's identity by restricting it to traumatic events (Lejeune & Ploton, 2012; Cyrulnik, 2012, 2014) or one's productivity. This "have/own" mode of being (Kagan & Pellerin, 2014; Malette & Oliver, 2006) prevents the older adult from building a new identity based on the "being mode," one that involves a more benevolent self-definition, in continuity with who they are in their essence and less with their productivity, performance or appearance. The factors favouring such building of resilience in older age will be discussed below.

Psychological Determinants of Resilience in Older Adults

Determinants refer to resources that foster resilience and buffer the impact of losses and trauma on one's self and life. We acknowledge that physical exercise, reduction of chronic stress (MacLeod, Musich, Hawkins, Alsgaard & Wicker, 2016; Mora, 2013) and the quality of the physical environment (Lejeune & Ploton, 2012) are important factors of resilience,[6] but we have chosen to focus on psychological determinants in the context of this chapter, i.e. personal characteristics, quality of attachments, beliefs and one's relationship with temporality (Delage, 2014; Lejeune & Ploton, 2012).

Personal Characteristics

Humour, mentalization (Delage, 2014), altruism (Lejeune & Ploton, 2012), creative and mindful choice on how to respond to unexpected events, sensitivity to others' needs and feelings, assertiveness (Del Corno & Plotkin, 2017 a) and self-awareness (Malette & Oliver, 2006) have been considered especially important characteristics in the later years. These attributes speak of the psychological maturity (Lejeune & Ploton, 2012; Wagnild, 2019) of individuals who have lived long enough to be able to take a step back, appraise a situation, learn from it and possibly transcend it (Del Corno & Plotkin, 2017 b). Based on her research and her nursing experience, Wagnild (2003, 2019) identified eight personal characteristics:

1 meaningfulness (purpose, direction and goals in life);
2 staying true to oneself, i.e. having beliefs, values which guide one on a daily basis, including in challenging period;
3 aiming for optimal health (sleep, nutrition, exercise) (2019);
4 equanimity (a balanced perspective of life), i.e. responding to stress with functional coping strategies[7];
5 perseverance, i.e. not giving up on activities and personal and social goals but adapting them to their current physical and psychological condition;
6 connections with friends and family members;
7 "existential loneliness (the recognition of one's unique path and the acceptance of one's life)";
8 "self-reliance, the belief in one's self and capabilities" (2003, p. 42), and consequently acknowledging one's accomplishment over a lifetime.

Quality of Attachment

According to Cyrulnik (2014), one of the most reliable factors of resilience in old age is affective relationships, and regular contacts with meaningful individuals. Indeed, as mentioned earlier, older adults retain the capacity to connect and relate with others despite sensory impairment due to illness, death and separation from friends and loved ones (Del Corno & Plotkin, 2017a). To connect is to be in contact emotionally, to share one's experience, to be heard and to hear the other. To relate, from the latin *relatus*, to stand in some relation, may include other human beings, animals, God or a higher entity, Nature, each of which bears the potential to bring meaning to one's life. The caveat, according to Wagnild (2019), is not to yield to loneliness and isolation, but to reach out. However, reaching out is easier for individuals who have experienced secure attachments.[8] Indeed, according to Lejeune and Ploton (2012), the quality of attachments is a fundamental determinant of resilience. They and Delage (2014) underscore how ageing, with its inherent changes, and one's own finitude, can be a source of insecurity, and increase the need to relate in a significant period of transition in order to feel safer. Further, because friends and loved ones may have departed, the attachment system may require the development of a new secure base. Delage (2014) talks about "circles of resilience" (p. 60) made up of persons, from spouse and children to friends, neighbours and health professionals, whose involvement will vary depending on the level of autonomy and sensory impairment of the older adult. Delage (2014) and Lejeune and Ploton (2012) also identify "tutors of resilience" ("tuteurs de resilience," in French), i.e. "a person of trust who helps the elderly to become aware of his own resources, and promotes their use" (Lejeune & Ploton, 2012, p. 121; free translation from the authors). The tutor journeys with the elderly, and forms a community of trust, empathy and hospitality with the elderly, thus promoting a more secure attachment style.

Finally, the capacity to connect and relate refers to the ontological need of being in relation, and to a movement described as spiritual by Basset (2006), where one allows others to get close; a movement that promotes altruism, increased self-awareness, self-knowledge and meaning (Mallet, Begat & Duchêne, 2012).

Ava's daughter, Helena, her social worker, Elisa, the "chauffeur," and her friends are tutors of resilience and have contributed to Ava's sense of relatedness. Each of them has also helped Ava to experience her autonomy and sociability a little differently in order to honour these personal characteristics, while at the same time adapting to ageing and the impact of her medical condition, e.g. using a walker to remain independent, and continuing to go for short walks, an activity she cherished; getting to the Centre via taxi and becoming friends with her "chauffeur"; Zooming with her friends.

Beliefs

According to Cyrulnik (2014), Griffith (2012) and Pargament and Cummings (2010), religious beliefs can be a resilience factor[9] following traumatic or challenging events as they can structure one's way of living, e.g. healthy diet and exercise, and promote a secure sense of belonging and togetherness that brings appeasement (physical and emotional support), hope, purpose and gratitude. Griffith and Gaby (2005) refer to hope, agency and communion as "existential postures" (p. 109; free translation from the authors) whereas Monod-Zorzi (2012 uses the terms "vital spiritual needs in the older adult" (p. 31) to refer to finding purpose in one's life, giving and receiving love, hope, and experiencing the Transcendent, e.g. God, nature, music.

Distinguishing between religious/spiritual beliefs/needs and existential postures is not our purpose. Nevertheless, let us mention Puchalski et al.'s (2009) definition of spirituality as it is inclusive of spiritual and religious beliefs: "Spirituality is the aspect of humanity that refers to the way individuals seek and express meaning and purpose and they experience their connectedness to the moment, to self, to others, to nature, and to the significant and sacred" (p. 887). Once again, meaning and purpose as well as connectedness stand out as inherent dimensions of one's being.

Del Corno and Plotkin (2017b) and MacKinlay (2012) do not mention the word resilience per se when addressing the role of spirituality in ageing. However, their respective models suggest that the belief in oneself, and in others, promote meaning and purpose, and the vocabulary they use closely resembles that of Cyrulnik (2014), Griffith (2012), Griffith and Gaby (2005), Monod-Zorzi (2012) and Puchalski et al. (2009). Del Corno and Plotkin (2017b) write:

> The capacity for meaning and purpose reflects a sense of belonging to and being an active member of a family, a society, a community … and the ability to not only accept but to work with the ongoing processes of change.
>
> (p. 769)

In her qualitative research, MacKinlay (2012) associates "continuing spiritual growth in later life" (p. 255) to three themes. First, it is associated to *Transformation and Transcendence*, as changes bring older adults to focus beyond themselves to attribute meaning to their experience. She suggests the use of arts, rituals, symbols and LR in assisting in the search for life meaning. Second, it is associated to *Relationships and Connectedness*: participants used the word relationships as a synonym to meaning. Third, participants identified prayer and friends as sources of *Hope* that help them experience the present while at the same time looking forward to tomorrow. Del Corno and Plotkin (2017b) and MacKinlay's models parallel research conducted by Brat (2000), Carstensen (2011), Malette and Pencer (2003), Monbourquette & Lussier-Russel (1992) and Wong (2019), who have found that personal growth and personal meaning making do take place during the later years, including during the last phase of a terminal illness.

Finally, Delage (2014) and Wagnild (2003, 2019) identify the belief in oneself as a source of resilience. Although it could be argued that this is true at every age, we postulate that this becomes even more so in the later years: believing in oneself means being self-aware and realistically hopeful of one's limitations, and adjusting accordingly while at the same time staying true to oneself.

To conclude this section, a determinant of resilience that has been implicit since the beginning of the chapter, temporality, or one's relationship with time, will be presented.

Temporality

According to Cappeliez (2018) and Ségal (2018), one's temporality is intimately associated to one's identity, self-awareness and continuity through time, and thus to one's autobiographical memory. In agreement with Cappeliez (2018) and Ségal (2018), Delage (2014) suggests that for temporality to be a resilience factor, it requires a fluid back and forth navigation between the present, the past and the future. Cappeliez (2018) suggests that remembering personal souvenirs can help to consolidate one's identity, and positive self-concept, especially during the ageing process when the person is confronted with a progressive physical and cognitive fragility, and with death. Indeed, with ageing comes a redefinition of time due to an increased awareness of one's physical finitude.

Despite this existential confrontation, might we put forward that the determinants of resilience (personal characteristics, quality of attachment, beliefs and temporality) contribute to instil meaning in the later years? In that vein, Malette and Oliver (2006), Malette and Pencer (2003) and MacKinlay (2012) suggest that old age is a period when one is more likely to appraise one's life and attribute meaning to the past, the present and the future. Being anchored in the present while at the same time revisiting the past and preparing for the future with a tutor of resilience who also becomes witness to the older adult's life narrative is at the core of LR, as we shall see.

Successful Ageing and Resilience

Considering the significant role resilience plays in the adaptation to ageing, it might be tempting to equate resilience in later life to successful ageing. In order to shed light on this question, successful ageing (SA), and conscious ageing (CA), will be defined, and nuanced with resilience in the older adult.

SA was originally defined as involving: "1) the ability to maintain a low risk of disease and disease-related disability, 2) high mental and physical functions, and 3) active engagement with life" (Rowe & Kahn, 1998, p. 38). A number of researchers have argued that such a definition is restrictive and devalues older adults who do not meet these criteria, and have aimed at expanding Rowe and Kahn's definition (1998) of SA. For instance, Wong (2000, 2019) developed the existential-spiritual model of ageing, which includes religiosity, personal meaning, optimism, commitment and coping. Wong (2019) found that personal meaning, relationship and religious and/or spiritual faith (the triad of meaning therapy), are the best predictors of happiness, perceived well-being and absence of psychopathology in older adults.

Aguerre and Bouffard (2003) argued that a definition of SA should also include spirituality, sexuality and emotional openness. They suggested that forgiveness towards oneself and the other, mindfulness-based stress reduction programmes and LR can promote SA. Instead of SA, Moody (2003) proposes the concept of CA, which does not focus on cultural ideals of success, but conceives of ageing as a developmental phase, the final possibility to become what and who one really wants to be. Autonomy, individuality, expressiveness and self-transcendence are important components of CA which underscore the potential for growth in the older adult. Moody (2003) suggests that one way to achieve personal growth, and possibly CA, is through LR. Therefore, SA is not a form of resilience, although resilience can encompass one, two or all three of the original defining characteristics of SA.

Life Review (LR)

Research suggests that LR promotes resilience in older adults and thus facilitates the adaptation to the ageing process (Aguerre and Bouffard, 2003; Cappeliez, 2018; MacKinlay, 2012; Malette & Oliver, 2006; Moody, 2003; Ségal, 2018; Wong, 2019). LR is a narrative technique that involves more than a remembering of past events:

> (It is) a review and "re-reading" or re-framing of these events. Thus, the individual may come to attribute new, different and possibly more benevolent meanings to past events during the course of LR, based on what he/she experienced in the present. The focus is not to dwell on the past, but to revisit and integrate it in order to live more fully in the present and prepare for the future.
>
> (Malette & Oliver, 2006, p. 31)

According to Cappeliez (2018), Del Corno and Plotkin (2017a), MacKinlay (2012) and Monod-Zorzi (2012), the sense of continuity and identity associated with personal souvenirs has the potential to deepen life meaning. Cyrulnik (2014) even goes as far as stating that an older adult "can only give meaning to past and present life events by sharing the narrative of his life with someone" (p. 9; free translation by the authors).

We believe that LR activates many determinants of resilience. By its very essence, LR implies temporality, an affective and cognitive back and forth between thoughts and emotions associated to the past, present and future. Although LR can foster resilience, it is not a panacea and is contraindicated with individuals who have experienced recent traumas and/or who have obsessive thoughts (Cappeliez, 2018). LR also participates in the weaving of links between events and the older adult, all the while creating a "community" with the tutor of resilience. The role of the story-listener/tutor of resilience is pivotal, not only in terms of his being a new attachment figure, but also because he helps the older adult to identify personal characteristics, experienced in a particular way in the past, that now need some adjustment in the way they are experienced. For instance, Ava's feeling fatigued after her dialysis treatments (adverse event), prevented her from visiting friends as often as she would have liked. Being a sociable person, this weighed heavily on her. Identifying means, e.g. using Zoom, through which she could still be sociable, was a way of honouring her sociability, while at the same time fostering resilience. Although she was not physically present with them, she could still see and hear them, and be present with and to them, and vice versa.

The LR process contributes to what Paul Ricoeur (1983) called the narrative identity where the construction of the narrative participates in the authorship of one's life, and thus in the meaning making of one's life. As Gazenvoort (2015) intently and most relevantly suggests, one's narrative promotes the personal identity, and the social identity, which underscores the importance of connecting, relating and the quality of attachments. LR has also shown to be a relevant tool to identify beliefs throughout one's life (Malette & Pencer, 2003; Malette & Oliver, 2006). For instance, through her LR, Ava identified her relationships, her faith in God, and the importance of taking care of her body as her fundamental values or beliefs which guided her decision-making, and brought meaning to her life. LR also helped Ava to redefine herself in her own eyes and in the eyes of people she cherishes: she is a woman who has *grown* older, not gotten older, i.e. she has integrated past trauma and physical limitations and has learned from them and transcended them. She is a resilient woman who has learned how to use Zoom at 75 years old!

Conclusion

Resilience in the older adult has been described, along with its psychological determinants (personal characteristics, quality of attachments, beliefs and temporality) and LR as a clinical tool promoting resilience. To these determinants, we suggest adding what the self-determination theory considers to be the three innate psychological needs which once satisfied allow one to flourish:[10] "autonomy (experiencing a sense of volition and psychological freedom), competence (feeling effective), and relatedness" (Van den Broeck, Vannsteenkiste, De Witte, Soenens & Lens, 2010, p. 981). These three needs are addressed in Ava's life story, at the beginning of the chapter. LR also speaks to these needs, and consequently contributes to the development and maintenance of resilience in the older adult. We consider LR to act as a bridge between the past, the present and the future; a bridge between a storyteller who narrates their life, including their losses, to a story-listener/tutor of resilience who co-creates meaning with the older person, with whom he forms a community. In a few words, LR addresses the aforementioned psychological determinants of resilience as well as the needs of autonomy, competence and relatedness, by helping the older adult to adapt personal characteristics to their current condition. LR also promotes the development of a narrative identity, and a social identity, both of which put losses and adversity in the broader perspective of one's entire life.

Ageing is normal and a fact of life. As Galton and Stinchcombe (n.d.) have shown, individuals who report fearing the process of dying of others also report more belief in stereotypes about older age. Such findings underline a common association between old age and deterioration. Nevertheless, it is important to distinguish between the dying process and the ageing process; the dying process is not age-bound, and the ageing process is not necessarily characterized by decline. The ageing paradox underscores how it is possible to flourish despite going through losses, and how closely it relates to resilience. Indeed, resilience reminds us that growing after having experienced adversity is possible, and that life is worth living regardless of losses because the human's intrinsic value transcends the latter.

Notes

1 Self-determination theory defines relatedness as the "inherent propensity to feel connected to others, i.e., to be a member of a group, to love and care and be loved and care for" (Van den Broeck et al., 2010, pp. 982–983).

2 Subjective well-being is the experience of emotions perceived as pleasant and positive, whereas psychological well-being is associated to the quality of our relationship with oneself, with others, and the environment, and the attribution of meaning to one's life (Shankland, 2004).

3 The reader will note that Jest (2016)'s definition of wisdom is not one of positive ageism where serenity is glorified.

4 The amygdala is a brain structure involved in the processing of memory, decision-making and emotional response (Amunts et al., 2005).

5 Addressing the debate on resilience as a process versus a personality trait is beyond the scope of this chapter. However, we echo MacLeod et al. (2016, p. 266): "a process versus a stable personality trait (often termed resiliency) suggests that people have the capacity to build and demonstrate resilience, regardless of their socioeconomic backgrounds, personal experiences, or social environments."

6 Contrary to popular belief, a high income has not been identified as a source of resilience (Jest et al., 2013; Thomas et al., 2016; Wagnild, 2003, 2019).

7 Coping strategies are "constantly changing cognitive and behavioral efforts to manage specific external and/or internal demands that are appraised as taxing or exceeding the resources of the person" (Lazarus and Folkman, 1984, p. 141). They are functional when they manage anxiety without having recourse to behaviours with their own side-effects, e.g. drug and/or alcohol use, self-harm.

8 A relationship where the other person is experienced as a secure base, a safe haven, dependable and available, and where one perceives oneself and the other person positively.

9 A nuance is warranted as Griffith (2012) suggests that religious beliefs can also exacerbate stressors when used to justify non-compliance to medical treatments, abuse, and to induce shame and guilt.

10 Flourishing is a concept from positive psychology and is associated with the experiencing of positive emotions, engagement, relationships, meaning and accomplishment (Seligman, 2011).

References

Aguerre, C., & Bouffard, L. (2003). Le vieillissement réussi: Théories, recherches et applications cliniques. *Revue québécoise de psychologie*, 24, 107–129.

American Psychological Association (2014). Guidelines for psychological practice with older adults. *American Psychologist*, 69(1), 34–65. doi:10.1037/a0035063.

American Psychological Association (2020). Building your resilience. Retrieved February 1, 2020 from www.apa.org/topics/resilience.

Amunts, K., Kedo, O., Kindler, M., Pieperhoff, P., Mohlberg, H., Shah, N.J., Habel, U., Schneider, F., & Zilles, K. (2005). Cytoarchitectonic mapping of the human amygdala, hippocampal region and entorhinal cortex: Intersubject variability and probability maps. *Anatomy and Embryology*, 210(5–6), 343–352. doi:10.1007/s00429-005-0025-5.

Basset, L. (2006). Oser faire confiance. *La chair et le souffle*, 1(1), 24–39.

Blazer, D.G. (2006). Spirituality, depression, and the elderly. *Southern Medical Journal*, 99(10), 1178–1179.

Brat, P.T. (2000). Logotherapy in the care of the terminally ill. *Journal of Religious Gerontology*, 11(3–4), 103–117. https://doi.org/10.1300/J078v11n03_09.

Butler, R.N. (1995). Foreword. In B.K. Haight & J.D. Webster (Eds.), *The art and science of reminiscence: Theory, research, methods, and application* (pp. 17–22). Washington, DC: Taylor & Francis.

Cappeliez, P. (2018). *À la lumière de mon passé. Mes souvenirs autobiographiques pour mieux me connaître et me comprendre*. Bruxelles: Éditions Mardaga.

Carstensen, L. (2011). *A long bright future*. New York: Random House.

Cyrulnik, B. (2002). *Un merveilleux malheur*. Paris: Odile Jacob.

Cyrulnik, B. (2012). Limites de la résilience. In B. Cyrulnik & G. Jorland (Eds.), *Résilience. Connaissance de base* (pp. 191–204). Paris: Odile Jacob.

Cyrulnik, B. (2014). Résilience âgée? In L. Ploton & B. Cyrulnik (Eds.), *Résilience et personnes âgées* (pp. 7–17). Paris: Odile Jacob.

Cyrulnik, B., & Jorland, G. (2012). *Résilience. Connaissances de base*. Paris: Odile Jacob.

de Hennezel, M. (2009). *La sagesse d'une psychologue*. Paris: L'oeil Neuf.

Deegan, P.E. (2005). The importance of personal medicine: A qualitative study of resilience in people with psychiatric disabilities. *Scandinavian Journal of Public Health*, 33(Suppl. 66), 29–35. doi:10.1080/14034950510033345.

Delage, M. (2014). Famille et résilience dans le vieillissement. In L. Ploton & B. Cyrulnik (Eds.), *Résilience et personnes âgées* (pp. 53–70). Paris: Odile Jacob.

Del Corno, F., & Plotkin, D. (2017a). Introduction to part V. In V. Lingiardi & N. McWilliams (Eds.), *Psychodynamic manual*, 2nd edn (pp. 751–754). New York: The Guilford Press.

Del Corno, F., & Plotkin, D. (2017b). Profile of mental functioning for the elderly. In V. Lingiardi & N. McWilliams (Eds.), *Psychodynamic manual*, 2nd edn (pp. 755–776). New York: The Guilford Press.

Fricchione, G., & Nejad, S. (2012). Resilience and coping. In M. Cobb, C.M. Puchalski, & B. Rumbold (Eds.), *Oxford textbook of spirituality and healthcare* (pp. 367–373). New York: Oxford University Press.

Gazenvoort, R.R. (2015). *Raconter pour vivre*. Montréal: Novalis.

Griffith, J.L. (2012). Psychiatry and mental health. In M. Cobb, C.M. Puchalski, & B. Rumbold (Eds.), *Oxford textbook of spirituality and healthcare* (pp. 227–233). New York: Oxford University Press.

Griffith, J.L., & Gaby, L. (2005). Brief psychotherapy at the bedside: Countering demoralization from medical illness. *Psychosomatics*, 46(2), 109–116.

Ho, J.Y., & Hendi, A.S. (2018). Recent life expectancy across high income countries: retrospective observational study. *BMJ*, 362, k2562. doi:10.1136/bmj.k2562.

Jacquemin, D. (2010). *Quand l'autre souffre: Éthique et spiritualité*. Bruxelles: Lessius.

Jest, D.V. (2016). The aging paradox: The older we get, the happier we are. Retrieved June 7, 2019 from www.latimes.com/science/sciencenow/la-sci-sn-older-people-happier-20160824-snap-story.html.

Jest, D.V., Savla, G.N., Thomson, W.K., Vahia, I.V., Glorioso, D.K., Martin, A.S., Palmer, B.W., Rock, D., Golshan, S., Kraemer, H.C., & Depp, C.A. (2013). Older age is associated with more successful aging: Role of resilience and depression. *American Journal of Psychiatry*, 170(2), 188–196. doi:10.1176/appi.ajp.2012.12030386.

Kagan, Y., & Pellerin, J. (2014). Grand âge, âgisme et resilience. In L. Ploton & B. Cyrulnik (Eds.), *Résilience et personnes âgées* (pp. 243–273). Paris: Odile Jacob.

Kenyon, G., Bohlmeijer, E., & Randall, W. (2011). *Storying later life: Issues, investigations, and interventions in narrative gerontology*. New York: Oxford University Press.

Lazarus, R.S., & Folkman, S. (1984). *Stress, appraisal, and coping*. New York: Springer.

Lejeune, A., & Ploton, L. (2012). Résilience et vieillissement. In B. Cyrulnik & G. Jorland (Eds.), *Résilience: connaissances de base* (pp. 115–135). Paris: Odile Jacob.

Little, W., & McGivern, R. (2014). Aging and the elderly. In *Introduction to Sociology*, 1st Canadian edition. BCcampus Open Textbook. Retrieved December 28, 2020 from https://opentextbc.ca/introductiontosociology/chapter/chapter13-aging-and-the-elderly/

MacKinlay, E. (2012). Care of elderly people. In M. Cobb, C.M. Puchalski, & B. Rumbold (Eds.), *Oxford textbook of spirituality and healthcare* (pp. 251–256). New York: Oxford University Press.

MacLeod, S., Musich, S., Hawkins, K., Alsgaard, K., & Wicker, E. (2016). The impact of resilience among older adults. *Geriatric Nursing*, 37(4), 266–272. doi:10.1016/j.gerinurse.2016.02.014.

Malette, J., & Oliver, L. (2006). Retirement and existential meaning in the older adult: A qualitative study using life review. *Counselling, Psychotherapy, and Health*, 2(1), 30–49.

Malette, J., & Pencer, I. (2003). Sens personnel, retrospective de vie et projet de creation chez une personne âgée cancéreuse. *Sciences Pastorales*, 22(1), 47–64.

Mallet, D., Begat, N., & Duchêne, V. (2012). Quel sens a le terme "sens"? *Les Cahiers francophones de soins palliatifs*, 12(1), 80–90.

Mather, M., Canli, T., English, T., Whitfield, S., Wais, P., Ochsner, K., Gabrieli, J., & Carstensen, L. (2004). Amygdala responses to emotionally valenced stimuli in older and younger adults. *Psychological Science*, 15(4), 259–263.

Monbourquette, J., & Lussier-Russel, D. (1992). *Mourir en vie!* Montréal: Novalis.

Monod-Zorzi, S. (2012). *Soins aux personnes âgées. Intégrer la spiritualité?* Bruxelles: Lumen Vitae.

Moody, H.R. (2003). Conscious aging: A strategy for positive change in later life. In J.L. Ronch & J.A. Goldfield (Eds.), *Mental wellness in aging: Strength-based approaches* (pp. 139–160). Winnipeg: Health Professions Press.

Mora, F. (2013). Successful brain aging: Plasticity, environmental enrichment, and lifestyle. *Dialogues Clin. Neurosci.*, 15(1), 45–52.

Palmore, E. (1999). *Ageism: Negative and positive*. New York: Springer.

Pargament, K.I., & Cummings, J. (2010). Anchored by faith: Religion as a resilience factor. In J.W. Reich, A.J. Zautra, & J.S. Hall (Eds.), *Handbook of adult resilience* (pp. 193–210). New York: Guilford Press.

Ploton, L., & Cyrulnik, B. (2014). *Résilience et personnes âgées*. Paris: Odile Jacob.

Puchalski, C., Ferrell, B., Virani, R., Otis-Green, S., Baird, P., Bull, J., Chochinov, H., Handzo, G., Nelson-Becker, H., Prince-Paul, M., Pugliese, K., & Sulmasy, D. (2009). Improving the quality of spiritual care as a dimension of palliative care: The report of the Consensus Conference. *Journal of Palliative Medicine*, 12(10), 885–904.

Reynolds, K., Pietrzak, R., El-Gabalawy, R., Mackenzie, C., & Sareen, J. (2015). Prevalence of psychiatric disorders in the U.S. older adults: Findings from a nationally representative survey. *World Psychiatry*, 14(1), 74–81. doi:10.1002/wps.20193.

Ricoeur, P. (1983). *Temps et récit* 1. Paris: Seuil.

Rovers, M., Malette, J., & Guirguis-Younger, M. (2018). *Touch in the helping professions: Research, practice, and ethics*. Ottawa: University of Ottawa Press.

Rowe, J.W., & Kahn, R.L. (1998). *Successful aging*. New York: Pantheon Books.

Rupp, D.E., Vodanovich, S.J., & Credé, M. (2005). The multidimensional nature of ageism: Construct validity and group differences. *Journal of Social Psychology*, 145(3), 335–362. doi:10.3200/SOCP.145.3.335–362.

Ségal, A. (2018). Le temps, le sens et la vie. *Les Cahiers francophones de soins palliatifs*, 18(2), 11–19.

Seligman, Martin (2011). *Flourish: A visionary new understanding of happiness and well- being*. London: Free Press.

Shankland, R. (2004). *La psychologie positive*. Paris: Dunod.

Statistics Canada (2018a). L'espérance de vie des Canadiens de 1920–1922 à 2009–2011. Retrieved June 7, 2019 from www150.statcan.gc.ca/n1/pub/11-630-x/11-630-x2016002-fra.htm.

Statistics Canada (2018b). Seniors. Retrieved June 7, 2019 from www150.statcan.gc.ca/n1/pub/11-402-x/2011000/chap/seniors-aines/seniors-aines-eng.htm.

Statistics Canada (2019). Leading causes of death, total population by age group. Retrieved June 7, 2019 from www150.statcan.gc.ca/t1/tbl1/en/tv.action?pid=1310039401.

Thomas, M.L., Kaufmann, C.N., Palmer, B.W., Depp, C.A., Martin, A.S., Glorioso, D.K., Thomson, W.K., & Jeste, D.V. (2016). Paradoxical trend for improvement in mental health with aging: A community study of 1546 adults aged 21–100 years. *The Journal of Clinical Psychiatry*, 77(8), e1019–e1025. doi:10.4088/JCP.16m10671.

Tkatch, R., Musich, S., MacLoad, S., Kraemer, S., Hawkins, K., Wicker, E., & Armstrong, D. (2017). A qualitative study to examine older adults' perceptions of health: Keys to aging successfully. *Geriatric Nursing*, 38, 485–490. doi:10.1016/j.gerinurse.2017.02.009.

United States National Library of Medicine (2019). Aging changes in the senses. Retrieved June 7, 2019 from https://medlineplus.gov/ency/article/004013.htm.

Van den Broeck, A., Vannsteenkiste, M., De Witte, H., Soenens, B., & Lens, W. (2010). Capturing autonomy, competence and relatedness at work: Construction and initial validation of the work-related Basic Need Satisfaction Scale. *Journal of Occupational and Organizational Psychology*, 83, 981–1002. doi:10.1348/096317909X481382.

Wagnild, G. (2003). Resilience and successful aging: Comparison among low and high income older adults. *Journal of Gerontological Nursing*, 29(12), 42–49. doi:10.3028/0098-9134-20031201–20031209.

Wagnild, G. (2019). Eight essential ingredients for resilient aging. Retrieved June 7, 2019 from www.resiliencecenter.com/articles/healthy-and-resilient-aging/eight-essential-ingredients-for-resilient-aging/.

Wong, P.T.P. (2000). Meaning in life and meaning in death in successful aging. In A. Tomer (Ed.), *Death attitudes and the older adult* (pp. 23–35). New York: Brunner/Mazel Publisher.

Wong, P.T. (2019). *Integrating meaning with growth through meaning therapy: Beyond psychological disorders*. Annual Spiritual and Cultural Care Conference, The Royal Mental Health Center, Ottawa, April 12, 2019.

Woo, A. (2019, May 30). Overdose crises lowering life expectancy: Statistics Canada. *The Globe and Mail*. Retrieved June 7, 2019from www.theglobeandmail.com/canada/british-columbia/article-overdose-crises-lowering-life-expectancy-statistics-canada/#comments.

5 Identity and Resilience in Victims of Trafficking for Sexual Exploitation

Willem F. Scholte, Rina S. Ghafoerkhan and Linda M. Verhaak

Introduction

This chapter addresses resilience and identity in victims of trafficking for sexual exploitation. We will consider sexual exploitation as defined by commercial sexual acts which are forced by either physical or psychological means, and for which one receives no or insufficient compensation. We will first introduce various concepts relevant for understanding what factors impact resilience in victims of sexual exploitation.

Dignity, Morality, Integrity, Shame and Identity

"All human beings are born free and equal in dignity and rights." These are the opening words of Article 1 of the Universal Declaration of Human Rights, as adopted in 1948 by the General Assembly of the United Nations (United Nations, 1948). The UN is the well-known intergovernmental organization which was established in response to the Second World War and is tasked to maintain international peace, harmony and cooperation. It officially came into existence in October 1945, after the signing of its charter earlier that year by 50 countries. Currently it is made up of 193 member states.

Although the declaration did not further define the concept of dignity, apparently all agreed that each and every person is entitled to dignity, simply by virtue of being a human being. In contrast, we all know that people do sometimes gain or lose dignity. Clear examples are regularly provided by certain public figures commanding great respect, and by others falling short. This, however, refers to another form of dignity, which may be called social dignity. While human dignity is considered to be grounded in human rationality and the ability to act as a moral agent, social dignity is determined by status, gravity and decorum but also by various forms of integrity (Shultziner, 2003).

Yet, morality and integrity are closely intertwined. Morality refers to values and related practices and institutions which prevent us from being selfish and harming others. Morality makes social life possible (Gert & Gert, 2017). The word integrity is often used in relation to consistency of people's norms and values, and thus to morality that is stable. In addition there is integrity in the physical sense of the word, referring to the unconditional experience of and respect for the boundaries of the human body – which points to consistency as well: the body as a consistent entity. Morality watches over our own integrity and urges us to respect the other's integrity. These processes serve human and social dignity, hence dignity relates to both morality and integrity.

Where morality fails one's personal boundaries may be disrespected, causing unwanted exposure, which in turn would elicit shame. Shame is an emotion universally experienced when one loses dignity, but also when such loss threatens to occur (Shen, 2018). So shame is regulatory and protective towards one's social position as well as towards one's own moral values. As both contribute to one's feeling of identity, shame can be considered as consolidating identity.

Sexual violence is one of the most extreme violations of personal boundaries possible. Trafficking for sexual exploitation adds slavery and often degrading, violent and cruel treatment to that. It may be self-evident that in such situations all the concepts and phenomena mentioned above apply, and bring about great distress.

Interpersonal Differences: Autonomy

As determined by culture and individual characteristics, there is great variety in the ways people handle physical boundaries, and to what degree one wishes or accepts closeness and exposure. Some always cautiously cover their bodies while others are at ease partly or fully showing it publicly. Likewise, some people readily seek and accept physical contact while others feel more comfortable keeping distance. By extension, great differences exist between people in openness to and around sexual activities. Hence there is variety in what individuals experience as their physical integrity, and what one would perceive as a violation of that integrity. In addition, one's drawing of boundaries depends on the other person(s) involved and on the actual situation.

Because of the latter anyone can be victimized by a violation of physical integrity, in the face of whatever cultural or individual factors, and however loosely one may usually handle personal boundaries. It is the discrepancy between the preferred closeness and what actually happens, the individually and situationally determined perception of the event as unwanted, which is essential. Thus the loss of self-determination, of the feeling of autonomy, is at the core of the experience of violation. As a result, emotional consequences such as the infringement of dignity and identity move in step with the degree to which one can preserve a feeling of autonomy in spite of what happens. While for many the violation of physical integrity is a seriously distressing event, some may have strategies available to nonetheless maintain a feeling of autonomy.

Appraisal, Sensemaking and Coping

The crossing of physical boundaries is a violation of integrity, and indeed sexual violence is one of the most extreme kinds, and thereby a major stressor possibly resulting in mental health problems. As laid out above, however, variance exists in how individuals cope with this stressor. As per the widely recognized appraisal model of Lazarus and Folkman, people's coping is highly influenced by their appraisal of the stressor, i.e. the way one assesses its impact on one's well-being and the sources one has available to deal with that impact (Lazarus & Folkman, 1984). The outcome of such impact assessment heavily depends on both personal and situational factors.

Clearly, on the personal level one's life history determines the solidity of basic trust, sense of identity and personal confinement, as will be elaborated later in this chapter. Such factors have great influence on one's appraisal of the external world and of individual experiences. In that way the impact on one's well-being of experiencing sexual violence, apart from physical damage, largely depends on the way one makes sense of that event. It may, for example, confirm one's existing negative self-image or, at the other end of the spectrum, it may evoke such outrage that it gives rise to an increased sense of autonomy.

Sensemaking in turn is related to available coping resources, be it inner sources like self-respect and a strong sense of identity (or rather autonomy) versus emotional instability and a negative self-image, or external ones such as a caring and supportive environment versus social insecurity and blaming.

The act of trafficking always means a deprivation of external resources for its victims. Their residence changes radically and, as will be elaborated in this chapter, some victims have been excluded from their usual social surroundings before being trafficked, or have reason to fear so upon reconnecting afterwards. Trafficking for sexual exploitation is oftentimes related to armed conflict, whether victims are trafficked by members of the conflicting parties or taken captive and exploited while fleeing the conflict area. In all situations mentioned social resources are actually lacking, and victims' resilience depends most on inner strengths previously gained in a nurturing environment.

Personal History

Trafficked sex workers form a heterogeneous group of individuals, and their personal histories vary widely. Therefore, clear-cut conclusions on their backgrounds cannot be formulated, and as a consequence no common characteristics of the formation of their identities either. However, various studies conducted into the personal histories of trafficked sex workers do provide some insight into their prior lives and experiences. In general the relevant literature paints a picture of trafficked persons being an already vulnerable population prior to the trafficking. The majority appear to be young women from low to middle-income countries who have limited educational backgrounds (e.g. Zimmerman et al.,

2006). It may be self-evident that both the naivety of young age and the limited knowledge of low education or intelligence render a person vulnerable to deception and exploitation.

Some common characteristics in personal histories reported in scientific and case studies need additional attention here, as precisely these factors may have caused victims to be at higher risk for trafficking, through impacting the formation of identity:

1 a high prevalence of childhood maltreatment; and
2 residing in a low or middle-income country (possibly affected by conflict or war).

Below we will address how these factors may negatively impact the development of a sense of personal integrity and identity, thereby inducing vulnerability.

Childhood Abuse and Interpersonal Functioning

Studies looking into life experiences of victims of sexual exploitation report high numbers of childhood maltreatment (Ottisova, Hemmings, Howard, Zimmerman & Oram, 2016). One study found that 71.7 per cent indicated having experienced emotional abuse during childhood (Abas, Ostrovschi, Prince, Gorceag, Trigub & Oram, 2013). Various studies looked into childhood physical and sexual abuse; depending on the study 30 to 65.8 per cent reported physical abuse, while this was 24 to 33 per cent for sexual abuse (Ottisova et al., 2016). Childhood maltreatment was mostly defined as experiences before the age of 15 or 17. Some studies only focused on parents or other adults in the household as possible perpetrators (Hossain, Zimmerman, Abas, Light & Watts, 2010; Oram et al., 2016); in other studies a perpetrator could be anyone, which yielded higher prevalence rates (Abas at al., 2013). At 24 to 33 per cent the rates of childhood sexual abuse among victims of trafficking are much higher than among females in the general population (around 18 per cent according to a meta-analysis of outcomes of worldwide studies (Barth, Bermetz, Heim, Trelle & Tonia, 2013)).

The long-term sequelae of childhood maltreatment, in particular sexual abuse, are numerous and continue in adulthood (Norman, Byambaa, De, Butchart, Scott & Vos, 2012). When growing up is undisturbed, constancy in a nurturing and caring family environment not only allows a child to confidently grow into an own identity; it also gives rise to the capacity to develop trust and stability in relationships. Otherwise, the absence of such constancy, or dependency on abusive caregivers, mostly leads to identity problems, emotional instability and a disturbed image of interpersonal relationships and intimacy (Collins, Guichard, Ford & Feeney, 2004; Murphy, Elklit, Hyland & Shevlin, 2016). It is not hard to imagine how such widely varying personal characteristics affect a victim's appraisal of sexual violence as a stressor. Obviously one's sense of identity, self-confidence, personal confinement and general expectations of intimacy are key factors in sensemaking here, as is the availability of a stable and supportive environment.

Appraisal is particularly impacted by two aspects of child abuse which raise the risk of becoming engaged in destructive relations with others in later life. First, perpetrators communicate to a child or youngster that one's physical boundaries are not to be determined by oneself, which as an unconscious conviction may settle in one's mind. In addition, child abuse may lead to the distorted cognition that violence and intimacy simply belong together in close relationships. Both factors may give rise to a greater susceptibility to relationships where moral and physical boundaries are easily violated, and new abusive liaisons and possibly exploitation lie ahead (Scholte, Verhaak, Lok & Ghafoerkhan, 2017).

Hence, sad though it is, when early child abuse has occurred, the violation of physical boundaries may feel familiar for its victims. This may mitigate the emotional impact of being forced into sex work in later life. For some of them the pathway towards exploitation is characterized by a promiscuous lifestyle gradually marked by increased coercion and violence. For others the entanglement of being valued as a person and as an object of sexual pleasure has become so intrinsic that even forced sex work may be somehow gratifying. Finally, in clinical practice people have come forward stating that compared to the prolonged abuse by family members during childhood, doing sex work felt like an improvement. Indeed, even in an exploitative situation some victims may have a certain feeling of control when performing, as will be elaborated later in this chapter.

Poverty, Agency and Identity

Reports on the demographics of trafficked sex workers indicate that many originate from low to middle-income countries, and have been trafficked to and exploited in high(er)-income countries (e.g. Zimmerman et al., 2006). Most individuals living in low-resource areas, where economic and social circumstances are poor and war and conflict often feature, have a limited say over the course of their lives. Not only is there a lack of means to effectuate possible aspirations and desires, future expectations are also constrained by a shortage of successful role models in the nearer circles.

Poverty is always a multifaceted problem. Bad living conditions result in poorer health outcomes, while opportunities to receive proper health-care are restricted. Poverty also comes with limited access to education, simply because school fees, school uniforms or travel costs cannot be paid, and from a certain age children/teenagers need to contribute to the household by earning money. In addition, as living in poverty in all likelihood means that those around are poor as well, family members depend on each other financially in times of sickness or old age, particularly if general social security is lacking.

Numerous studies have established the link between poverty and poor mental health. However, even without a mental health disorder as such, one has a disadvantaged position in life when living in poverty in a low-resource area. Having limited perspectives and opportunities for change has a strongly disempowering impact, and deprives a person from a sense of agency. Then, the resulting feelings of worthlessness and powerlessness may get incorporated into one's self-image, beliefs and sense of identity: "I am powerless," or "It is my fate to be of lower ranking."

One strategy to try to escape poverty and maybe being able to support one's family financially, is to go along with persons offering a solid income-generating opportunity somewhere else. Through this, many have been misguided into sexual exploitation. Admittedly, some may have had a hunch or actually knew about the nature of the job they would be doing, i.e. sex work. Given the (perceived) lack of options, however, there was hardly any choice (Ghafoerkhan, Scholte, de Volder & de Brouwer, 2019).

Armed conflicts, most of which take place in low-resource areas, sharpen the divide between the poor, relatively powerless and the powerful. In ongoing conflicts the powerless frequently are members of a persecuted group. In addition, in traditional cultures the conflict may only add to a pre-existing perception of marginalized persons and women as less worthy and dignified. In such context the danger of sexual violence always lurks, and many possible victims will develop strategies to avoid violence or limit its severity. If sexual violence seems inevitable, one may try to partly regain control by proactively setting conditions for surrender. One may even go along with the wishes of a perpetrator in order to prevent further harm to oneself or loved ones. In other cases one may try to sexually engage with a prominent figure (e.g. a high-ranking soldier, a humanitarian aid worker) to ensure the provision of basic needs like food, shelter or protection. When fearing for conflict-related (sexual) violence and being forced to flee, one often becomes dependent on criminal networks of human traffickers. Then, seeking refuge may take the course of being trafficked, and sexual exploitation may lie ahead (Ghafoerkhan et al., 2019).

The Actual Experience

Multisided Horror

The experience of being trafficked for sexual exploitation entails multisided horror. Victims may be seduced to leave behind their homes and relatives, to later discover that promises were false and that they have been trapped by exploiters. They may also be forced to follow a trafficker by all forms of threats or harm to themselves or their loved ones. In either case the journey ends in social isolation and deprivation, often shaped as full captivity at an unknown location and in deplorable living circumstances. Interaction with exploiters or abusers may be frightening, dehumanizing and violent. Sometimes victims remain in a locked room for a long time, not knowing if this will ever come to an end and whether more aggression will follow. At unpredictable moments one or more persons may enter the room for sexual purposes, after which the victim may be exposed to extremely degrading acts.

Hence a victim of trafficking for sexual exploitation is confronted with a multi-headed monster. During captivity one has to cope with threats and disenchantment, isolation, disorientation as regards one's location and future perspective, and bad living conditions. Sexual abuse comes with repeated assaults on one's dignity at the very least, and implies an absolute denial of both morality and one's integrity and sense of self-determination.

Resilience while being Trafficked

Being trafficked thus comes with deprivation of one's familiar surroundings, culture and social resources. Here, a certain level of self-confidence, flexibility and smartness helps for psychological survival. Resilience partly depends on one's capacity to not only orient and adapt to physical and non-material characteristics of the new situation – however gruesome it may be – and to detect its rules and regularities, but also to figure out whether there is space for creating some (sense of) freedom and how to manipulate the situation towards this end. One may also gain strength from bonding with fellow-victims if these are present, or find hope in seeking possibilities to escape. Some victims bond with an abuser ("customer") and elicit compassion, which may even lead to being helped to escape. For all such strategies intelligence will help, provided that it goes along with flexibility and self-confidence. Therefore the streetwise rather than the intellectual kind of intelligence may serve best.

Meanwhile, missing one's family and friends can cause great grief, which is obviously more so for those who feel strongly attached to others back home. This may be less problematic for those with many but varying and loose contacts, but such persons often have difficulty enduring real solitude. For those who feel strong bonds with loved ones far away, solace and perseverance may come from fantasizing about being close to them and aspiring to a future reunion. It may be self-evident, however, that traffickers' threats of hurting a victim's relatives or friends in case of non-collaboration work the opposite way, by both inducing fear and reducing a victim's margin for manoeuvre. In addition to thinking about loved ones, many in solitude and fear also find support in religion, prayer and the conviction that their God is near.

One possible combined effect of captivity, threat and isolation is a psychological constellation often referred to as Stockholm Syndrome (Adorjan, Christensen, Kelly & Pawluch, 2012). This is a state wherein victims develop affection for and an alliance with their captors. Given the fear and complete dependency as likely experienced, a victim's emotional bond with a trafficker may be understood as an ultimate survival mechanism, whereby powerlessness gradually transforms via strategic submissiveness to identification with the trafficker's ideas. A victim's isolated position prevents external correction, and a process called cognitive distortion takes over: the development of illogical reasoning, e.g. about affection from the trafficker's side. Although serving survival, and in that sense a coping strategy indeed, this psychological process is obviously detrimental to one's sense of identity in the longer term.

Resilience while being Sexually Exploited

As regards to the sexual exploitation we surprisingly learn from clinical experience that a minority of victims of trafficking do show to be psychologically more or less resilient to the extreme condition of sexual exploitation. Some display specific kinds of appraisal, enabling them to maintain a certain dignity in the face of degrading acts and to not fall apart despite loss of integrity.

Indeed, some victims succeed in experiencing superiority over (rather than fear for) their abusers, thereby only feeling sheer contempt and, in effect, being morally untouchable. Others seem to have a primal sense of dignity and autonomy which is unshakable and absolute, and which they can continue to draw upon while actually being subdued: "They may take my body, but they'll never have my mind." Such strong sense of identity and dignity may originate from a loving and nurturing upbringing during childhood.

Others again have been more or less familiar with restraint and abuse throughout their lives, hence the trafficked situation sadly does not make a huge and shocking difference: "Business as usual – life just sucks." Familiarity may also play a role in appraisal by those who have habitually been leading a promiscuous life, not caring too much about physical boundaries and integrity. For the categories of victims just mentioned, neglect or abuse during childhood and identity-related and interpersonal problems in later life may be common characteristics.

If, however, a victim's appraisal of the trafficked and exploited condition is not protective against its potential distressing impact as just described, specific coping strategies may still be helpful. Some strategies are risky but may nonetheless help in bearing the misery for the time being, such as numbing oneself or escaping to an imaginary world through taking drugs. Victims may continuously be provided drugs by their exploiters, thereby rendered non-sensitive and non-resistant. Obviously this results in addiction, which may later act as a secondary problem complicating recovery and facilitating revictimization.

Another mechanism temporarily preventing victims from fully experiencing what is happening is psychological dissociation (Schalinski, Elbert & Schauer, 2011). It should be noted, however, that this is not so much a strategy as an involuntary inner process. Dissociation ensures that elements of an intense experience, e.g. its emotional impact, are kept outside one's full awareness. Although a dissociative state may be considered an adaptive psychological response under very distressing circumstances, it may cause problems in later life (Ross-Gower, Wallace, Tyson & Elliott, 1998; Scholte et al., 2017). It may, for instance, lead to the inability to remember certain things. Also, stimuli linking to the event(s) in question – whether on a conscious level or not – may lead to inadequate and undesirable emotional states in the actual post-abuse situation. Such states may be triggered by sensory perceptions like images or smells that were associated with the event(s), but also by certain conversation topics. In addition, dissociative states during abuse may cause later sexual dysfunction, as any intimacy may bring about the re-experiencing of emotions originally associated with the assault(s) suffered, such as great fear and rage. And lastly, research shows that those experiencing a dissociative state during abuse are at higher risk of later developing a posttraumatic stress disorder – which in turn raises the risk of revictimization (Nöthling, Lammers, Martin & Seedat, 2015; Klanecky, McChargue & Tuliao, 2016).

The Psychological Aftermath

Psychological and Physical Problems

In recent years evidence on the psychological impact of sexual exploitation has been emerging from the scientific literature (Ottisova et al., 2016). Due to constraints in study methodologies, the estimated prevalence rates of various mental health disorders and psychological problems vary greatly. Nonetheless it can be concluded that many victims of sexual exploitation are seriously suffering. Victims visiting post-trafficking services mainly report symptoms of anxiety, depression and posttraumatic stress disorder. In addition to psychological issues several physical, including sexual, problems are reported as well.

Predictors for mental health outcomes after sexual exploitation have also been studied. Such research looked into factors occurring prior to, during and after trafficking. It was found that higher levels of post-trafficking support were likely associated with a reduced risk of mental disorders (Abas et al., 2013). Meanwhile, poorer mental health outcomes were associated with: pre-trafficking childhood maltreatment; sexual and physical violence; poor living and working conditions; restrictions of movement; and longer duration of exploitation while being trafficked; and unmet social needs after the exploitation period (Abas et al., 2013; Hossain et al., 2010; Kiss et al., 2015).

As outlined before, victims of sexual exploitation have often experienced adverse or traumatic events before being trafficked. Solely attributing psychological issues and problems in daily functioning to the recent experience of sexual exploitation would not do justice to the cycle of violence many have lived through. Many regard the recent sexual exploitation as another confirmation of pre-existing negative beliefs about oneself, others or the world in general: "I am just not a valuable person," or "The world is as it is: a dangerous jungle."

Reconnecting with Home

After escaping the trafficked situation victims have the opportunity to reconnect with relatives or friends, and maybe return home. Although doing so may seem self-evident, it may also be problematic. First, shame may prevent one from seeking contact. Here, shame relates to non-fulfilled expectations about good fortune in the country of destination when one left "voluntarily," and, of course, to the sexual exploitation itself (see below). In addition, already before being trafficked victims may have been marginalized or even excluded from their communities because of some social stigma, e.g. related to homosexuality. This may be a reason to build a new life in the present country rather than to reconnect with what was home.

Another group of victims, in particular among those originating from Western African countries, fear vengeance from Voodoo spirits when opening up about their experiences. This relates to an overwhelming magical ritual they have undergone, initiated by traffickers. Such ritual often comprises the taking of body tissues and fluids to be kept by the procedure's executers, which makes victims believe that they remain within their magical power. During the ritual they are told that escaping from and talking about the exploitation will be severely punished, e.g. through sending a horrible disease to them or, less magical, through the harming or killing of relatives back home.

Dealing with Shame

Feelings of shame are common in people who have endured sexual violence, and these are often prominently present after sexual exploitation. Sexual exploitation may have shattered possibly existing implicit moral values, e.g. that sexual contact should only happen between intimate partners, or that the naked body should be respected as reserved to the private domain. Here, sexual morals and taboos in the culture of origin play an explicit role.

Sexual violence may have been extreme and prolonged, physical boundaries and integrity grossly violated, and dignity affected. As a result, one may internalize feelings of shame and integrate these into beliefs about oneself: "I am soiled," or "I am disgusting." Such beliefs, originating from either the recent sexual exploitation or prior abuse, may prevent victims from later engaging in healthy relationships. One may fear rejection by family members, or may actually be rejected by one's relatives or communities because of the sex work one has been engaged in – the latter sadly happens all too often. Such exclusion in turn may lead one to either becoming socially isolated or getting involved in unhealthy relationships, which obviously would reinforce the negative beliefs one holds about oneself, and might result in revictimization.

As shame originating from sexual abuse represents violated dignity and makes a victim feel a soiled person as a whole, shame and self-deprecation may only be countered by focusing one's attention on the own qualities, resources and positive life events. Amazingly, some persons are capable of doing that by themselves, and gradually regaining what apparently was strongly present before: self-respect and pride – which, as outlined before, is rooted in childhood experience of love and care. Others may need someone else's help here. Although shame, by its very nature, makes it hard to open up about humiliations one has been subjected to, sharing with trusted confidants can alleviate the feeling and help one to reconnect with one's strengths, that is, when sharing the story is met with understanding and compassion. Seeking social support or, if needed and available, professional counselling may then help overcome shame.

Dealing with Guilt

As victims of sexual exploitation often originate from low resource regions, many may have had little other choice than "agreeing" to a job abroad. In addition, some may have known or suspected that sex work could be involved. However, its extent and nature, the violence encountered, and the insufficient or lacking financial compensation were obviously not expected. Still the fact that one initially agreed and trusted the people involved, may give rise to later feelings of guilt: "I agreed with it to some extent" and "I should have known better."

One may also feel guilty towards people left behind. Traffickers involved, often part of larger criminal networks, may have made threats towards one's family members or loved ones. In some cases relatives live in fear, are even forced to move to another area, or are actually being harmed. The burden thus put on one's loved ones often causes great guilt in a victim.

The simple truth, however, obviously is that victims never expected or wanted such outcomes, and this insight helps to overcome feelings of guilt. Coping strategies comparable to those relating to shame may help to counter guilt as well. Resilience here requires such processing of guilt feelings that one changes one's judgement from self-blame to self-acceptance or even self-appreciation.

Settling in a New Country

Despite all distressing circumstances, the majority of victims trafficked for sexual exploitation do not develop serious mental health problems, and find strength in rebuilding their lives in a new country. After escaping captivity many experience a sense of great relief and a strong urge to radically leave the past behind, and look towards the future. Research among visitors of post-trafficking services has established that this may result in relatively better psychological well-being right after sexual exploitation than during follow-up at later stages (Abas et al., 2013).

In some European countries, being a victim of sexual exploitation and filing a formal complaint can grant access to a residence permit. However, the involved legal process often proves challenging and puts a psychological strain on the victims. Unfortunately, in the majority of cases, perpetrator(s) cannot be sentenced due to lack of evidence (Nationaal Rapporteur

Mensenhandel en Seksueel Geweld tegen Kinderen, 2018), which for victims leads to losing the residence permit just recently acquired. One then has to live in illegality or return to one's country of origin, facing potential disappointment and blame by family members, or even criminal networks that have made threats against one's life. In some cases, however, victims fortunately succeed in obtaining a residence permit on other grounds (e.g. belonging to a persecuted group).

Paradoxically, when finally allowed to settle in the country indeed, mental health problems tend to start emerging. Moving out of a psychological survivor mode, one has to re-orient and rebuild a "normal life." Emotional exhaustion may then become manifest. In addition, one may face difficulties properly processing and integrating the past horrific experiences in one's life history, balancing these with one's present life and wishes for the future. Such challenges may play a disturbing role when entering a first romantic relationship, e.g. due to painful sexual memories, but also because of uncertainty over how to trust one's own setting of personal boundaries and maintaining integrity. Distressing memories may come to the surface in an intrusive way, for some leading to posttraumatic stress symptoms.

In general, most people who have experienced trauma (e.g. victims of violence, refugees) do not develop a stress-related psychiatric diagnosis. Likewise, most victims of sexual exploitation manage to cope with past experiences and look forward. Although not scientifically established yet, from clinical experience we learned that relevant factors promoting resilience in the post-trafficking phase are social support, religious dedication, daily routine and study or work opportunities. In addition, past victims report that having children to take care of is a major source of strength.

Concluding Remarks

There is no doubt that victims of sex trafficking are confronted with some highly distressing conditions, such as repeated humiliation and abuse, threats to life, and prolonged isolation. Emotional survival depends on the severity and duration of such horror, but victims' resilience is heavily impacted by personal characteristics. While the main stressors represent a violation of self-determination and dignity, a strong sense of identity and agency are essential characteristics for coping.

Here, individual life histories are key, as safety, love and care while growing up are conditional for the development of a sense of self-respect and autonomy. Many personal backgrounds of victims, however, are characterized by a lack of safety and reliable care, often resulting in a negative self-image and interpersonal problems. This accounts for this group's vulnerability for being trafficked, but also for emotional bending under the strain of exploitative abuse.

As this chapter may have brought forward, resilience in trafficked and sexually exploited victims is either based on a strong feeling of identity and dignity originating from a nurturing upbringing, or on strategies developed to cope with a miserable previous life, and both conditions may successfully shape sensemaking of current abusive experiences.

References

Abas, M., Ostrovschi, N.V., Prince, M., Gorceag, V.I., Trigub, C., & Oram, S. (2013). Risk factors for mental disorders in women survivors of human trafficking: A historical cohort study. *BMC Psychiatry*, 13(1), doi:10.1186/1471-244X-13-204.

Adorjan, M., Christensen, T., Kelly, B., & Pawluch D. (2012). Stockholm syndrome as vernacular resource. *The Sociological Quarterly*, 53(3), 454–474.

Barth, J., Bermetz, L., Heim, E., Trelle, S., & Tonia, T. (2013). The current prevalence of child sexual abuse worldwide: A systematic review and meta-analysis. *International Journal of Public Health*, 58(3), 469–483.

Collins, N.L., Guichard, A.C., Ford, M.B., & Feeney, B.C. (2004). Working models of attachment: New developments and emerging themes. In W. Rholes & J.A. Simpson (Eds.), *Adult attachment: Theory, research, and clinical implications* (pp. 196–240). New York: Guilford Press.

Gert, B., & Gert, J. (2017). The definition of morality. In E.N. Zalta (Ed.), *The Stanford encyclopedia of philosophy*, Fall 2017 edn. Stanford University. Retrieved from https://plato.stanford.edu/archives/fall2017/entries/morality-definition.

Ghafoerkhan, R., Scholte, W., de Volder, E., & de Brouwer, A-M. (2019). The nexus between conflict-related sexual violence and trafficking for sexual exploitation in times of conflict. *Journal of Trafficking and Human Exploitation*, 3(1), 9–33. doi:10.7590/245227719X154762350965172452–2775.

Hossain, M., Zimmerman, C., Abas, M., Light, M., & Watts, C. (2010). The relationship of trauma to mental disorders among trafficked and sexually exploited girls and women. *American Journal of Public Health*, 100(12), 2442–2449.

Kiss, L., Pocock, N. S., Naisanguansri, V., Suos, S., Dickson, B., Thuy, D., … & Borland, R. (2015). Health of men, women, and children in post-trafficking services in Cambodia, Thailand, and Vietnam: An observational cross-sectional study. *The Lancet Global Health*, 3(3), e154–e161.

Klanecky, A.K., McChargue, D.E., & Tuliao, A.P. (2016). Proposed pathways to problematic drinking via post-traumatic stress disorder symptoms, emotion dysregulation, and dissociative tendencies following child/adolescent sexual abuse. *Journal of Addictive Diseases*, 35(3), 180–193.

Lazarus, R.S., & Folkman, S. (1984). *Stress, appraisal and coping*. New York: Springer.

Murphy, S., Elklit, A., Hyland, P., & Shevlin, M. (2016). Insecure attachment orientations and posttraumatic stress in a female treatment-seeking sample of survivors of childhood sexual abuse: A cross-lagged panel study. *Traumatology* 22(1): 48–55.

Nationaal Rapporteur Mensenhandel en Seksueel Geweld tegen Kinderen (2018). *Slachtoffermonitor Mensenhandel 2013–2017*. Den Haag: Nationaal Rapporteur.

Norman, R.E., Byambaa, M., De, R., Butchart, A., Scott, J., & Vos, T. (2012). The long-term health consequences of child physical abuse, emotional abuse, and neglect: A systematic review and meta-analysis. *PLoS Medicine*, 9(11), e1001349.

Nöthling, J., Lammers, K., Martin, L., & Seedat, S. (2015). Traumatic dissociation as a predictor of posttraumatic stress disorder in South African female rape survivors. *Medicine*, 94(16), e744.

Oram, S., Abas, M., Bick, D., Boyle, A., French, R., Jakobowitz, S., ... & Zimmerman, C. (2016). Human trafficking and health: A survey of male and female survivors in England. *American Journal of Public Health*, 106(6), 1073–1078.

Ottisova, L., Hemmings, S., Howard, L.M., Zimmerman, C., & Oram, S. (2016). Prevalence and risk of violence and the mental, physical and sexual health problems associated with human trafficking: An updated systematic review. *Epidemiology and Psychiatric Sciences*, 25(4). doi:10.1017/S2045796016000135.

Ross-Gower, J., Waller, G., Tyson, M., & Elliott, P. (1998). Reported sexual abuse and subsequent psychopathology among women attending psychology clinics: The mediating role of dissociation. *British Journal of Clinical Psychology*, 37(3), 313–326.

Schalinski, I., Elbert, T., & Schauer, M. (2011). Female dissociative responding to extreme sexual violence in a chronic crisis setting: The case of Eastern Congo. *Journal of Traumatic Stress*, 24(2), 235–238.

Scholte, W.F., Verhaak, L., Lok, A., & Ghafoerkhan, R. (2017). The mental health of trafficked persons. In R. Piotrowicz, C. Rijken, & B.H. Uhl (Eds.), *Routledge handbook of human trafficking* (pp. 291–302). London: Routledge.

Shen, L. (2018). The evolution of shame and guilt. *PloS ONE*, 13(7), e0199448. doi:10.1371/journal.pone.0199448.

Shultziner, D. (2003). Human dignity: Functions and meanings. *Global Jurist Topics*, 3(3), 1–21. doi:10.1007/978-1-4020-6281-0_7.

United Nations (1948). *Universal declaration of human rights*. Retrieved from www.un.org/en/universal-declaration-human-rights/index.html.

Zimmerman, C., Hossain, M., Yun, K., Roche, B., Morison, L., & Watts, C. (2006). *Stolen smiles: A summary report on the physical and psychological health consequences of women and adolescents trafficked in Europe*. London: London School of Hygiene and Tropical Medicine.

Part II

Resilience and Identity During Adversities

6 Resilience, Spirituality and the Imaginary in the Context of Chronic Pain

Christian R. Bellehumeur and Laure-Marie Carignan

When I was five years old,[1] *while crossing a residential street in my hometown, I was hit by a careless driver. The accident left me with a moderate lordosis*[2] *as well as a mild scoliosis,*[3] *conditions which impeded recovery from various subsequent sports injuries which occurred during my teenage years.*

Undaunted, I continued to be active and pursued various sports as a healthy young adult. Then one day while biking, at the age of 30 years old, I was hit by another careless driver. This accident could have killed me; instead, it left me with chronic pain in my upper back and neck for about 18 months, during which time the pain slowly dissipated as a result of various treatments which I doggedly pursued.

Then, almost pain-free a few years later, I was tobogganing with friends when I fell violently on my back. The pain was excruciating. A constant "burning" sensation (with a consistent subjective score of 7 or 8 out of 10) became part of my daily life for over five years. It was as if my back had simply taken too many hits …

Overall, for about seven years, chronic back pain characterized my daily life. As I write this today, I can still remember the pain I was experiencing while working on my doctoral dissertation in my early thirties: there was not a single sitting position in which I felt comfortable. For every 30 minutes spent on the computer, I needed to lie down for 30 minutes or more. There were no relaxing positions. Even going to the movies was not relaxing – it was an exercise in constantly adjusting my position.

Living with chronic pain has had a significant impact on my life. As much as the physical pain in my back was debilitating, associated losses became a source of real psychological and moral suffering. I struggled with the grief of losing my pain-free life. I had the impression I was living a life of constant losses: beyond the loss of health were also many relational and financial losses. During those challenging years, I remember experiencing a whole range of negative emotions: denial, anger, sadness, anxiety, powerlessness, vulnerability and even despair. I spent thousands of dollars in the hope of even a partial recovery. Managing my pain became one of my first priorities during this seven-year period, and I met many different specialists in chiropractic, physiotherapy, acupuncture, pain management, and so on. I also tried various forms of self-care: medications, exercise and meditation, along with psychotherapy.

As other people I knew were living vibrant and meaningful lives, my chronic pain was a curse that dulled my life. Limiting my activities and delaying projects led to feelings of frustration and stress at the best of times. At the worst, I was overcome by feelings of depression and anxiety. Even though I had been able to almost fully recover from the biking accident and had learned and practiced effective coping strategies for dealing with chronic pain, the physical recovery from the tobogganing accident took much longer than I had anticipated. This second period of chronic pain also left me in dire financial straits, impeding my most cherished dream of beginning a family. Because it never really went away, the chronic pain became anxiogenic, and I had to try hard to keep a positive attitude. The physical pain was invisible to most people. Many family members, friends and even some doctors simply did not understand what it was like for me to live with chronic pain. On many occasions, I often felt completely isolated, even if I knew other people also had to live with chronic pain. How could I learn to cope with the pain? How could I harbour hope for eventual healing despite contradictory medical prognoses?

These questions echo concepts of resilience, spirituality and the imaginary. The relevance of studying resilience and spirituality may seem obvious when someone is facing traumatic experiences, painful situations and adversity (Anaut, 2015; Bellehumeur, 2011; Hood, Hill & Spilka, 2009). Such situations often lead to existential questioning related to meaning systems[4] (Carignan & Bellehumeur, 2018). As soon as one's meaning system is destabilized, one is called to adapt and imagine new ways of being and coping with an unexpected situation (Paloutzian, 2005). In this chapter, we postulate that human beings turn to the potential of the imaginary to access spirituality and resilience in developing a new way of being (Bellehumeur, 2011). This posit is based on two premises: that optimal resiliency is related to healthy spirituality, and that resilience and spirituality can be seen as concomitant processes that rely on and require the imaginary (Bellehumeur, 2011; Bellehumeur, Deschênes & Malette, 2012; Nguyen, Bellehumeur & Malette, 2018).

This chapter is divided into five sections. The first section paints a summary of the biopsychosocial model of chronic pain and its consequences on quality of life. The second section defines the concept of resilience, and includes a description of Wong's (2012, 2013) "pathway to resilience." The third section proposes an operational definition of spirituality according to Benson et al. (2003), and then discusses the points of convergence between resilience and spirituality. The fourth section presents Gilbert Durand's (1960, 1992) theory of Anthropological Structures of the Imaginary (ASI), and argues that the three main Durandian structures are at work when a person is dealing with chronic pain. Finally, the last section outlines how Durand's theory of ASI constitutes a conceptual framework which can embrace and consolidate various notions such as the emotional consequences of living with chronic pain, as well as components of resilience and spirituality required to deal with such. Furthermore, the final section suggests interventions to help people living with chronic pain.

The Biopsychosocial Impact of Chronic Pain

Living with chronic pain can be overwhelming. According to a recent health report from Statistics Canada, six million people in Canada (19 per cent of the population) and 25 million in the United States (11 per cent of the population) report experiencing some form of chronic pain (Cragg et al., 2018).

> [The] experience of pain interferes with different aspects of the patient's life … negatively affecting their daily activities, physical and mental health, family and social relationships, and their interactions in the workplace … This problem also affects the health care system and what is known as economic well-being … the strong burden associated with CP[5] not only deriving from health care costs but also from the loss of productivity and from compensatory payments to patients as a result of the disability that pain produces.
>
> (Dueñas, Ojeda, Salazar, Mico & Failde, 2016, p. 457)

In their biopsychosocial model of pain and its impact on quality of life, Dueñas et al. (2018) propose that chronic pain extends from the biological dimension (nociception,[6] injury, trauma, infection, illness and nerve damage) to the psychological (mental health, coping skills, anxiety and depression) as well as the social (workplace environment and impact on relationships, family and social functioning), thus affecting overall quality of life from many standpoints.

Although each person experiences chronic pain in a unique way, some people have stronger reactions and experience more intense psychological distress. This distress can manifest itself in a number of ways (Rusinek, 2018):

1. at the somatic level (e.g. headache, stomach ache, loss of concentration, etc.);
2. at the behavioural level (e.g. social avoidance, aggression);
3. at the emotional level (e.g. sadness, anger, guilt, anxiety, etc.); or
4. at the cognitive level (e.g. "it's my fault if I'm in pain").

To this list, we could also add the spiritual level, through existential questioning, such as: "is God punishing me?" (Dedeli & Kaptan, 2013; Rolland, 2012).

According to Moyle (2016), chronic pain has a fluctuating and unstable progression that leads to feelings of uncertainty about the future. Furthermore, according to experts from the organization Pain Australia (2015), chronic pain can even constitute a severe and distinct disease entity since it has a distinct pathology, causing changes throughout the nervous system that often worsen over time. The most common psychological consequences of chronic pain and their manifestations include insomnia, fatigue, anxiety, depression, guilt, social stigma and pain catastrophizing (Block & Cianfrini, 2013; McAllister, 2015; Moyle, 2016; Salazar et al., 2013; Turner-Cobb, Michalaki & Osborn, 2015).

Chronic pain makes sleeping difficult, which can be due in part to the pain itself (Moyle, 2016). Insomnia adversely impacts concentration, digestion, memory, fitness, relationships, and can also exacerbate psychological disorders like depression or anxiety (Moyle, 2016). Fatigue, a by-product of insomnia, is different from simply being tired, a condition which can be resolved by resting (Moyle, 2016). Feeling fatigued cannot be relieved by resting and, if anything, resting might worsen the feeling of being withdrawn from loved ones and normal daily activities.

Anxiety associated with chronic pain often revolves around the medium and long-term impact of taking time off work and the financial repercussions arising from that (Moyle, 2016). Since pain often leads to insomnia, anxiety at night might take the form of rumination about future scenarios (Moyle, 2016). There is a strong link between chronic pain and depression, yet depression often remains under-diagnosed in individuals with chronic pain (Salazar et al., 2013). A person suffering from both chronic pain and undiagnosed depression will have an increased level of pain compared to that of an individual receiving treatment for their depression (Salazar et al., 2013). Furthermore, the insomnia caused by chronic pain exacerbates symptoms of mood disorders and prompts one to nap frequently instead of engaging with others, thus increasing isolation (Salazar et al., 2013).

Feelings of guilt can overwhelm a person suffering from chronic pain, since it prevents them from participating in activities that most people take for granted like socializing, working and exercising (Moyle, 2016). As Moyle (2016) points out, one might feel angry at oneself and harbour feelings of self-blame for no longer being able to engage with the world. Indeed, Moyle (2016) calls guilt one of the most insidious mental side effects of chronic pain. Turner-Cobb et al. (2015) indicate that people with chronic pain experience higher levels of shame and guilt than people who are healthy.

According to McAllister (2015), chronic pain is also associated with social stigma related to the perception that the individual is not strong enough to cope with the pain. This can lead to impatience on the part of observers, and a belief that the individual should be doing better than what they are (McAllister, 2015). Social stigma can also keep the patient from seeking out treatment as they fear that they will be perceived as not coping well enough with the pain (McAllister, 2015).

Pain catastrophizing involves the magnification of pain symptoms leading to increased levels of depression, an increased sense of helplessness, anxiety and consequent functional loss (Block & Cianfrini, 2013). It occurs as a result of the manifestation of negative feelings such as anxiety, and can also lead to the individual displaying avoidance behaviours which, in turn, only lead to further increased levels of disability, disuse and depression (Block & Cianfrini, 2013). Eventually, the person will physically stop doing things because they have catastrophized their pain to such a level that they truly believe they cannot perform certain activities (Block & Cianfrini, 2013).

According to Sturgeon, Dixon, Darnall and Mackey (2015), social consequences of chronic pain are also very important to consider. Examples of these refer to:

1 difficulties connecting with others and/or impaired interpersonal functioning in various relational contexts, such as relations with family, relatives, friends or significant others;
2 difficulties in romantic and sex life;
3 loss of social roles and social identity and associated issues with employment;
4 reduced participation in family events/activities and in recreational and social activities (Turk et al., 2008).

In Sturgeon et al.'s (2015) study – conducted on 675 individuals with chronic pain – they found that the disruption of emotional well-being of people living with chronic pain involves both physical and social factors; however, the disruption of social relationships seems to be even more important than the global physical impairment per se.

According to Ausloos (2010), in the context of a serious illness (such as cancer), two major types of opposite emotional reactions may be encountered: (a) emotional cut-off (as manifested through defence mechanisms such as denial[7]); or (b) emotional flooding (as manifested through a sense of feeling overwhelmed, leading to resignation to the suffering and to an attitude of victimization). We suggest that by extension, chronic pain can also lead to these two opposing emotional responses. Finally, the most troubling or worrisome concern is suicidal ideation, which can become more explicit in the person suffering from chronic pain (Séguin, Beauchamp, Robert, DiMambro & Turecki, 2014). The negative consequences of living with chronic pain are multiple; resilience is needed.

Resilience

The concept of resilience is multifaceted: *recovery* (bounce back to previous level of functioning); *resistance* (stand strong against adversity); *reconfiguration* (changed, transformed or bounce forward to new functioning) (Cunningham, 2009; Lepore & Revenson, 2006). According to Richardson's (2002) meta-analysis on studies on resilience, three streams of research emerge from these studies. The first one is the identification of characteristics (e.g. normal or superior intelligence, self-esteem) and protective factors (e.g. quality of social support) presented by resilient people. The second stream looks at the description of resilience as a process. Finally, the third current perceives resilience as an inner motivational force pushing an individual to grow despite the encountered adversities or difficulties.

In this chapter, we focus on the last two streams of individual resilience, the motivational process and the resilience force. This resilience process is "in permanent co-construction. It results from an interactive and multifactorial exchange located at the intersection between the individual, the family and the social environment" (Anaut, 2009, pp. 71–72, as cited by Bellehumeur, 2011). According to Anaut (2009), resilience is an adaptive and dynamic process that is never definitively acquired; this process is variable during the development of the person throughout his life according to factors such as life circumstances and environment (Anaut, 2009). As such, an individual who might not have been resilient at one stage of life might become so at a later stage. Similarly, a person who might have been resilient at an earlier life stage might become less resilient in later years.

The ABCDE Strategy for Overcoming Adversity

Wong and Wong (2012) and Wong (2013) propose the ABCDE intervention strategy for dealing with negative life experiences, a strategy referred to as a "pathway to resilience." This strategy, based on a cognitive-behavioral approach, unfolds in a series of five distinct steps:

Accept the reality
Believe in possibilities
Commit to achievable goals
Discover new resources and solutions
Evaluate and enjoy the progress.

These five components refer to five corresponding principles, which are summarized along with their descriptions in Table 6.1.

Table 6.1 ABCDE strategy

Principles	*Descriptions*
Accept and confront the reality (the reality principle).	"Acceptance does not refer to giving up or to resigning, rather it simply means accepting what cannot be changed, such as the dark side of the human condition."
Believe that life is worth living (the faith principle).	"This refers to the three basic tenets of logotherapy: (1) there is always some area of freedom in which we can act responsibly and courageously; (2) in the worst-case scenario, we still have the freedom to take a stand, adopt a defiant attitude, or maintain faith in a higher being or others, or simply put, to take action, (3) it also involves affirming one's ideals, core values, worthwhileness, and competence."
Commit to goals and actions (the action principle).	"Commitment means moving forward and carrying out one's responsibility with resolve, regardless of feelings or circumstances."
Discover the meaning and significance of self and situations (the "Aha!" principle).	"Discovery involves learning something new about the self and life. It means that as we dig deeper into our resources and explore further, we discover hidden strengths and resources."
Evaluate the above (the self-regulation principle).	"Evaluation means continuing to monitor and make the necessary adjustments to ensure progress. If nothing seems to work and there is no improvement in the pursuit of positive life goals, then some adjustments will be necessary."

Source: These brief definitions are partly direct citations (and/or partially paraphrased) from Wong (2012, 2015).

The importance given to accepting, believing and discovering meaning echo the notion of spirituality. Since spirituality is complex to define, we do not pretend to be exhaustive in our efforts to describe it. However, we aim to refer to it because we believe optimal resilience is related to healthy spirituality (Bellehumeur, 2011).

Spirituality

But what is "spirituality"? In fact, there are many definitions. "Attempts to define [spirituality] … can be sure of one thing: misrepresenting spirituality's complexity, depth, and fluidity. Spirituality is like the wind – though it might be experienced, observed, and described, it cannot be 'captured'" (Nye, 1999, p. 58).

While they recognize the fundamental truth of Nye's (1999) metaphor of spirituality as ungraspable as the wind, Roehlkepartain, Benson, Ebstyne King and Wagener (2006) nonetheless propose a definition of spiritual development derived by a previous research team (Benson et al., 2003), which include the five most common elements found in the multiple definitions of spirituality available at that time:

> the process of growing the intrinsic human capacity for self-transcendence, in which the self is embedded in something greater than the self, including the sacred. It is the developmental "engine" that propels the search for connectedness, meaning, purpose and contribution. It is shaped both within and outside of religious traditions, beliefs, and practices (Roehlkepartain et al., 2006, pp. 205–206)

But, how is optimal resilience related to healthy spirituality? Bellehumeur (2011) has demonstrated the common processes that are encountered in both resilience and spirituality. Let us present processes by which spirituality (and religion) can promote resilience and vice versa. Spirituality can present itself as a condition facilitating the development of resilience. Indeed, Crawford, O'Dougherty Wright and Masten (2006) propose four processes by which spirituality and religion can promote resilience. We summarize them briefly:

1 relationships of attachment: these are relations with the Divine, conjugal relations or family cohesion, peers and mentors;
2 social support: this refers to the feeling of belonging to the community;
3 guidelines of conduct and moral values: this refers to integrity, compassion, forgiveness, empathy, altruism, kindness, benevolence, love and so forth;
4 personal development and growth or opportunities for transformation: this refers to the regulation of affect and states of exaltation, prayer and meditation, liturgies, celebrations, strengthening family values and rules, the meaning of life and the philosophy of life, reframing one's understanding of trauma, acceptance of the will of God, conversion and transformation.

Farley (2007) refers to the Wolin and Wolin model (1993), which also focuses on spiritual components that promote individual resilience. Among these components, five of them – insight, independence, relationships, initiative, morality – echo the processes identified by Crawford et al. (2006), while two other components which can also be qualified as spiritual – creativity and humour – complete this picture (Farley, 2007).

Conversely, resilience processes influence spirituality as well (Lesser, 2007). For example, resilience processes proposed by Vinay (2004) can echo some processes encountered in spirituality (Bellehumeur, 2011). Furthermore, where resilience processes allow for finding new meanings about traumatic events (Delage, 2010), or for creating new rituals of significance (Walsh, 2016), the result is the development of one or several components of spirituality as identified by Benson et al. (2003).

Beyond the Psychological Perspective: The Need for the Imaginary

Resilience and spirituality appear as two concomitant processes. We postulate that these two processes rely on another essential psychic reality which contributes to their emergence and manifestation, a reality which partly encompasses both resilience and spirituality. The latent dimension of resilience implies that it can potentially exist in the person without, however, manifesting itself. As Anaut (2009) clearly points out:

> all individuals have a potential for resilience but this can be developed differently depending on the person and socio-environmental contexts … In the face of adversity, the process of resilience can take place spontaneously or, conversely, remain in a latent state.
>
> (p. 71)

But in the human psyche, what activates this latent dimension of resilience? In our opinion, one activating resource could be the person's imaginary,[8] which can be defined as the repertoire of images and symbols and the relationships between those images and symbols that define for an individual and their cultural collective what is possible to imagine. We will expand further on the imaginary in the next section.

Furthermore, the way in which we define resilience and spirituality in our Western context is often dependent on a psychological perspective that is essentially centred on the individual. In doing so, according to Bellehumeur (2011), the social dimension seems to be forgotten in favour of a psychologizing[9] individualism. If even considered, the social dimension seen as a common process to both spirituality and resilience is reduced almost exclusively to support of the individual. But the social dimensions of resilience and spirituality actually go well beyond this, since it is within the social dimension that any culture is elaborated; cultures which carry myths, legends and collective narratives that convey the universes of meaning to which individuals have access (Durand, 1960; Bellehumeur, 2011).

Bellehumeur (2011) argues that during times of adversity, "human beings, in addition to appealing each to one's own resilience and spirituality, also draw on the potential of their imaginary to rebuild a new way of being" (p. 47). This imaginary potential makes it possible to envisage a dimension outside the adversity, either by anticipating a victory over it or by accepting it, and then through their imaginary/their envisaged dimension growth becomes possible. According to Durand (1960), the imaginary is always at work in any conscious or unconscious human act. Let us now briefly consider how the imaginary may be used by a person suffering from chronic pain.

A Brief Overview of Durand's Theory of Anthropological Structures of the Imaginary

Philosopher and cultural anthropologist Gilbert Durand[10] developed his theory of the Anthropological Structures of the Imaginary (ASI) as an attempt to encompass what it is to be completely "human" – the "whole human universe" (Durand, 1979, p. 23, our translation). His theory addressed issues of existence, meaning and the imaginary. In his view, *homo sapiens* survive and even thrive not by means of a predetermined nature from basic instincts, but by symbolic structures that create meaning. For Durand, *homo sapiens* was more accurately identified as *homo symbolicus* because of the existence of the imaginary.

The imaginary refers to the repertoire of images symbols and archetypes and the relationships between those aspects that define for an individual and their cultural collective what is possible to imagine, or use to make sense of existential issues such as suffering, death and the passing of time. Durand (1960, 1992) argues that these images and symbols (and archetypal patterns), common to anyone, deploy in an "anthropological trajectory" defined as a ceaseless exchange taking place on the level of the imaginary between the subjectivity (psyche) and the objectivity (culture); in other words, this trajectory oscillates as a constant back and forth between the internal or subjective influences (person's drives and motivations) and the external or objective influences arising from the cosmic and social milieu (Durand, 1999).

According to Laprée (2017), to fully grasp the depth and heuristic potential of Gilbert Durand's thought, we can first refer to the stories describing human activity, to which we increasingly have access through the media via the internet and virtual communication.

> The media is full of stories about everything from society, culture, human life, both individual, national and international … Thanks to access to universally available information, we can increasingly put ourselves in the presence of all contemporary human culture. We thus have access to

stories from here and elsewhere that are part of a culture and testify to human activity.

(Laprée, 2017, p. 8, our translation)

Durand (1960, 1992) created a classification of mental images and visual narratives relevant to most cultures, which is divided into two main regimes or polarities in opposition to one another: the "diurnal," in which the structure of the imaginary is "heroic"; and the "nocturnal," in which the structure of the imaginary is "mystical."

However, a "synthetic" structure arising also from the "nocturnal" is needed to create a synthesis between the two opposing regimes, allowing them to co-exist and to maintain balance between them (Durand, 1999). Note that the synthetic structure was later seen more precisely belonging to the "crepuscular" regime. Let us now consider the heroic, mystical and synthetic structures or universes of meaning. Figure 6.1 offers an abridged version of Durand's classification of anthropological structures of the imaginary.

The Heroic Universe

Through contemporary media, we are witnessing reports of an endless list of humanity's misfortunes in the form of natural, economic or socio-

Regimes	Diurnal	*Nocturnal (could be called Crepuscular)*	Nocturnal
Structures	heroic	synthetic or "systemic"	mystical
Verbal schema	to distinguish	to link	to confound
Reflexive gesture	postural	oscillating, rhythmic or cyclical	digestive or absorbing
Visual representations		 	
St-Arnaud (1989)'s three axes of group dynamics[1]	Axis of productivity	Axis of regulation	Axis of solidarity

1 The relevance of these axes with ASI are well explained in Laprée (2013).

Figure 6.1 Durand's classification of structures of the imaginary.[11]

political disasters (Laprée, 2017). To this, we can add health disasters like the current COVID-19 pandemic. In this great concert of human setbacks, the good results often go unnoticed, as if evil makes more noise than good (Bellehumeur, 2019). However, it also happens that contemporary social media highlights and celebrates the records of champions, the causes won, the remarkable courage and kindness of certain individuals or groups in the midst of humanity's misfortunes (Laprée, 2017).

> Gilbert Durand proposes the term heroic in order to qualify the structures of the imaginary which underlie all these realities and human activities. It shows that this type of activity is so familiar to us that it stems from our condition of homo sapiens; this type of activity whose ancestors once stood on their two feet to face life … Think of the little child who, after spending time on all fours, begins to walk and then runs down the aisle of the store. It is as if he suddenly becomes lighter once he stands on his own two feet.
>
> (Laprée, 2017, p. 9, our translation)

But as Laprée (2017) points out, we are not usually heroes without defining some type of adversity to overcome. "[W] hen we defend a cause, we bring it to light, we highlight it, we clarify the issues, we specify the argument used to defend it" (Laprée, 2017, p. 9, our translation).[12] The idea of combat and the presence of tension is fundamental here. To better qualify this type of activity or gesture, Durand uses verbs such as distinguishing, separating, elevating and purifying to name the essentials of human life when it calls upon the heroic imaginary (Laprée, 2017). Indeed, the heroic structure's dominant postural position is that of getting up, standing or ascending (Bellehumeur, Lavoie, Malette, Laprée & Guindon, 2013).

The heroic structure, in its postural reflexive gesture, predisposes to stand up against adversity, to distinguish or clarify between what is good and bad, to decide between what is true and what is false, and to elevate us from what makes us fail (Laprée, 2000, 2017). It carries the notion that heroes have to struggle to victory, to stand and fight to overcome any challenges they face (Xiberras, 2002). In the context of someone living with chronic pain, this could refer to all efforts being deployed to learn new information about his or her health condition, along with the courage to stand up, to resist the temptation of giving up one's goals despite ongoing feelings of vulnerability.

The Mystical Universe

As Laprée (2017) points out, living endlessly in the heroic universe can be exhausting, so we must also rest and take care of ourselves. Once again, contemporary media appeals to this aspect of human life by providing us with an endless list of what is needed to make a good life, more comfortable, more relaxing, abandoning oneself to the present moment.

> It's like going back to paradise in the womb! To be convinced, it is a question of admiring the infant huddled against his mother, who draws food from the mother's breast, a complete and voluptuous happiness. And then, the sated child will fall asleep heavily (provided that his digestive system works well!). This whole process … comes [also] from the heritage of *homo sapiens*.
>
> (Laprée, 2017, p. 10, our translation)

This dominant sucking reflex, which appears from birth and is essential to the survival of the newborn, is the reflexive gesture identified by Durand (1999) which comes to condition the entire inner universe. Indeed, Durand (1960) names this structure of the imaginary "mystical" to allude to the mystery of our selves. Arising from the nocturnal regime, the mystical structure tends to receive within oneself, absorbing and digesting so that two entities are no longer separate but blended together, indistinguishable. In this state of fusion everything is friendly, gentle, peaceful, warm, harmonious and internalized. "[W]ords are softened by figures of speech, euphemisms … the fall is slowed to a descent" (Xiberras, 2002, p. 66, our translation). To further illustrate, consider euphemisms such as "passing away" or "putting to sleep."

> It is important, however, to be careful not to restrict the nocturnal vocabulary and its intimate meaning to interior life alone. The calm, the warmth, the secret, the slow and deep descent can just as easily take root in an environment external to oneself; in the secret of one's own room, one's home ["home sweet home"], an excursion in a peaceful forest, a delightful campfire with friends. These are all examples of this intimate atmosphere. So, there is no need to be exclusively alone, because we can just as easily be among ourselves, in a welcoming and inclusive group of all. We can also live in such gatherings in times of electoral victories where the winners celebrate together and the losers are united in desolation.
>
> (Laprée, 2017, pp. 10–11, our translation)[13]

In the context of chronic pain, the mystical structure would refer to the ability to let go when needed, or to attempt to relax in a convenient manner. It may also involve embracing one's limitations, not in the sense of giving up or resignation, but in the sense of acceptance.

The Synthetic Universe: The Place of Wisdom and Optimal Resilience

In presenting the characteristics of the heroic and mystical structures of the imaginary, we recognize the importance of each polarity in its own time and circumstance. Why? In absolute terms, the sun never shines at night, the temporal kingdom of the moon. However, day breaks over night, to be regularly reabsorbed by it at the end of the daytime (Laprée, 2017). In his theory, Durand

(1999) identified a third structure called "synthetic," arising from the nocturnal, and what he called in later writings the "crepuscular" regime, occurring between the nocturnal and diurnal polarities. The crepuscular regime is not a polarity as are the nocturnal and diurnal regimes, but refers "rather to an imaginary place of connection between these first two [heroic and mystical structures]" (Laprée, 2013, p. 157). This structure refers to the third path, where both the diurnal and nocturnal regimes co-exist harmoniously.

> Human activity, to make life bearable or to compensate for its excesses, usually follows an alternating cycle from day to night or vice versa … This state is formed when the two opposite polarities (diurnal and nocturnal) are facing each other with sufficient vigor not to give up too much territory to the other … It comes from the depths of *homo sapiens* and summons polarities to conciliation, compromise or mutual fascination. Those who have dealt with depth psychology … [and] phenomenology of religions … have often used, to name this phenomenon … the expression *coincidentia oppositorum* (which means coincidence of opposite elements).
>
> (Laprée, 2017, p. 12, our translation)

The key verb chosen by Durand (1999) to convey the fundamental idea of this bipolarity is "to link," and its reflexive gesture is oscillating, rhythmic or cyclical, tending to synthesize or hold opposites together in harmony without any will of exclusion. The synthetic structure of the imaginary has a historian side, seeking coherence in contrasts repeating themselves over time, like seasons and other rhythms of life. In this structure, distinctions are safeguarded because their complementarity are essential: without winter, there is no spring. In Christianity, one cannot have a resurrection without death. The icon of Taoism, the ubiquitous yin/yang symbol, represents the perfection of this idea. Judeo-Christian thought as expressed in the wisdom "for everything there is a season, a right time for every intention under heaven"[14] provides a temporal illustration of the synthetic structure.

Laprée (2017) invites us to consider other examples brought to us through contemporary media of the synthetic structure in action, such as diplomatic endeavours (mystical structure) during times of war (heroic structure). Other examples specifically result from media efforts to galvanize communities into caring behaviours (mystical structure) to alleviate inequities (heroic structure) exacerbated by many of humanity's misfortunes.

Finally, at the global level, let us mention the crisis linked to the COVID-19 pandemic. As contemporary media subjects the entire world to endless updates on death tolls, and medical research teams frantically attempt to develop a vaccine whilst most levels of governments urge their constituents to adopt extreme preventive measures, individuals scramble to face the "new normal." Cheering on health workers, our new societal heroes, we live in a resounding reflection of the heroic structure. Paradoxically, the crisis surrounding the COVID-19 pandemic has resulted in many families rediscovering the pleasure of spending time together. Not allowed to work outside the home, many families manage to find the comfort and pleasure of indulging in fun recreational activities and hobbies, reflecting the mystical structure.

In the context of chronic pain, the task of self-regulation between the heroic and mystical structures becomes a daily endeavour. If one becomes too heroic, the tendency to over-resist may be associated with excessive stress; if one becomes too mystical, there may be a lack of personal engagement to overcome the adversity, with a resulting tendency to giving in to short-term comfort and ignoring healthy challenges. As mentioned previously, the synthetic structure has a historian side, seeking coherence in contrasts repeating themselves over time, like the rhythms of life. Indeed, the crepuscular regime is reflected in many religions and ideologies, where the representation of the future is mastered by hoping in a better world coming after the tribulations of life, which is really the case with chronic pain. Last but not least, the synthetic structure is related to a holistic (physical, psychological and spiritual) and optimal health (Bellehumeur, 2011; Durand, 1980; Laprée, 2000).

Applications of Durand's ASI to the Situation of Chronic Pain, Resilience and Spirituality

In Table 6.2, we regroup various notions discussed in this chapter according to how they are reflected in Durand's Anthropological Structures of the Imaginary (ASI).

Let us now consider certain elements as they are classified in Table 6.2. Regarding the notion of emotional consequences and attitudes towards chronic pain, emotional cut-off, anger, a desire to conquer by every means possible, and being overwhelmed by striving belong to the heroic structure, because the heroic structure is characterized by a constant tension that seeks to stand up against adversity, to resist and to overcome it. In that resistance, one can cut oneself off from vulnerable emotions that may accentuate defeat. Anger is a secondary emotion that makes oneself feel powerful and less at the mercy of vulnerable emotions (Johnson, 2004).

Furthermore, anger is often what fuels heroic solutions to adversity.[15] The desire to conquer by every means possible is clearly heroic, and as previously discussed, to remain in that state perpetually can lead to exhaustion and a sense of being overwhelmed. In contrast, acceptance, letting go, and mindfulness practices belong to the mystical structure, which is characterized by absorption and taking into oneself. The synthetic structure allows a balance between these opposite emotional consequences or attitudes, as reflected in tendencies which recognize the "good and bad days" of chronic pain, as well as the hope that relief will come in its time.

With respect to resilience, it is important to note some key points to better understand the content of Table 6.2. Cunningham (2009) uses the English expression "bounce forward" – in contrast to "bounce back" – to refer to

Table 6.2 Durand's ASI as a framework regrouping emotional consequences and attitudes related to chronic pain, and various elements of resilience and spirituality

Regimes	*Diurnal*	*Crepuscular*	*Nocturnal*
Structures	Heroic	Synthetic	Mystical
Emotional consequences, attitudes and /coping (Ausloos, 2010)*	• Emotional cut off* • Anger • Desire to conquer by every means possible • Overwhelmed by striving*	• Balance in tensions • Oscillation between good and bad days • Belief in relief after pain	• Acceptance • Letting go (as a positive coping strategy) • Mindfulness practices
Resilience (Lepore & Revenson, 2006)	Resistance (stand strong)	Reconfiguration (changed, transformed, grow or bounce forward to new functioning)	Recovery (bounce back to previous level of functioning)
Wong's ABCDE pathway to Resilience (Wong, 2012)	Step C (for committing to goals and actions)	Step B (for believing in other life possibilities); Step D (for Discovering the meaning and significance of self and situations); Step E (for Evaluating steps A–D, the self-regulation principle)	Step A (for Acceptance of the reality)
Components of spirituality (Benson, Roehlkepartain & Rude, 2003)	Self-transcendence (as aspiration of the self, transcending oneself and/or one's limits)	Self-transcendence	Self-transcendence (as social dimension of embeddedness in others or comfort in the Divine)
			Connectedness (as social dimension of mystical structure)
		Meaning (as wisdom born of adversity)	
	Purpose (as self-definition)	Purpose	Purpose (as social dimension of sacredness of one's home, family)
	Contribution (as sense of giving of oneself)	Contribution	Contribution (as social dimension of providing relief)

people's ability to not only "bounce back" in the face of adversity, but to be able to *"bounce forward" before an uncertain future*, especially since one is unlikely to return to the exact state in which they were before the adversity occurred. For example, in the case of an accident followed by a long period of chronic pain, not only the physical body may endure residual effect or weakness, but the whole person can be transformed for better or worse. In Table 6.2, one can see the relevance of matching the three types of identified processes related to resilience: (1) Resistance (standing strong); (2) Reconfiguration (changing, transforming, growing, or bouncing forward); and (3) Recovery (bouncing back, as a reversal to previous level of functioning) with the three main corresponding structures of the imaginary.

Wong's ABCDE pathway to resilience is fairly easy to follow in ascribing its steps to their corresponding structure of the imaginary. While it might be clear as to why step A (for Acceptance of the reality) belongs to the mystical structure and step C (for Committing to goals and actions) echoes the driving force of accomplishment that is encountered in the heroic structure, the classification of steps B, D and E in the synthetic structure may require more explanation. Step B (for Believing in other life possibilities) reflects the cyclical aspect of the synthetic structure, as it requires the capacity to envisage a reality which can exist outside of the current adversity, a reality which can come in its own time. Step D (for Discovering the meaning and significance of self and situations) represents a truce between the heroic and the mystical, where wisdom that embraces paradox resides. In the context of chronic pain, while one is doing everything possible to be proactive in managing pain, this action needs to be tempered with acceptance of one's limits. The paradox of "doing by being" or "being active while resting" is resolved by linking the two in perpetual meaning-making. Step E (for Evaluating steps A–D)is a principle of self-regulation, which allows for oscillation between Step A (Acceptance of reality) and Step C (Commitment to goals and actions). It is the Serenity prayer of wisdom in discerning the difference between what can be changed and what cannot,[16] and belongs to the synthetic structure that harmonizes the two opposites.

Finally, in regard to spirituality, we previously presented Benson et al.'s (2003) definition encompassing the five most commonly identified elements found in the multiple definitions of spirituality. Of these five elements, connectedness belongs to the mystical structure, as it refers to connectedness to others and to the environment in harmonious relationship, which Laprée (2017) describes as the social dimension of the mystical structure. Meaning as wisdom born out of adversity belongs to the synthetic structure as it consolidates without confusing the various aspects of meaning systems – global meaning, situational meaning, meaning-making processes and meanings made (Carignan & Bellehumeur, 2018; Paloutzian & Park, 2015; Park, 2005, 2010). Furthermore, meaning-making processes tend to embrace polarities harmoniously rather than accentuating (heroic) or eliminating (mystical) them. The three remaining elements of spirituality – self-transcendence, purpose, and contribution – are considered to have dimensions that reflect all three structures of the imaginary.

When self-transcendence reflects an aspiration of the self towards surpassing one's limits, going beyond oneself, it echoes the heroic structure's verbal schema of standing up, of distinguishing oneself. However, when self-transcendence reflects embeddedness in something greater than the self, including the sacred, it belongs to the mystical structure of absorption, of comfort, of taking into oneself or becoming one with the other, as in contemplation of the divine or considering one's home or family to be sacred. Self-transcendence reflects the synthetic structure when it oscillates between these two dimensions, between surpassing oneself and losing oneself in the sacredness of the other.

Purpose likewise can be classified in all three structures of the imaginary. Where purpose relates to self-definition (as in "my personal mission statement"), it parallels the heroic action of distinction. However, when purpose relates to an action conferred upon or for the sake of others (as in a mother making sacrifices for her children because her family is sacred to her, or a person living out a vocation for the good of humankind), it reflects the social dimension of the mystical structure. Purpose can also reflect the synthetic structure, in that both dimensions of self-definition and action towards or for the sake of others can be linked in a harmonious balance.

Contribution, like purpose, can also be classified as a synthetic structure in that it can reflect a harmonious balance between the giving of oneself (the heroic act of self-sacrifice) and the provision of assistance or relief (the social dimension of the mystical in contributing to alleviating suffering or bringing joy to those with whom one is connected).

In Table 6.3, we match the three main imaginary structures with several practical tips to deal with chronic pain.

In following Table 6.3, one can see how all three structures of the imaginary are involved in positive ways of dealing with chronic pain. For those who wish to help someone living with chronic pain, we suggest the following:

1 to accompany this person in his fight against chronic pain and resignation by listening to him (or her) and supporting him (or her) in his (or her) treatment;
2 to maintain a reassuring emotional connection by allowing verbalizations of fears and doubts;
3 to encourage and stimulate physical and intellectual activities;
4 to help when it is necessary to let go, as living as before may not be possible anymore;
5 to lead the person to look to the future;
6 encourage him (or her) to use his (or her) creativity;
7 to support him (or her) projects and dreams;
8 to offer him (or her) moments of happiness, such as trips or other festive activities, among many other things (Ausloos, 2010).

Table 6.3 Durand's ASI as a framework classifying common processes to resilience and spirituality along with various tips to deal with chronic pain

Heroic structure (Diurnal regime)	*Synthetic structure (Crepuscular regime)*	*Mystical structure (Nocturnal regime)*
Common processes to resilience and spirituality		
Directing guidelines and moral values/virtues (as opposed to vices)	Personal growth	Attachment relationship (based on safety)
		Social support
Tips or strategies[17]		
Educate yourself about your condition to reduce fear of the unknown.	Learn biofeedback to decrease migraine and tension headache pain. (regulates between "accepting the pain" and actively controlling it)	Learn deep breathing or meditation to help you relax.[18]
Boost chronic pain relief with the natural endorphins from physical exercise.	Consider seeing a mental health counsellor for talk therapy. (contributes to acquiring the wisdom of recognizing limitations and courage to change what can be changed)	Reduce stress in your life; Practice mindfulness: focus on the here and now. Get a massage for chronic pain relief.
Cut back on alcohol. Don't smoke. Eat a healthy diet.	Some people might need medication to treat insomnia, depression, or anxiety[19] (regulates between "accepting the pain" and actively controlling it).	Join a support group. Meet others living with chronic pain.
Track your pain level and activities every day.		Find ways to distract yourself from pain so you enjoy life more.

Conclusion

In this chapter, we have expanded on Bellehumeur's (2011) ideas of linking resilience, spirituality and Durand's Anthropological Structures of the Imaginary (ASI). As we have suggested, Durand's ASI can serve as a framework for understanding various notions at play when someone is struggling with chronic pain. In these situations, it is most important to call upon various means to promote sufficient quality of life and preserve it in order to maximize a person's resilience. These various means ideally do not exclusively reflect either heroic or mystical polarities of Durand's ASI, as optimal health is reflected in the synthetic structure of the imaginary which allows for oscillation between the heroic and the mystical (Bellehumeur, 2011; Durand, 1980).

Like Ausloos (2010), it is interesting to note that the Chinese character for the word "crisis" uses two ideograms:

1 injury, suffering and sometimes death;
2 chance or opportunity.

If one can easily understand all the suffering and anguish of death related to chronic pain, it may seem harder to perceive "opportunities" in the difficult situation. The way the Chinese character illustrates "crisis" echoes according to us, the systemic structure of imaginary, as within a paradox lies a possible fruitful transformation. All situations of chronic pain are unique, special and different. Everyone has their own life story with adversity. As we began this chapter with the first co-author's testimonial, it is fair to say that today, life has become a real blessing for him …

Following the second accident, after two years of living with chronic pain as a constant companion, I attended a three-day retreat weekend. I remember a special moment during this retreat when I was in so much pain that I couldn't sit down quietly to listen to the preacher. I decided to take a slow walk outside instead. These words came to me like an epiphany: "Au coeur de la douleur, j'ai rencontré la douceur".[20] *In French, only one middle letter differentiates the words "douleur" (pain) and "douceur" (tenderness), the "L" and the "C", and this intrigued me. Clearly to me, it appeared that I had to "C"hange my perspective on my "L"onely situation. The pain would not go away, I could not fight it anymore, I just had to learn to live with it … With a new attitude of full acceptance of my reality, while remaining open and proactive to explore new ways of healing, I got better over the years. Today, I am almost pain free. I cannot really play volleyball or basketball anymore; jumping is just not a wise thing for me to do … But still, life has pleasantly surprised me in many ways. Today, I enjoy my professional life, and above all, I am a happily married man, and a blessed father of two precious young children, a son and a daughter, who very much enjoy jumping on their beds from time to time!*

Notes

1 First co-author.
2 Inward curvature of the spine.
3 Lateral curvature of the spine.
4 A meaning system is a worldview which encompasses *global meaning* (broad beliefs such as the global sense that one's life has meaning), *situational meaning* (assigned meaning of a given stressful event), *meaning-making processes* (processes which restore global life meaning after it has been disrupted by a stressful event), and *meanings made* (results of meaning-making processes such as perceived growth) (Carignan & Bellehumeur, 2018; Paloutzian & Park, 2015; Park, 2005, 2010).
5 CP: chronic pain.
6 Sensory nervous system's response to certain harmful or potentially harmful stimuli.
7 In the case of chronic pain, this could be seen as taking medication in an abusive way, to numb one's pain in order to engage in a physical activity that could aggravate one's condition, e.g. an elite athlete who abuses painkillers during a sports competition.
8 "Imaginary" can be used as noun (see the translated book of Durand, 1999). "Imaginary" is not to be confused with "imagination." The "imaginary" is the ability to create images, whereas "imagination" refers to the dynamics of image creation.

9 To psychologize (as a verb) refers to speculate, explain or interpret (only) in psychological terms or motivations (www.merriam-webster.com/dictionary/psychologize). Carignan and Bellehumeur (2019) argue that there is a risk in discussing religion and spirituality as an exclusively psychological matter.

10 Born in 1921, Gilbert Durand early engaged in resistance (an example of resilience) during the Second World War. Founder of the *Cahiers internationaux du symbolisme* and the *Cahiers de l'hermétisme* (Souty, 2006), Gilbert Durand was professor emeritus of cultural anthropology and sociology at the University of Grenoble II. In 1966, he participated in the creation of the network of Imaginary Research Centers (CRI). Today, there are around 50 laboratories in various countries.

11 The visual representations in Figure 6.1 demonstrate the main differences between the three structures. from the diurnal regime, reflecting the energy of constant tension in life. In Durand's original classification of anthropological structures of the imaginary, a darker (midnight blue) circle is used to represent the mystical structure, as it echoes the nocturnal polarity, reflecting the energy of absorption, comfort and a peaceful life. Finally, in the middle, a swirling circle with both the bright and the dark colours is used to represent the synthetic structure with its verbal schema "to link." Note that in the synthetic structure, there is no "blending" of the two polarities (which would best be represented by a green circle, blending yellow and midnight blue); instead, the swirl illustrates the harmonious co-existence of opposites

12 Note that all these gestures of clarification and precision are also omnipresent in any therapeutic approach, it is very often important to specify the reason for the consultation, to confront a client in his contradictions to help him elucidate points of confusion, to give himself a direction.

13 Psychotherapists are well aware of the importance of creating a safe climate and a strong alliance to allow a person in distress or trauma to be reassured to better explore their experience with confidence.

14 Kohelet 3:1–8: "For everything there is a season, a right time for every intention under heaven – a time to be born and a time to die, a time to plant and a time to uproot, a time to kill and a time to heal, a time to tear down and a time to build, a time to weep and a time to laugh, a time to mourn and a time to dance, a time to throw stones and a time to gather stones, a time to embrace and a time to refrain, a time to search and a time to give up, a time to keep and a time to discard, a time to tear and a time to sew, a time to keep silent and a time to speak, a time to love and a time to hate, a time for war and a time for peace."

15 One needs only consider movements like MADD (Mothers Against Drunk Driving) which were initiated through the constructive anger of parents against a phenomenon that led to the deaths of their children.

16 Reinhold Niebuhr's Serenity Prayer: "God, grant me the serenity to accept the things I cannot change, courage to change the things I can, and wisdom to know the difference."

17 Sources: Florida Medical Clinic (2018); Lava (2018); Molitor, Keck and Nordal (2019).

18 Several techniques can help reduce stress and promote relaxation. Listening to soothing, calming music can lift your mood and make living with chronic pain more bearable. There are even specially designed relaxation tapes or CDs for this. Mental imagery relaxation (also called guided imagery) is a form of mental escape that can help you feel peaceful. It involves creating calming, peaceful images in your mind. Progressive muscle relaxation is another technique that promotes relaxation.

19 Do not fall into self-medication! Using substances might temporarily alleviate physical or emotional pain, but this is never a good long-term solution.

20 In English: "At the heart of pain, I met tenderness."

References

Anaut, M. (2009). La relation de soin dans le cadre de la résilience. *Informations sociales*, 70(156), 70–78.

Anaut, M. (2015). La résilience: évolution des conceptions théoriques et des applications cliniques. *Recherche en soins infirmiers*, 121(2), 28–39.

Ausloos, G. (2010). De la crise à la résilience face au cancer. In M. Delage & B. Cyrulnik (Eds.), *Famille et resilience* (pp. 165–179). Paris: Odile Jacob.

Bellehumeur, C. (2011). Rapprochements entre la résilience, la spiritualité et l'imaginaire Durandien. *Counselling et spiritualité*, 30(1), 45–70.

Bellehumeur, C.R. (2019). Psychologie Positive et Psychothérapie Positive: Un Bilan Synthèse des Contributions Majeures. In C.R. Bellehumeur & J. Malette (Eds.), *Psychologie Positive et Spiritualité en Psychothérapie: Fondements, Recherche et Applications* (pp. 41–69). Québec: Presses de l'Université Laval.

Bellehumeur, C.R., Deschênes, G., & Malette, J. (2012). L'imaginaire au Cœur du Développement Psychospirituel des Jeunes: Une Réflexion Interdisciplinaire sur la Spiritualité de l'Enfance et de la Préadolescence. *Sciences Religieuses*, 41(1), 68–92.

Bellehumeur, C.R., Lavoie, L.-C., Malette, J., Laprée, R., & Guindon, M. (2013). An empirical study of young French Quebecers' imagination using the archetypal test with nine elements: Exploring the links between interpersonal style and socioeconomic status. *International Journal of Interdisciplinary Cultural Studies*, 7(3), 11–25.

Benson, P.L., Roehlkepartain, E.C., & Rude, S.P. (2003). Spiritual development in childhood and adolescence: Toward a field of inquiry. *Applied Developmental Science*, 7, 204–212.

Block, C., & Cianfrini, L. (2013). Neuropsychological and neuroanatomical sequelae of chronic non-malignant pain and opoid analgesia. *NeuroRehabilitation*, 33, 343–366.

Carignan, L.-M., & Bellehumeur, C.R. (2018). Journeys from shattered dreams to meaning-making in a resilience framework: Families with special needs children. In L. Armstrong (Ed.), *Existential elements of the family* (pp. 183–214). Leuven: Peeters.

Carignan, L.-M., & Bellehumeur, C.R. (2019). Bilan-synthèse de l'historique des rapports entre la psychologie, la religion et la spiritualité. In C. Bellehumeur & Judith Malette (Eds.), *Psychologie positive et spiritualité en psychothérapie: Fondements et applications*. Quebec : Presses de l'Université Laval.

Cragg, J.J., Warner, F.M., Shupler, M.S., Jutzeler, C.R., Cashman, N., Whitehurst, D.G.T., & Kramer, J.K. (2018). Prevalence of chronic pain among individuals with neurological conditions. *Health Reports*, 29(3), 11–16.

Crawford, E., O'Dougherty Wright, M., & Masten, A.S. (2006). Resilience and spirituality in youth. In E.C. Roehlkepartain, P. Ebstyneking, L.M. Wagener, & P.L. Benson (Eds.), *The handbook of spiritual development in childhood and adolescence* (pp. 355–370). Thousand Oaks, CA: Sage Publications.

Cunningham, B. (2009). Resiliency: The art of bouncing forward! Resilience in the individual and the family system. Retrieved from: www.cunninghamtherapy.com/Resiliency.en.html.

Dedeli, O., & Kaptan, G. (2013). Spirituality and religion in pain and pain management. *Health Psychology Research*, 1(3), e29. doi:10.4081/hpr.2013.e29.

Delage, M. (2010). La famille confrontée au traumatisme. Déchirure des liens et résilience. In M. Delage & B. Cyrulnik (Eds.), *Famille et resilience* (pp. 17–38). Paris: Odile Jacob.

Dueñas, M., Ojeda, B., Salazar, A., Mico, J.A., & Failde, I. (2016). A review of chronic pain impact on patients, their social environment and the health care system. *Journal of Pain Research*, 9, 457–467.

Durand, G. (1960). *Les structures anthropologiques de l'imaginaire. Introduction à l'archétypologie générale.* Paris: Dunod.

Durand, G. (1979). *Figures mythiques et Visage de l'œuvre: De la mythocritique à la mythanalyse.* Paris: Berg International.

Durand, G. (1980). *L'Ame tigrée, les pluriels de Psyché*, Paris: Denoël.

Durand, G. (1992). *Les structures anthropologiques de l'imaginaire. Introduction à l'archétypologie générale*, 11th edn. Paris: Dunod.

Durand, G. (1999). *The anthropological structures of the imaginary* (translated by M. Sankey & J. Hatten). Brisbane: Boombana Publishing.

Farley, Y.R. (2007). Making the connection: Spirituality, trauma and resiliency. *Journal of Religion & Spirituality in Social Work*, 26(1), 1–15.

Florida Medical Clinic (2018). The psychological impact of chronic pain. Retrieved from: www.floridamedicalclinic.com/blog/psychological-impact-chronic-pain/.

Hood, R.W.J., Hill, P.C., & Spilka, B. (2009). *The psychology of religion: An empirical approach*, 4th edn. New York: The Guilford Press.

Johnson, S. (2004). *The practice of emotionally focused couple therapy: Creating connection.* New York: Routledge.

Laprée, R. (2000). *La psychagogie des valeurs: Symbolique et imaginaire en education.* Montréal: Logiques.

Laprée, R. (2013). La dynamique de groupe et les structures anthropologiques de l'imaginaire. In R. Laprée & C.R. Bellehumeur (Eds.), *L'imaginaire durandien: Enracinements et envols en Terre d'Amérique* (pp. 149–165). Quebec City: Presses de l'Université Laval.

Laprée, R. (2017). *La sagesse des 9–12 ans: 30 vies chez monsieur Lazhar.* Quebec City: Presses de l'Université Laval.

Lava, N. (2018). Tips for living with chronic pain. WebMD Medical Reference. Retrieved from: www.webmd.com/pain-management/guide/11-tips-for-living-with-chronic-pain#1.

Lepore, S.J. & Revenson, T.A. (2006). Resilience & posttraumatic growth: Recovery, resistance, & reconfiguration. In L.G. Calhoun & R.G. Tedeschi (Eds.), *Handbook of posttraumatic growth: Research and practice.* Mahwah: Lawrence Erlbaum Associates, pages 24-46.

Lesser, E. (2007). *Le big-bang intérieur: Quand les épreuves guérissent l'âme.* Montréal: Le Jour.

McAllister, M. (2015). Understanding chronic pain. Retrieved from: www.institutefor chronicpain.org/un[...]ma.

Molitor, N., Keck, A., & K. Nordal (2019). Coping with chronic pain. Retrieved from: www.apa.org/helpcenter/chronic-pain.

Moyle, S. (2016). The emotional and psychological impacts of chronic pain. Retrieved from: www.ausmed.com/cpd/articles/chronic-pain-emotional-psychological-impacts.

Nguyen, T.T., Bellehumeur, C.R., & Malette, J. (2018). Images of God and the imaginary in the face of loss: A quantitative research on Vietnamese immigrants living in Canada. *Mental Health, Religion & Culture*, 21(5), 484–499.

Nye, R. (1999). Relational consciousness and the spiritual lives of children: Convergence with children's theory of mind? In H. Reich, F.K. Oser, & W.G. Scarlett (Eds), *Psychological studies on spiritual and religious development* (pp. 57–83). Lengerich: Pabst.

Pain Australia (2015). What is pain? Retrieved from: www.painaustralia.org.au/about-pain/what-is-pain.

Paloutzian, R.F. (2005). Religious conversion and spiritual transformation. In R.F. Paloutzian & C.L. Park (Eds.), *Handbook of the psychology of religion and spirituality* (pp. 331–347), New York: The Guilford Press.

Paloutzian, R.F., & Park, C.L. (2015). Religiousness and spirituality: The psychology of multilevel meaning-making behavior. *Religion, Brain & Behavior*, 5(2), 166–178. doi:10.1080/2153599X.2014.891254.

Park, C.L. (2005). Religion and meaning. In R.F. Paloutzian & C.L. Park (Eds.), *Handbook of the psychology of religion and spirituality* (pp. 295–314). New York: The Guilford Press.

Park, C.L. (2010). Making sense of the meaning literature: An integrative review of meaning making and its effects on adjustment stressful life events. *Psychological Bulletin*, 136(2), 257–301.

Richardson, G.E. (2002). The metatheory of resilience and resiliency. *Journal of Clinical Psychology*, 58, 307–321.

Roehlkepartain, E., Benson, P.L., Ebstyne King, P., & Wagener, L. (2006). Spiritual development in childhood and adolescence: Moving to the scientific mainstream. In E. Roehlkepartain, P. Ebstyne King, L. Wagener, & P. Benson (Eds.), *The handbook of spiritual development in childhood and adolescence* (pp. 1–15). Thousand Oaks: Sage Publications.

Rolland, J.S. (2012). Mastering family challenges in serious illness and disability. In F. Walsh (Ed.), *Normal family processes*, 4th edn. New York: Guilford Press.

Rusinek, S. (2018). Douleur chronique. In F. Chapelle, B. Monié, R. Poinsot, & S. Rusinek (Eds.), *Aide-Mémoire: Thérapies Comportementales et Cognitives en 37 notions*, 3rd edn (pp. 141–148). Malakoff: Dunod.

Salazar, A., Dueñas, M., Mico, J.A., Ojeda, B., Aguera-Ortiz, L., Cervilla, J.A., & Failde, I. (2013). Undiagnosed mood disorders and sleep disturbance in primary care patients with chronic musculoskeletal pain. *Pain Medicine*, 14, 1416–1425.

Séguin, M., Beauchamp, G., Robert, M., DiMambro, M., & Turecki, G. (2014). Developmental model of suicide trajectories. *British Journal of Psychiatry*, 205(2), 120–126.

Souty, J. (2006). Gilbert Durand: La réhabilitation de l'imaginaire. *Sciences Humaines*, 176. Retrieved from: www.scienceshumaines.com/gilbert-durand-la-rehabilitation-de-l-imaginaire_fr_14969.html.

Sturgeon, J.A., Dixon, E.A., Darnall, B.D., & Mackey, S.C. (2015). Contributions of physical function and satisfaction with social roles to emotional distress in chronic pain: A Collaborative Health Outcomes Information Registry (CHOIR) study. *Pain*, 156(12), 2627–2633.

Turk, D.C., Dworkin, R.H., Revicki, D., Harding, G., Burke, L.B., Cella, D., Cleeland, C.S., Cowan, P., Farrar, J.T., Hertz, S., Max, M.B., & Rappaport, B.A. (2008). Identifying important outcome domains for chronic pain clinical trials: An IMMPACT survey of people with pain. *Pain*, 137(2), 276–285.

Turner-Cobb, J.M., Michalaki, M., & Osborn, M. (2015). Self-conscious emotions in patients suffering from chronic musculoskeletal pain: A brief report. *Psychology & Health*, 30, 495–501.

Vinay, A. (2004). Repérer et développer les comportements résilients: Maël, un adolescent adopté. *Revue québécoise de psychologie*, 25(1), 171–185.

Walsh, F. (2016). *Strengthening family resilience*, 3rd edn. New York: Guilford Press.

Wolin, S., & Wolin, S. (1993). *The resilient self.* New York: Willard Books.
Wong, P.T.P. (Ed.). (2012). *The human quest for meaning: Theories, research, and applications*, 2nd edn. New York: Routledge.
Wong, P.T.P. (2013). A meaning-centered approach to addiction and recovery. In L.C.J. Wong, G.R. Thompson, & P.T.P. Wong (Eds.), *The positive psychology of meaning and addiction recovery*. Birmingham, AL: Purpose Research. Retrieved from www.drpaulwong.com/meaning-centered-approach-addiction-recovery/
Wong, P.T.P. (2015). Meaning therapy: Assessments and interventions. *Existential Analysis*, 26(1), 154–167.
Wong, P.T.P., & Wong, L.C.J. (2012). A meaning-centered approach to building youth resilience. In P.T.P. Wong (Ed.), *The human quest for meaning: Theories, research, and applications*, 2nd edn (pp. 585–617). New York: Routledge.
Xiberras, M. (2002). *Pratique de l'imaginaire: Lecture de Gilbert Durand.* Québec: PUL.

7 A Resilient Identity

Myth or Reality?

Stephanie Massicotte

21-year-old Dylan sat facing his therapist for the umpteenth time and sighed frustratingly. Week after week, he sat in the same chair and talked about his problems, but nothing ever seemed to change. "I'm not saying I'm against the occasional pity-party," his therapist was saying gently "I'm simply saying that we can't still call it a 'pity-party' if it's your permanent state of mind. I'm starting to wonder if maybe what you're wrestling with is a full-blown victim identity. After all, it would be normal if you saw yourself as a victim after what he did to you –" Dylan bolted up in his chair, "I'm NOT a victim!" he interrupted. "I'm a man, not some damsel in distress! Life has just been harder for me, you don't understand." But the therapist sat perfectly still until the silence made Dylan squirm. "Well, if I did have this victim identity thing … what would I need to do to get rid of it anyways …?"

"Finding yourself" and "reinventing yourself" are very popular topics in the world of pop psychology and self-help books; a quick Google search can certainly substantiate this observation. The topic of identity is a fascinating subject which intrigues not only mental health professionals, but sociologists, anthropologists, economists, political scientists and even your average Joe (Oyserman, Elmore & Smith, 2012). Famed Canadian philosopher Charles Taylor argues that the self "ought to be an object of study like any other" (1989). But why is identity of such interest? Have you ever considered studying your "self"? Is our identity really important? The answer is yes; having an identity is very important in order to function through life.

An "identity" is a broad concept encompassing the sense of self which includes roles in relationships, how an individual relates to oneself and perceives oneself in different contexts, different beliefs about oneself, and "ideal self-representations" (Agnew, Ciarán, Ryan, Storey & Mcdonnell, 2016). Our identity is the lens through which we make sense of ourselves and the world in which we live (Oyserman et al., 2012). It is important to have a coherent sense of self because our behaviour flows consequently from our perception of self. Changing how we think about ourselves will alter ensuing behaviours in order to remain coherent in our sense of self.

According to Erickson, constructing a personal identity is a lifelong journey (Feist, Feist & Roberts, 2013). It is a process that requires time, effort and a sense of self-awareness in a multitude of circumstances which provide self-relevant information. Thus, one's identity has the opportunity to either flourish under positive circumstances or wither under unfavourable ones. That being said, having a healthy and coherent sense of self implies having a positive attitude towards self which is crucial for good mental health (Poujol, 2007). It could be argued that the role and function identity plays in people's lives often go unnoticed and thus when identity issues surface, the source may be difficult to identify. How can someone have a coherent sense of self after experiencing something as traumatizing as victimization?

How can one's identity not be overwhelmed and negatively redefined by the adversity? Some publications have coined the term "resilient identity" in passing, but without attempting to define it. A significant amount of attention has been granted to the topic of resilience in the field of psychology (Luthar, Cicchetti & Becker, 2000), however the concept of a "resilient identity" has not benefited from such attention thus far. This leaves a gap in understanding how people can overcome the "victim label" while others succumb to it. If an identity can change for the worse, could it also change for the better? What is the relationship between identity and resilience? And is a resilient identity possible for everyone or just the lucky few? Does a resilient identity even exist in the first place? The purpose of this chapter is to explore the specific relationship between identity, trauma and the possibility of adopting a resilient sense of self in spite of adversity.

Defining Identity

In our quest to discover this illusive "resilient identity," we must begin with the basics and understand what an identity is. However, an identity differs from similar concepts such as personality, which is defined as "a pattern of relatively permanent traits and unique characteristics that give both consistency and individuality to a person's behaviour" (Feist et al., 2013). In other words, personality is innate and more permanent than an identity. Although one's personality can influence one's identity, the two are not interchangeable even though they can certainly be interactive.

Identity can be a complex concept prone to varying definitions according to culture and historical era (Taylor, 1989). Fortunately, it can be explained simply as the way we see, evaluate and feel about ourselves (Poujol, 2007). This understanding of identity is a very modern and Western way of thinking which promotes individuality and inwardness as core values (Taylor, 1989). After defining identity in those terms, Poujol (2007) goes on to state that having a coherent identity is crucial in order to have a good quality of life because it can be the difference between being "at home" or "at war" with ourselves. Identity, along with a sense of self, plays an important role in one's mental health. In fact: "findings suggest that identity is an integral aspect of [difficulties with mental illnesses such as] Borderline Personality Disorder" (Agnew et al., 2016). Lacking a coherent identity can be linked to poor psychological well-being and of course increases the risk of having an identity crisis (Andrew, Fisk & Rockwood, 2012).

This begs the question, what makes our identity coherent? Charles Taylor elaborates eloquently on this topic by asserting that the question "who am I?" is best answered by understanding what is of fundamental value to the individual (Taylor, 1989). What is "of crucial importance" for an individual constitutes a point of reference by which we can evaluate and determine "what is good, or valuable, or what ought to be done" (1989). However, the importance of culture's influence upon us must not be under-estimated; our values can be framed within a cultural understanding. If we use the example previously mentioned of the men who were victimized by hate crimes, their understanding of what it meant to be a "man" and a "victim" was thoroughly tainted by cultural, therefore external, norms and definitions (Dunn, 2012). Therefore, our values are understood and interpreted within a cultural and temporal context. Taylor explains that if we were to lose one or many of these points of reference, then we would experience an "acute form of disorientation" leading to an identity crisis often characterized by "a radical uncertainty of where they stand" and "not knowing who [we] are" (1989). Indeed, our identity provides an "orienting … meaning-making lens" because we make choices based on our identity and who we perceive ourselves to be (Oyserman et al., 2012). In other words, one's identity influences the way one interprets the world and assigns value and priority differently than another person would. Therefore, an identity is the frame which structures the sense of self into a coherent understanding that can shape and orient our behaviour, our choices and our interpretation of the world.

But before venturing farther on the subject, a crucial question has to be addressed in order to validate the fundamental premise of our quest; is identity a stable construct? In other words, can our identity change or does it consistently remain the same? This point is of crucial centrality to this chapter, because if identity is immutable, then the concept of a resilient identity is more than improbable – it is utterly impossible. Therefore, the next step in exploring if a resilient identity is possible is to examine if our identity is stable or malleable.

Interestingly, whether or not identity is malleable was a popular intriguing mystery in ancient Greece. An example commonly used is Plato's philosophical thought experiment often referred to as "Theseus' ship." The analogy narrates that after some years a single plank on Theseus' ship became rotten and was subsequently replaced. However, over time the ship continued to undergo reparations when needed and the owner did so by only replacing one plank at a time. After the last of the original planks was replaced, the following question emerged; is it still the same ship or is it considered a new one? Clearly this thought-provoking analogy has no simple answer; but it does illustrate identity's paradox of being both the same in essence yet changing over time. Some identity theorists support this view and speculate that the self is paradoxically both stable and fluid (Oyserman et al., 2012). However, this is a highly controversial topic.

On one hand, some theorists speculate that a stable identity is crucial for a good mental health while instability is a sign of mental illness (Schachter, 2004; Agnew et al., 2016). Research typically demonstrates that people often "go to great lengths to protect the images they have of themselves" and avoid change by "ignoring or reinterpreting contradictory information and distancing themselves" from the threat of changing their identity (Oyserman et al., 2012). Having a stable sense of self is certainly reassuring to the individual and the people around them because maintaining a sense of continuity and "sameness" is important not only for the individual's well-being, but also for society's welfare (Schachter, 2004). Since people are naturally very attached to their self-image, if or when it is threatened, that threat becomes a source of great stress. The ability to remain essentially the same is undoubtedly of crucial importance to frame the sense of self into a coherent understanding that can guide one's life.

On the other hand, some theorists question whether "personal continuity" might be a socially imposed construct restricting the self and resulting in "fragmentation and incoherence [within the self]" (Schachter, 2004). In the same vein, Mishler (2004) challenges the objectivity of our perception of reality and the subsequent interpretation of information about self. He argues that one's narrative or life-story is continually revised and updated and thus influenced by various aspects of one's environment and experiences. As "historians of their own lives," people can amend and modify their personal story over time and when "they tell and retell their stories in variant ways [they] continually revise their identities" (Mishler, 2004). Poujol (2007) adds that human beings unconsciously juxtapose symbolic significance to the real world in order to assign meaning to their lives and the world around them. Those symbols are endowed of the values the individual attributes to it. Thus, personal interpretation brings a highly subjective and malleable view of self, others and the world.

Having the ability to change is necessary in order to adapt to various situations and contexts. One's identity must be context-sensitive in order to be efficient in its role because it orients the individual in his or her perception of self, others and the world and consequently behaviour and interaction. Thus, if the concept of self was incapable of adapting, it would lose its efficiency as a tool over time (Oyserman et al., 2012). This approach would therefore recognize the importance of stability while still advocating, not for a randomly changing sense of self, but for a need to adapt as a strategic response to new information. In other words, while maintaining a sense of continuity, adapting is essential in an ever-changing world.

Clearly, either theory is difficult to prove empirically because "self and identity may appear quite stable or quite changeable depending on how they are assessed" (Oyserman et al., 2012). Therefore, we will adopt a paradoxical stance which claims that identity is both fluid and stable because the identity needs to be stable enough to orient the individual yet changeable enough in order to adapt strategically and be context-sensitive.

Identity and Attachment Theory

The next step in our exploration is to understand how we develop our identity and how it is subject to change. A multitude of theoretical frameworks have been produced in the field of psychology which define the conception of our identity. But for the purpose of our exploration, Bowlby's attachment theory will be favoured in order to examine how the concept of self can be altered in response to significant external influences. John Bowlby (1907–1990) was a psychoanalyst, like Freud, who believed that mental health and behavioural problems could be attributed to early childhood (Feist et al., 2013). The attachment theory speculates that through the relationship with the child's primary caregiver, the child learns lessons such as: he is loved, his needs are important and can be satisfied or that the opposite is true (Bowlby, 1969).

A secure attachment style will allow and even encourage the child to explore because he or she feels safe and able to return to the safe haven that is the primary caregiver. By exploring his or her surroundings, the child can learn self-relevant information and experiences which are in turn adopted into the internal working models (Bowlby, 1969). These internal working models, or I.W.M., are cognitive frameworks to which Bowlby referred as "cognitive maps" which lay the foundation for the child's perception of the world so he may comprehend "how the physical world may be expected to behave, how his mother and other significant persons may be expected to behave, how he himself may be expected to behave, and how each interacts with the other" (Bowlby, 1969). Therefore, the I.W.M. store and contain valuable information that the child accumulates through time and personal experiences which serve him to be better equipped as he manoeuvres through life (Guedeney & Guedeney, 2015). Because the I.W.M. are developed within a relationship with the primary caregiver, the quality of that relationship will determine the kind of messages and meanings the child internalizes about self and others (Demasure, 2014). The comparison between I.W.M. and "cognitive maps" is in line with the previous discussion on the importance of having a stable yet fluid identity (Oyserman et al., 2012), though a map provides concrete directions, it must still be revised and updated with new information in order to stay relevant.

Indeed, these "cognitive maps" begin to develop from birth when the information has a pre-linguistic nature and is acquired through sensorimotor skills (Bowlby, 1969). From childhood onward, an individual perceives and interprets his or her surroundings, relationships and self through the lens of the I.W.M. initially developed as a result of the individual's experiences within the relationship with the primary caregiver which continue to develop in complexity and nuances throughout a lifetime (Guedeney & Guedeney, 2015). Indeed, the ways the primary caregiver perceives and interacts with the child provide the child with important information about him or herself (Jousselme, 2008). However, the initial I.W.M. which were conceived in childhood can be altered by later significant relationships either for the better or for the worse

(Demasure, 2014). After all; "the self-concept is a social, flexible construct that shifts in response to the salience of a relationship partner" (Gabriel, Carvallo, Dean, Tippin & Renaud, 2005). Hence identity is a cognitive construct informed by a social environment.

In fact, a thorough psychological study was conducted to determine whether or not an individual's identity changed within the context of a close friendship (Gabriel et al., 2005). The study consisted of experimenting with undergraduate students at the State University of New York at Buffalo, and the results were compared with their personal attachment style. The study demonstrated that those with a secure attachment style tend to adopt similarities with close friends whereas those with an unsure attachment style did not. Indeed, they concluded that "friends not only lead to shifts in self-perception but they also lead to shifts in actual behaviour" (Gabriel et al., 2005). Because one's identity is not only a cognitive construct, but also a social product in need of social support, thus "being a self requires others who endorse and reinforce one's selfhood, who scaffold a sense that one's self matters" (Oyserman et al., 2012).

Contrasting Traditional and Modern Identity: Inward versus Outward

Because "self and identity are social products," it is important to consider the role that society plays in the development of identity (Oyserman et al., 2012). As discussed with Bowlby's Attachment Theory, the self first develops within the context of a relationship with a primary caregiver, but relationships continue to play an important role throughout the various stages of life. After all, humans are social creatures and we "cannot discover or create an identity in isolation, merely through some kind of internal dialogue" (Keller, 2016). The previously mentioned experiment from the State University of New York at Buffalo demonstrated our subconscious desire to resemble those with who we are in close relationship (Gabriel et al., 2005). This can be applied on a greater scale with societal norms and values. Indeed, it is a well-known "fact about human beings that they care that their image matches up to certain standards, generally socially induced" (Taylor, 1989). The individual will thus be prone to define herself according to what is valued in her culture and her place within society (Oyserman et al., 2012). For example; "family roles, looks, school attainment, athletic prowess should matter more or less depending on what is valued in one's culture" (Oyserman et al., 2012). Those values change according to the culture and the time period. Taylor expanded on the topic of self and emphasized how much time and culture influences the values through which the sense of self is constructed. He provides the example of the "warrior morality" in what might be considered ancient cultures such as the Celts and primitive Scandinavians. These cultures had "externally oriented values" including courage, strength and action, enabling people to execute great deeds which would be demonstrated or proven on a battlefield. The ultimate achievement of success in that time and culture was to attain immortality by accomplishing famous and long-celebrated feats (Taylor, 1989). Taylor contrasted this externally oriented warrior culture to modern society which he described as "internally oriented." Indeed, dying on a battlefield after accomplishing feats exhibiting great strength and courage is far from today's "American Dream." Therefore, identity is very much a product of its time. In fact, Taylor speculates that since the olden days of "warrior morality" great philosophers, such as Descartes and Locke and Plato, had a hand in reinforcing certain values and opinions which shaped entire cultures, thus making the modern concept of identity the product of a rich socio-historical heritage which influences the way the self is perceived today (Taylor, 1989).

Modern Identity

Just as culture influences identity, the same can be said about the time period. As stated, today's modern identity greatly values an internal and individualistic orientation (Taylor, 1989). While basing his arguments on the works of thinkers such as Taylor, Keller underlines the irony of our paradoxical dilemma when it comes to our modern-day search for identity. Keller asserts that "we must look outside ourselves and connect to something else first, before we can descend into ourselves" (2016). This view of cultivating an identity through an outward connectedness fits perfectly with Bowlby's Attachment Theory. However, Keller makes the distinction that modern identity, unlike traditional identity, bought into the belief that a sense of self is created in a private sphere (2016). Indeed, books, movies, television shows and even social media influence the way people see themselves (White & Perrone, 2001), and these often circulate the message to look for "internal validation" without external approval of others (Keller, 2016). Taylor names this a "buffered" concept of self which has very clear and firm borders not only between different people as individuals, but also within the individual; between mind and body, and internal and external worlds (Taylor, 2007). This individualist point of view is drastically contrasted by the community-oriented "traditional identity" of ancient Western cultures as well as today's non-Western cultures (Keller, 2016). Although modern-day people proudly claim to have emancipated themselves from traditional restrictions dictating their identity, Keller points out that people still require some kind of external validation. He remarks that identity cannot be shaped through "an internal monologue" in seclusion. On the contrary, an identity evolves "through dialogue with the moral values and beliefs of some community" (2016). Instead of developing our identity within a community, modern individuals now aspire to find a sense of self and worth in their chosen area of interest whether it be a profession, a particular relationship, sport, or any other achievement (Keller, 2016). But the need for validation from others still remains; it only shifted to those directly involved in the area of interest (Keller, 2016).

Of course, either opposite is of equal danger. Just as isolation is detrimental for the development of the self, extreme external attachment, to a relationship, a goal or even a dream can have devastating results on our identity. Indeed, "the self-made identity, based on our own performance and achievement … makes our self-worth far more fragile in the face of failure and difficulty" (Keller, 2016). In fact, this quest of finding validation through a specific achievement can take on the characteristics of an addiction; "more and more is required to obtain the same high, and the compulsion of the pursuit prompts a growing sense of the despair and unworthiness it is meant to solve" (Schwartz, 2015). Therefore, this type of unilateral identity seeking is extremely vulnerable and unstable, not to mention unsatisfying.

Fortunately, recent findings reveal our identity as a plural and flexible concept (Agnew et al., 2016). This signifies that the self can demonstrate multiple facets and roles which are not singularly defined by a relationship, career or achievement.

Definition of Victim and the "Victim Label"

The definition of "victim," according to the Merriam-Webster dictionary, describes "one that is acted on and usually adversely affected by a force or agent; (1) injured, destroyed, or sacrificed under any of various conditions (2) subjected to oppression, hardship, or mistreatment" (n.d.). In other words, to identify an individual as a victim is to emphasize the effect of an external harmful incident on the individual. Indeed, the word "victim" is distinctly linked with both the abuse experienced and the abuser responsible (Demasure, 2014). The term "victim" can be a heavy and loaded label which holds many different implications to a given individual. The Red Cross speculated in one of its publications that the term "victim" can evoke adverse psychological effects such as shame and helplessness and suggests a sense of weakness, vulnerability, passivity, subjugation and an inability to meet one's own needs either for protection or for the restitution in the aftermath (Meredith, 2009). This "victim label" can be experienced as an invasive new identification imposed upon the affected individual's sense of self, it can be seen by some as a reminder of one's own weakness and that "the offender had prevailed" (Dunn, 2012). Other individuals may consider it useful in understanding their own innocence in the traumatic incident (Dunn, 2012). Thus, as the Red Cross indicates, the concept of "victim" is inescapably tied to self-perception (Meredith, 2009). As previously mentioned in the introduction, Dunn's research with men who were victims of hate crimes struggled with the "victim label" because it undermined their identity as "men" as though one cancels out the other (Dunn, 2012). In situations of victimization, certainties are shaken and the identity is questioned (Poujol, 2007). Therefore, an individual who suffers can find himself in an "identity crisis" because he is at a loss of symbolic meaning when forced to interpret his new state of being unwell. The frame which identity provides in order to interpret ourselves and the world around us is shaken and less coherent than before (Poujol, 2007).

The Effects of Abuse and Victimization on Identity

As previously mentioned, having a coherent and healthy sense of identity is inescapably linked to our quality of life and mental health; it is the difference between being "at home" or "at war" with ourselves (Poujol, 2007). Thus, when our sense of self is subjected to negative consequences in adverse situations, the tool through which we understand and evaluate everything is damaged, because our identity is the lens through which we perceive everything.

As previously established, an identity is a cognitive and social construct that cannot be developed in isolation; hence the magnitude of the impact abuse imposes on its "victim" because it is a form of relationship. According to research, one of the greatest triggers of cortisol, a stress-related hormone, was in response not only to "threats to one's social self" but also to a "threat to one's social acceptance, esteem and status" (Schwartz, 2015). In the context of victimization, one's "social acceptance, esteem and status" are certainly in peril or at the very least being jeopardized. In cases of abuse these I.W.M. which were conceived in childhood adjust in the aftermath of trauma in the interest of self-protection and self-preservation (Demasure, 2014). Therefore the I.W.M. contain new information about the world and how safe or threatening it is which either reinforces previous information or contradicts it in which case an adjustment will ensue. Unfortunately, it is equally true that the information on the self is also affected and consequently altered for better or for worse.

A study on the effects of bullying on teenage students in the northern United States examined the "association between adopting or denying the label of bully victim and students' psychosocial functioning" (Sharkey et al., 2015). The findings demonstrated that students who are frequently bullied internalize the experience of victimization which altered their self-perception and their identity adopted a "victim label" (Sharkey et al., 2015). The study explains that the process of internalizing the victimization comes through a need to question why this is happening to them and arriving to the unfortunate conclusion that *they* are the problem and the cause of the frequent victimization (Sharkey et al., 2015). Adopting a victim label was linked to a "more general self-deprecating self-identity" which was consequently associated with loneliness, self-blame, low self-esteem, anxiety and depression as well as suicidal thoughts and attempts (Sharkey et al., 2015). The solitude and alienation felt by the individual only reinforce the emotional distress (Poujol, 2007). On the other hand, students who denied being victims of bullying, even though their peers considered them as such, perceived themselves and functioned as "nonvictims" and thus avoided the negative psychological consequences of the victim label (Sharkey et al., 2015).

According to research examining the life narrative of survivors from victimization, abuse and trauma, there seems to be "an internalization of the perpetrator's view and an interference with positive identity development" (Brown, Kallivayalil, Mendelsohn, Harvey & Steven 2012). In fact, abuse is considered a form of "meta-communication" between the perpetrator and the injured party, which can be internalized and consequently influence the individual's self-perception (Croll, 2008). Such meta-communication "can get to your very core" (Dunn, 2012), and damage "fundamental beliefs about the world, self and others" (Roth & Newman, 1992). The consequential alterations in regard to the self can be quite complex and harmful. It has been described by some survivors as "an annihilation of self" with repercussions including self-blame, helplessness, and "a fearful, shameful, and generally powerless self" (Roth & Newman, 1992). In addition to the cognitive and affective ramifications, there also exist somatic consequences to the concept of self in the aftermath of trauma. Depending on the nature of the trauma, the individual's body can be a reminder of the abuse (Brown et al., 2012). In some cases, the individual can even have a dissociative relationship with their body by not feeling quite in control of it or not feeling a sense of ownership and personal belonging (Roth & Newman, 1992). "Anger, depression, fear, shame, loss of self-esteem, and onset of posttraumatic stress disorder" are all frequent and common consequences of victimization (Dunn, 2012).

Black, Curran and Dyer (2013) argue that "profound or cumulative aversive life experiences can instil negative core beliefs/attitudes about the self (e.g., worthlessness, badness) which morph into shame-related cognitive biases, emotional states, and behaviours." Therefore, the integrity of one's identity can be compromised and introduced to a painful intruder – shame. Consequently, shame's detriment on personal development harms and even corrupts the identity which will in turn pollute the individual's relationships with self, others and the divine (Caine, 2016).

Shame and Identity

Shame is essentially a self-conscious emotion requiring "self awareness and a sense of self-identity" (Black et al., 2013). It can be seen as "an authentic manifestation of being human" because it is a common painful by-product of being aware of our own human fragility and limitations as mere mortals (Martinez De Pisòn, 2006). However, there exists a toxic type of shame that seeps into an individual's life and corrupts the way they see themselves. When shame takes up residency, it manipulates its host's identity because it contaminates "the very image we have of ourselves" (Anderson, 2016). Their identity becomes shackled to their own perception of being "inferior, inadequate or defective" (Mendes, Ferreira, Marta-Simoes & Trindade, 2016). If "who they are, where they fit in and what might be possible for them" is processed through a thick filter of shame, then their whole life will inevitably bear marks of its affliction (Munford & Sanders, 2015).

Unfortunately, shame has been linked to a multitude of psychological disorders ranging from violence and rage to depression and posttraumatic stress disorder (Black et al., 2013). Certainly, the most devastating result of shame is suicide (Martinez-Pilkington, 2007). Shame can put down roots and thrive in virtually any stage of an individual's development regardless of their age (Martinez De Pisòn, 2006). However, if the issue of shame is not addressed in a timely fashion, it can then be repressed and its destructive effects postponed, manifesting itself more strongly at a later stage of personal development (Martinez-Pilkington, 2007). Some psychologists believe that depression is one of the more severe results of delayed or even "bypassed shame" (Martinez-Pilkington, 2007). Therefore, the best course of action when dealing with shame is to first acknowledge the issue at hand in order to avoid delayed reaction or bypassed shame. As made evident by the list of related psychological disorders, it might seem easier to address the symptoms while ignoring or overlooking the root problem of shame. As threatening as shame can be, it still remains a nebulous issue which can sometimes be overlooked, misunderstood or even misdiagnosed by clinicians. In fact, misdiagnosing shame is frequent in our Western culture because shame and guilt are often erroneously considered to be similar, if not interchangeable (Martinez-Pilkington, 2007). Even though both guilt and shame can cause great psychological and emotional distress, they remain fundamentally different and must be addressed accordingly as to not worsen the suffering of the afflicted individual. The important distinction to be made between guilt and shame is that guilt stems out of the perception of committing a condemned action while shame stems out of perceiving oneself to be flawed and condemned (Martinez-Pilkington, 2007). "Simply put, guilt says 'I did something bad.' While shame says 'I am (fundamentally) something bad'" (Martinez-Pilkington, 2007). Although guilt can be a healthy "internal alarm" signalling a need to stop and assume responsibility for a specific action, shame on the other hand is an emotionally painful state of being (Caine, 2016). Blurring the lines between shame and guilt has created an environment where captives of shame are not recognized as such. Instead, they are treated as if they are afflicted with guilt like any other wrongdoer. The danger here is the possibility to add insult to injury by labelling victims as perpetrators and therefore worsen the suffering instead of helping in the healing process (Martinez-Pilkington, 2007).

In 2016, a study conducted with women struggling with severe eating disorders claimed that shame was the underlying culprit of the addictive disorder and that a strong correlation exists between the coping mechanism and a lack of self-compassion (Mendes et al., 2016). The less compassion women had towards themselves the more severe their eating disorder was and the more pressure they took upon themselves to achieve the "perfect body" (Mendes et al., 2016). Regrettably, one of the most common maladapted ways to cope with shame is to "attack the self" which already feels inadequate and flawed (Black et al., 2013). Therefore, self-compassion makes way for the shame-afflicted individual to practice self-acceptance in spite of feeling inferior and the vicious cycle of self-debasing can end. Thus, the second important step, after acknowledging the issue with shame, is to respond with self-compassion.

Unfortunately, shame's damage goes beyond someone's personal development. Low self-worth will inevitably affect a person's relationships and interaction with the external world around them. At its core, shame is essentially a fear of being rejected by others and thus has deep-seated social ramifications tied to a dread of "negative evaluation from others" (Black et al., 2013). When shame erodes the identity by diminishing our perceived worth, it is only natural that relationships would suffer. In fact, "shame and shame-proneness predict poorer relationship satisfaction, quality, and functioning, decreased perceived social rank, and increased fear of intimacy" (Black et al., 2013). In fact, a "shame model" has been theorized with four basic coping responses to shame which include: "attacking the self, attacking others, withdrawing, or avoiding" (Black et al., 2013). These four shame-induced reactions provide a false sense of comfort and security leading the defensive person to believe that there is nothing safe outside of these maladapted coping mechanisms and therefore encourages the individual to cling to these (Caine, 2016).

Building a Resilient Identity: A Discussion

With the key elements explored in depth in the previous pages, a discussion about the concept of a "resilient identity" can ensue. Since identity plays a significant role in providing a frame to understand and interpret self, others and the world, having a coherent sense of self is crucial for good mental health. As previously mentioned, the rationale held in this discussion is that if an identity can change for the worse, it could also change for the better. Therefore, the question "how is resilience applicable to identity?" should be investigated. The first step in addressing this question has been explored in the previous pages; it was determined that identity is an evolving construct and resilience is also a process which involves abilities that can be learned. Because both are proven to be active and ongoing processes, they could possibly overlap and produce a resilient identity.

A Working Definition of a Resilient Identity

Because so little is known about the concept of resilient identity, it is difficult to conceptualize a proper definition. But since its existence has been established as being plausible, a definition would be required in order to have a working understanding of the parameters of this concept, before pursuing the topic any further. Resilience can be taught, yes, but in order to determine, or even explore whether or not a *resilient identity* can be taught, or how, one must first know what a resilient identity is.

A few guiding principles might be helpful in this task. First of all, even though a strong definition of resilience exists, there still seems to be "a wide range of opinions regarding what objectively constitutes resilient behaviour" (Alvord, Rich & Berghorst, 2016). A reason for this diversity of opinion is the role culture plays, not only in determining the values and areas in which individuals will prioritize to develop resilience, but also in judging if the adaptation is at all successful. What constitutes a successful adaptation would likely differ from one culture to another because of the prevailing values and the behaviour encouraged. Therefore, cultural expectations play an important role in "how one defines a resilient response to life challenges" (Alvord et al., 2016). Just like identity will develop according to what is valued within a society, so will resilience also develop in order to meet the standards and expectations of a given society. Thus, a resilient identity is doubly governed by cultural norms. For the sake of this chapter, a Western influence will prevail in the making of this definition.

That being said, a resilient identity might be what Charles Taylor called a "porous" concept of self which is both open to "external social roles and ties" while still valuing internal desires (Keller, 2016). This balance between the internal and the external mitigates the influences exercised upon the sense of self. After all, an individual's understanding of "being does not exist strictly within our psyches. It is interdependent upon meanings and relationships that we locate and create inside and outside of ourselves" (Croll, 2008).

The previous sections already mentioned briefly a few typical characteristics and abilities commonly associated with resilience, however an individual with a resilient identity would not only possess those attributes, he or she would perceive and know himself or herself to have those attributes which would signify a deeper integration of resilience as being incorporated within the framework of the self. He or she would not simply react in a way that might be considered as resilient by other people; instead he or she would knowingly identify themselves as a resilient person. It would imply a strength-based recognition of self and the attribution of resiliency would not only come from the external, it would also be internally validated. Since one's identity is the lens through which one makes sense of the world, a resilient identity would mean a resilient perception of self in relation to others. Considering the conceptualization of identity, it is conceivable that someone identifying as resilient would also react and behave consistently with their global perception of self. In turn, this belief about self would evoke consistent behaviour in line with that way of perceiving the self, thus creating a balance between the individual's internal and external world. A resilient identity would signify an internalized message of resilience stipulating that one is capable of adapting positively in the face of adversity which is reflected in one's selfhood and actions.

Therefore, a resilient identity would represent a deeper integration and assimilation of resilient abilities through the process of internalization. By appropriating those resilient abilities as their own, one's personal values, belief systems and outlook on life starts to incorporate resilience as part of its "DNA."

Therapy, the Aftermath of Victimization and Identity

The logical next question is "how can we rebuild a positive self-identity"? How can clinicians help clients build a resilient identity through the therapeutic process? As a general rule, Brown (2015) encourages all those who teach resilience to focus on three spheres: "natural resilience" which involves exploring what is "as-yet undiscovered components of resilience" within the client; "strategies" which include coping mechanisms such as self-regulating techniques; and finally "values" which promote and encourage resilience such as courage or endurance.

Because resilience is often more common than expected, it is important for clinicians to identify the resilient tendencies already within the individuals in order to support, strengthen and validate natural abilities. Affirming this can help the person see him or herself in a more positive light and thus begin the process of adopting a resilient identity. One way of achieving this is through "Psychoeducational resilience enhancement" which is a practical approach to "reduce maladaptive coping mechanisms [and] foster adaptive coping skills" as a way to defer the consequences of stress and encourage resilience (Southwick, Pietrzak & White, 2011).

A crucial asset to the concept of resilient identity is having a "growth mindset" instead of a "fixed mindset." As already discussed, the common conception that identity is a fixed, stable and a singular construct is being replaced with an empirically supported belief that identity is fluid and individuals have a multiplicity of identities (Agnew et al., 2016). The "multiplicity of identities" could possibly be demonstrated differently by various people; for example, it could refer to multiple roles that are important to the person, or it could also represent different stages of growth achieved by the person; past, present and future. Indeed:

> identities can be focused on the past – what used to be true of one, the present – what is true of one now, or the future – what one expects or wishes to become, the person one feels obligated to try to become, or the person one fears one may become.
>
> (Oyserman et al., 2012)

This chronological perspective of the self can help the client explore who they were before or during the trauma, who they perceive themselves to be today, and who they hope to become in order to start building a favourable future identity. This can invite the client to explore possible "alternative views [of the self] as a result of other life experiences and their experience in therapy" and thus start defining him or herself "in a way other than by what others had done to her [or him]" (Roth & Newman, 1992).

Conclusion

Is a resilient identity possible? Yes, findings do support its existence. There exists a creditable intersection between identity and resilience which can produce a resilient identity. The concept of identity, or the sense of self, is a cognitive construct which collects its guiding information from the social sphere. It has been considered as a paradoxically stable yet malleable construct capable of adapting to new information when needed. Correspondingly, experts on the topic of resilience claim that resilience is not an innate trait only inherited by the few, but rather an ability to be acquired or learned through time and experience. Thus, resilience can be integrated within one's concept of self and consequently influence one's perceptions, actions and relationships not only with oneself but also with others and one's environment. A resilient identity could arguably represent a deeper integration of resilience by internalizing a message of one's ability to adapt despite adversity, which goes beyond a simple skill set.

References

Agnew, G., Ciarán, S., Ryan, T., Storey, L., & Mcdonnell, C. (2016). Self and identity in women with symptoms of borderline personality: A qualitative study. *International Journal of Qualitative Studies on Health and Well-being*, 11(1), 30490.

Alvord, M.K., Rich, B.A., & Berghorst, L.H. (2016). Resilience interventions. In J.C. Norcross, G.R. VandenBos, D.K. Freedheim, N. Pole, & L.H. Berghorst (Eds.), *APA handbook of clinical psychology*. Vol. 4, *Psychopathology and health* (pp. 505–519). Washington, DC: American Psychological Association.

Anderson, T.L. (2016). God our father as a script of intimacy for those suffering shame. *Journal of Spiritual Formation and Soul Care*, 9(2), 247–269.

Andrew, M.K., Fisk, J.D., & Rockwood, K. (2012). Psychological well-being in relation to frailty: A frailty identity crisis? *International Psychogeriatrics*, 24(8), 1347–1353.

Black, R.S.A., Curran, D., & Dyer, K.F.W. (2013). The impact of shame on the therapeutic alliance and intimate relationships. *Journal of Clinical Psychology*, 69(6), 646–654.

Bowlby, J. (1969). *Attachment and Loss*. Vol. 1, *Attachment*. New York: Basic Books.

Brown, N.R., Kallivayalil, D., Mendelsohn, M., Harvey, R., & Steven, N. (2012). Working the double edge: Unbraiding pathology and resiliency in the narratives of early-recovery trauma survivors. *Psychological Trauma: Theory, Research, Practice, and Policy*, 4(1), 102–111.

Brown, R. (2015). Building children and young people's resilience: Lessons from psychology. *International Journal of Disaster Risk Reduction*, 14, 115–124.

Caine, C. (2016). *Unashamed*. United States: Zondervan.

Croll, M.C. (2008). *Following sexual abuse: A sociological interpretation of identity re-formation in reflexive therapy*. University of Toronto Press.

Demasure, K. (2014). *Se relever après l'abus sexuel: accompaggnement psycho-spirituel des survivants*. Bruxelles: Lumen vitae.

Dunn, P. (2012). Men as victims: "Victim" identities, gay identities, and masculinities. *Journal of Interpersonal Violence*, 27(17), 3442–3467.

Feist, J., Feist, G., & Roberts, T-A. (2013). *Theories of personality*, 8th edn. New York: McGraw-Hill.

Gabriel, S., Carvallo, M., Dean, K.K., Tippin, B., & Renaud, J. (2005). How I see me depends on how I see we: The role of attachment style in social comparison. *Personality and Social Psychology Bulletin*, 31(11), 1561–1572.

Guédeney, N., & Guedeney, A. (2015). *L'attachement: approche théorique: Du bébé à la personne âgée*, 4th edn. Issy-les-Moulineaux: Elsevier Masson.

Jousselme, C. (2008). Souffrance dans la construction identitaire de l'enfant atteint de maladie chronique: place du regard parental. *Neuropsychiatrie de l'enfance et de l'adolescence*, 233–236.

Keller, T. (2016). *Making sense of God: An invitation to the sceptical.* New York: Viking.

Luthar, S.S., Cicchetti, D., & Becker, B. (2000). The construct of resilience: A critical evaluation and guidelines for future work. *Child Development*, 71, 543–562. doi:10.1111/1467-8624.00164.

Martinez De Pisòn, R. (2006). *Death by despair: Shame and suicide.* Germany: Peter Lang.

Martinez-Pilkington, A. (2007). Shame and guilt: The psychology of sacramental confession. *The Humanistic Psychologist*, 35(2), 203–218.

Mendes, A.L., Ferreira, C., Marta-Simoes, J., & Trindade, I.A. (2016). The effects of shame, self-compassion and perfectionist self-presentation of body image on eating psychopathology. *European Psychiatry*, 33(S1), 428.

Meredith, V. (2009). Victim identity and respect for human dignity: A terminological analysis. *International Review of the Red Cross*, 91(874), 259–277.

Merriam-Webster Dictionary (n.d.). Retrieved September 15, 2017 from www.merriam-webster.com/.

Mishler, E. (2004). Historian of the self: Restorying lives, revising identities. *Research in Human Development*, 1(1–2), 101–121.

Munford, B., & Sanders, J. (2015). Negotiating and constructing identity: Social work with young people who experience adversity. *British Journal of Social Work*, 45(5), 1564–1580.

Oyserman, D., Elmore, K., & Smith, G. (2012). *Handbook of self and identity.* New York: Guilford Press.

Poujol, J. (2007). *L'accompagnement psychologique et spiritual.* France: edition-empreinte.

Roth, S., & Newman, E. (1992). The role of helplessness in the recovery process for sexual trauma survivors. *Canadian Journal of Behavioural Science/Revue canadienne des Sciences du comportement*, 24(2), 220–232.

Schachter, E.P. (2004). Identity configurations: A new perspective on identity formation in contemporary society. *Journal of Personality*, 72, 167–199.

Schwartz, T. (2015, May 1). The enduring hunt for personal value. *New York Times.* www.nytimes.com/2015/05/02/business/dealbook/the-enduring-hunt-for-personal-value.html.

Sharkey, J., Ruderman, M.A., Mayworm, A.M., Green, J.G., Furlong, M.J., Rivera, N., Purisch, L., & Jimerson, S. (2015). Psychosocial functioning of bullied youth who adopt versus deny the bully-victim label. *School Psychology Quarterly*, 30(1), 91–104.

Southwick, S.M., Pietrzak, R.H., & White, G. (2011). Interventions to enhance resilience and resilience-related constructs in adults. In S.M. Southwick, B.T. Litz, D. Charney, & M.J. Friedman (Eds.), *Resilience and mental health: Challenges across the lifespan* (pp. 289–306). United Kingdom: Cambridge University Press.

Taylor, C. (1989). *Sources of the self: The making of the modern identity.* Cambridge, MA: Harvard University Press.

Taylor, C. (2007). *A secular age.* Cambridge, MA: Harvard University Press.

White, R., & Perrone, S. (2001). Racism, ethnicity and hate crime. *Communal/Plural*, 9(2). 161–181.

8 Resilience as it Relates to the Young Adults with a Sudden Onset of Chronic Illness

Melanie Morin

Campbell's opening testimony for this book provides us with an open and honest perspective of what resilience looks like in the face of adversity and hardship. Her decision to find a new sense of purpose and to continue choosing positivity and humour speaks to the power an individual can have over their life despite uncontrollable external factors. Her testimony also brings to light the true face of resilience, shown by highlighting the downfalls and hardships that she has faced and continues to face throughout her journey. Resilience itself was fostered and developed when facing her demons and openly admitting and accepting her fears. Campbell's positive outlook and her humour definitely helped her during this difficult time, but her path to resilience also include her authentic and real experience of her lowest moments, these seem to have provided the building blocks of her resilience.

Her story is one of many: individuals showing courage, determination and hardiness when faced with adversities. Resilience has been studied many times over from various perspectives. On the individual level studies have explored resilience within the trauma experience (Southwick & Charney, 2012), within the military (Sinclair & Britt, 2013) and within the context of severe mental health (Meyer & Mueser, 2011). On the institutional and organizational levels, studies have explored family resilience (Slezackova & Sobotkova, 2017) and community resilience (Price-Embry, 2017). Despite the large amount of research dedicated to the study of resilience, its fluidity and abstract nature can make it difficult for us to pinpoint, especially in instances of trauma, adversity, fear or pain. In these moments, it is difficult to find resilience within ourselves or to believe that we have the capability to survive the experience, questioning our ability to sustain the trauma not only emotionally but also physically and spiritually. Campbell's experience with resilience is unique, although she is not the only young adult to have faced health issues. Her values, goals and ambitions are particular to her. What resilience looks like and feels like to Campbell may be very different to others in a similar position. The purpose of this chapter is to better understand the elements that enable resilience to foster within each of us. In the end, resilience does not come in a "one size fits all" or a perfectly wrapped package with instructions, resilience is fostered in a way that is individual and unique to each of us, helping to survive and thrive in times of difficulty. This chapter specifically focuses on identifying the gap in the resilience literature available to young adults with a sudden onset of chronic illness. However, the review of resilience and the elements that encompass it can be applicable to all demographics and in various scenarios.

This chapter provides insight on how young adult clients suffering from chronic illness can build a sense of resilience through therapy and daily practice. While keeping in mind the unique challenges and specific goals young adults may have difficulty achieving due to their illness, increasing their sense of resilience could not only help buffer the negative impact of chronic disease symptoms (Manning, Carr, & Kail, 2014) but also help maintain a more positive mental health status (Gao et al., 2017). This could also help them better navigate the negative and at times difficult psychological symptoms, such as depression and anxiety that may be an aftereffect of their chronic disease. As people with chronic disease continue to live longer with the help of medical advancements, it is possible to assume that young adults with a strong sense of resilience may be better able to manage the ongoing symptoms of their chronic disease in comparison to young adults with a lower sense of resilience.

Chronic illness will be defined based on the definition provided by Kralik (2002): "a chronic illness is one that persists over time, usually without an easily definable beginning, middle or end" (p. 187). This definition, although broad in nature, was used in a study by Kralik, van Loon and Visentin (2006) that facilitated group discussion among adults aged 21–65 who had experienced adult-onset chronic illness and multiple medical diagnoses that included chronic fatigue syndrome, diabetes, psoriatic arthritis, osteoarthritis, fibromyalgia, depression, Crohn's, ulcerative colitis, multiple sclerosis, cardiomyopathy and chronic pain.

In order to gain a better understanding of resilience itself and its applicability, not only to young adults with a sudden onset of chronic illness, but also to the general population, it is important to examine the different types of definitions and conceptualizations of resilience. A look at the different components of resilience, such as cognitive factors, social ties and spirituality, will be examined to help further illustrate the various factors that can increase resilience and help individuals maintain their positive mental health status. In addition, a compilation of resilience increasing therapeutic frameworks will be explored to help therapists and clients.

What about Young Adults?

Campbell's story shows resilience in the face of chronic illness, but she is not alone in her struggles. According to Statistics Canada, more than one in five Canadian adults live with one of the following four chronic diseases: cardiovascular diseases (CVD), cancer, chronic respiratory diseases (CRD) or diabetes. Also, one in 25 Canadian adults aged 20 years and older reported having a mood and anxiety disorder and at least one of the four above-mentioned diseases (Statistics Canada, 2017). Although these statistics do not encompass the full range of chronic diseases, they provide us with a generalized overview of the overall health of Canadians.

In addition, there has been a significant increase in the prevalence of Canadian adults with an anxiety disorder and co-morbid chronic illnesses, from 2.7 per cent in 2005 to 3.9 per cent in 2014, which corresponds to an increase of 3.8 per cent every year. Among the young adult population, ages 20–34, 2.4 per cent are affected by a mental health disorder and co-morbid chronic illness (Statistics Canada, 2016). With a growing number of Canadians living with a chronic disease it is understandable that there have been significant efforts placed on collecting data and information aimed to further help individuals and their families better cope with the challenges that come hand in hand with chronic disease.

More specifically there has been a significant amount of research dedicated to the younger population in an effort to understand the difficulties of transitioning from the childhood medical care system to the adult system, and the impact this has on the emerging adults and their families (Gorter, 2009; Gorter, Stewart & Woodbury-Smith, 2011). Additionally, research has considered resilience as a tool to help children with chronic illness adjust to adolescence (Lennon, Psihogios, Murray, Holbein & Holmbeck, 2016) and build resilience; not only within the children affected by disabilities due to illness but also within the families who serve as the primary support system and caregivers (Munford, 2016). Furthermore, research has explored how to build resilience in the chronic illness experience for individuals and family systems (Smith & Bailey, 2017).

Both spheres of research have provided ample information on the different challenges these demographics face. Research has also gone beyond observing the challenges individuals face by putting an emphasis on investigating individual's ability to adjust and adapt to a life with chronic disease. One example of this is the 2016 study done by Heaton, Räisänen and Salinas, who explored how young adults with a childhood history of chronic illness are able to reach a sense of mastery when managing symptoms of their illness. They found that emerging adults are able to foster a sense of mastery over their illness through years of experience. Their study identified control and autonomy to be two major topics that were often presented by the young adults. By achieving good medical control of their condition, such as taking the right medication, knowing their limits and being able to manage their condition themselves, young adults obtained a sense of control over their chronic illness. The participants also talked about whether or not the onset of their disease had hindered their ability to live what they called a normal life for their age. The presence of a positive or negative outlook on their autonomy depended on the specific personal goals that they had been able to achieve or pursue. However, it was noted that these goals also had to be prioritized and balanced separately as their lives changed over time (Heaton et al., 2016). Though there is a possibility for young adults to achieve mastery of their chronic illness, young adults with a childhood history of chronic illness may have had more experience and opportunities to develop these skills compared to young adults with a sudden onset of chronic illness.

With regards to the older adult population, their adjustment to chronic illness may also be experienced differently. There is evidence that shows chronological age is responsible for a small yet consistent positive correlation with better coping and psychological adjustment in the face of chronic illness. Furthermore, accumulated life experiences are also important components that are often stated to be a part of the reason why older adults may experience an easier transition to a life with health problems (Bombardier, Ehde, Stoelb & Molton, 2010; Rybarczyk, Emery, Guequierre, Shamaskin & Behel, 2012). Rybarczyk et al. (2012) use the concept of the inoculation hypothesis which suggests that past experience with a negative event helps to establish preventative measures from a strong emotional response in the face of a similar experience in the future. When considering the stress inoculation theory as it relates to ageing, it is expected that older adults have more past experience with stress and adversity than would the younger adult demographic, and therefore, could be less impacted and more prepared to face stressors in their future. The past experiences with stressors and adversity the older adult demographic have faced over their lifespan is now a source of strength and resilience that they can rely on when confronting the new challenges and issues caused by chronic illness.

Unfortunately, there seems to be a pretty significant gap in the research that has been made available, as young children and older adults seem to be priority groups when it comes to chronic illness research. Because of the limited research available for this specific demographic, it is imperative that mental health practitioners be aware of the limitations young adults may face when diagnosed with a sudden onset of chronic disease. It seems that young adults with a history of childhood chronic illness, as well as the older adult demographic, both have time and past experience that can facilitate a better adjustment to their chronic illness. The young adult population lacks these fundamental elements due to their limited life experiences that could have helped them during this difficult life transition. In addition, adolescence and early adulthood are critical periods for self-development, independence and exploration of romantic relationships; these needs could be greatly affected by a sudden onset of chronic disease.

More specific to this demographic, a 2004 study conducted by Schulenburg, Bryant and O'Malley established seven developmental tasks that correlated with higher levels of well-being among young adults, specifically education, work, financial autonomy, romantic involvement, peer involvement, substance abuse avoidance and citizenship. Achievement of these, specifically success in work, romantic involvement, peer involvement and citizenship, were strongly correlated with increasing and maintaining high levels of well-being among young adults. These developmental tasks may be difficult to attain or maintain for young adults who need to adjust to their new diagnosis. In addition to having difficulty reaching or maintaining these tasks, young adulthood, like adolescence, is a time period in which mental health is critical. Research indicates that depressive symptoms fluctuate during these critical years of development: symptoms increase from early to late adolescence, and decrease from late adolescence to early young adulthood, but then increase again during the later part of young adulthood. Furthermore, depressive symptoms increase with the presence of chronic illness, such that youth and young adults with chronic illness have higher depression scores and less favourable trajectories over time in comparison to their healthy counterparts (Pinquart & Shen, 2010; Ferro, Gorter & Boyle, 2015).

To further illustrate the difficulties faced by young adults when limited by a chronic illness, Schwartz and Drotar (2009) explored how young adults' goals could be hindered by their health status. Their research showed that health-related hindrances (HRH) had a direct impact on young adults' personal aspirations. Their study focused on assessing participants' personal goals; participants listed 10 or more personal projects (goals), these were described as: plans, undertakings, or activities in the pursuit of some valued goal or outcome. The HRH items asked to which extent the management of their health, pain and other physical symptoms affected their ability to pursue or attain each of the personal projects listed. These items were chosen to represent potential health-related burdens of all individuals, independent of disease status. Their findings show that one's ability to establish personal goals and the pursuit of these goals are directly related to one's well-being, especially during emerging adulthood, which is a critical period for self-development.

In addition to establishing the positive correlation between personal goal pursuit and a young adult's well-being, Schwartz and Drotar (2009) also found that despite differences in HRH (pain, management of health and other physical symptoms), there were no significant differences in the content of goals between the healthy group and their peers suffering from chronic illness. This suggests, despite their illness history or health-related barriers, that young adults seek to accomplish goals within the seven developmental tasks that are normative for their age group (Schulenberg, Bryant & O'Malley, 2004) rather than focusing on disease-specific goals (Schwartz & Drotar, 2009).

There is limited research available that focuses solely on the adjustment process of young adults affected by a sudden onset of chronic illness. Based on the research presented above, it is safe to assume that this population would list the same generalized types of psychosocial goals, such as success in work, education and interpersonal relationships. Furthermore, not only are these psychosocial goals consistent across the spectrum of young adults, whether healthy or suffering from illness-related issues, the pursuit and achievement of these goals is directly correlated with the well-being and life satisfaction of this population. In the context of a chronic illness diagnosis for young adults, not only do they face the difficulties of a natural fluctuation of depressive symptoms resurging throughout emerging adulthood, they also lack the life experience that older adults and young adults with a history of childhood chronic illness have obtained to help them better adjust and adapt to their new diagnosis during this critical time of independence and self-development. Some young adults with a childhood history of chronic disease have the ability to reach a sense of mastery over their chronic illness, during or maybe even before this time of development, but a sudden onset of chronic illness during this developmental stage may be more challenging, which has yet to be fully explored and researched by the psychological community. When combining all of these factors, it is possible that this demographic may face more mental health issues, such as depression and anxiety, and more difficulty reaching acceptance of their sudden change in health. The 2006 study done by Kralik et al. perfectly describes the emotional impact that a sudden chronic illness diagnosis can have on an individual. The authors state:

> the emotional trauma of chronic illness is caused by loss of a valued level of functioning in everyday life. A person with chronic illness experiences the loss of immediate competency and is also deprived of a predictable future. While no person's future is ever guaranteed, we can become accustomed to the taken-for-grantedness of the future as we envisage ourselves moving in a particular direction.
>
> (Kralik et al., 2006, p. 194)

In the context of chronic illness, therapists may feel limited in the help that they can provide to chronically ill clients. Often, therapists do not have access to clients' medical records, and in the event that they do, many of them do not have the medical background that can provide additional information that could help the client. Additionally, chronic illness is a lifelong challenge for these clients, and depending on the illness itself, there could be many challenges ahead which the therapist and the young adult might not predict. With this information in mind, it is important that therapists work towards finding an appropriate and productive treatment plan for clients of this demographic. By focusing on developing clients' ability to withstand and overcome the ongoing adversities that await them, clients may be able to experience more positive mental health, which could better help them in achieving their personal goals.

Resilience research provides us with many examples in which individuals have been able to overcome adversities and challenges. Campbell, for instance, is a young adult who had to face a sudden onset of chronic disease, and her goals were set aside for the benefit of her health. How can therapists help other young adults who face similar adversities and difficulties either maintain or regain a positive mental health status throughout this challenging experience? As some older adults face the similar problem of having a sudden onset of chronic illness, therefore experiencing a time period of adaptation, researchers have investigated the concept of resilience and looked to find ways to help the older adult population further develop a sense of resilience to help maintain positive mental health. By studying the impact of resilience on the relationship between the onset of new chronic conditions and subsequent changes in disability among older adults, it was found that higher levels of resilience can protect against the harmful impact of new chronic conditions in older adults. In particular, results showed that having higher levels of resilience protects against the negative impacts of the onset of a new chronic condition and the effect on activities of daily living (ADL) and instrumental activities of daily living (IADL) limitations in later life (Manning et al., 2014). Although this is aimed towards older adult functioning, this can also be relevant for young adult clients as their chronic disease could become degenerative or worsen over time. Furthermore, research also indicates that positive affect at the critical point of a diagnosis can also contribute to more resilient psychological and physical health trajectories for people dealing with chronic illness (Moskowitz, 2010). If resilience provides a protective shield against the negative impacts of new onsets of chronic conditions in older adults, this could also be the case for young adults.

Resilience Definition as it Relates to Chronically Ill Young Adults

While keeping in mind the history of resilience research, it is clear that although the definition of resilience has evolved over the course of the development of the concept, it has not yet obtained a standardized definition. There is a wide range of definitions available and each varies depending on the study, context or researcher. In addition to the variability in the definition of the outcomes of resilience, the way in which resilience is conceptualized is also a subject of debate among researchers. Resilience has been conceptualized as a process, an outcome or a trait (Hariharan & Rana, 2017). As explored previously, in the early stages of resilience research, some researchers focused on finding individual traits that at risk children used to help them overcome their adversities (Murphy & Moriarty, 1976). As research evolved, so did the definitions of protective factors and protective mechanisms, implying that resilience can be fluid throughout different contexts (Rutter, 1987), which leaned more towards a process-oriented conceptualization.

Although there are variations in the definitions of outcomes of resilience as well as its conceptualization, there are two factors that remain constant within the numerous definitions: adversity and positive adaptation (Fletcher & Sarkar, 2013; Hariharan & Rana, 2017). These two factors are consistent across studies of resilience; however, inconsistencies in their definition have led to confusion about their meaning (Fletcher & Sarkar, 2013). When defining adversity within the context of a specific study, there is an element of subjectivity; the degree of adversity, such as the frequency and duration, must be taken into consideration (Hariharan & Rana, 2017). Furthermore, positive adaptation is indicative of the degree to which an individual is able to adjust to their surrounding environment, but if the environment is unhealthy, the individual will not experience positive adaptation.

These variations are important to note when resilience is defined within the chronic illness experience, specifically for the young adult demographic with a sudden onset of chronic illness. Therapists should keep in mind the specific challenges and limitations faced by this population and adjust what resilience would look like for them. In turn, individuals should also take into consideration their particular situation and what resilience could feasibly look like. Setting appropriate expectations is vital in the context of resilience building. As we look back on Campbell's story, we can see that she represents an exceptional example of resilience. It may not be realistic to expect everyone to achieve such an accomplishment; therefore, providing a reasonable and practical definition of resilience for chronically ill young adults may be important when establishing personal goals and developing therapeutic treatment plans, not only in the context of therapy, but also in people's day to day lives.

Resilience Components

As we continue to explore the history and the complexity of resilience it is clear that there have been many ways in which resilience has been conceptualized over the course of its research and development. For the purpose of this chapter, the components that will be further examined will relate specifically to a process-oriented conceptualization of resilience, meaning that we are looking primarily at components that can be learned, altered and improved; therefore, this research is limited to exploring cognitive factors, social ties/relationships and spirituality. These are the components that can be implemented into daily practice to help further develop and strengthen resilience.

Cognitive components, such as cognitive reappraisal, causal attributions, self-regulation and self-efficacy (Benight & Cieslak, 2011), as well as active coping, positive emotions and optimism (Feder, Nestler, Westphal & Charney, 2010) have all been seen to improve resilience outcomes. Benight and Cieslak (2011) found that these cognitive components could easily be applied through other available theoretical approaches to help increase our understanding of resilience. Primary appraisal allows individuals to assess the importance of a specific need or demand for their well-being; in this step, it can be labelled as irrelevant (not important to the person's needs), positive (there could be positive consequences without the need for additional resources) or stressful (there could be positive or negative consequences and resources will be needed). The primary appraisal helps interpret the stressful situation as harm/loss, a threat or a challenge. Benight and Cieslak (2011) further explain that this evaluation helps assess positive or negative consequences and if they are important to the individual. If the individual perceives it to be positive, despite the amount of resources that must be invested, the stressful situation will be interpreted as a challenge. On the other hand, harm/loss or threat appraisals are made in circumstances in which the stress demands overtake the available resources, leading to negative outcomes. The context of available resources is the secondary appraisal. The combination of these appraisals provides an evaluation of the physical, psychological, social and material resources available to the individual. Causal attributions refer to the stability, controllability and generalizability related to the stressors (Benight & Cieslak, 2011).

In addition, the interaction between external and internal factors, specifically the environment, the person and their behaviour is also important to consider. When this dynamic interaction between internal and external factors is fostered, individuals are able to better adapt to changing demands. This feedback system encourages self-regulating behaviour. Furthermore, self-evaluation is also an important component within this feedback process. By evaluating one's successes and failures, individuals are able to modify their cognitions (thoughts) and behaviours in order to shape a more desired environmental condition. Self-efficacy, along with self-evaluative processes, provide individuals with the ability to perceive competence to achieve a certain behaviour (Benight & Cieslak, 2011). As self-efficacy is developed and fostered through the interactive feedback system, individuals can evaluate their success or failure as they strive towards valued goals. More specifically, Benight and Cieslak (2011) introduce the concept of coping self-efficacy while using the same feedback loop; it relates to the beliefs surrounding one's abilities to manage demands that are specific to coping with trauma or stressful events.

Active coping is another cognitive component that has been linked to resilience. Through planning and problem-solving, these strategies help individuals better manage the stressors related to their adverse experience. In addition, facing one's fears allow for proper cognitive appraisal to better assess the threat of the stressful situation and helps evaluate the appropriate actions to take; whereas maladaptive strategies such as avoiding or escaping the stressful situation can leave an individual blind to the full scope of the adverse situation (Feder et al., 2010). Positive emotions and optimism have also been linked to improving psychological resilience. Feder et al. (2010) refer to the broaden-and-build model by Friedman (2000) which explains that positive emotions can offer a buffering effect against adverse consequences of stress. This decreases the arousal produced by negative emotions which allows more flexibility for thinking and problem-solving (Feder et al., 2010).

In addition to cognitive factors, *social ties* have been an important component of resilience research. A large number of studies have found that social support can be a protective factor in stress-related disorders (Feder et al., 2010). Deverts and Cohen (2011) found that the component of social ties/relationships can be divided into two separate categories: social support and social integration. Social support relates specifically to an individual's social network and the resources (material or psychological) that can be provided through these connections, which can help the individual's ability to cope with stress. Support can be provided in three different ways: instrumental (through material aids such as financial assistance), informational (offering valuable information aimed to help the individual during a difficult or stressful time) and emotional (the expression of empathy, compassion, trust and reassurance). Social integration is to have an active commitment in social activities and relationships, and cognitive components, which relate to a sense of commonality and identification with one's social roles (Deverts & Cohen, 2011). Social support is thought to provide a defence against negative effects of stressor exposure. In comparison, social integration, the feeling of being a part of something, helps with better adjustment regardless of an individual's current stress levels (Deverts & Cohen, 2011).

Finally, *religion and spirituality* have also been linked to helping promote psychological resilience in the face of challenges and adversity (Pargament & Cummings, 2010). Pargament and Cummings (2010) refer to Pargament's (1997) research that reported on the efficacy of religion, which offers four different functions in building resilience. The first function explores that religion is regularly linked to the search for meaning and purpose. The second function relates to the relationship between religion and emotional comfort or reduced anxiety. Studies over the years have supported the notion that religion is linked to positive emotional outcomes and may play a role in promoting resilience through this function. The third function relates to its ability to encourage a sense of social connectedness. As presented above, social ties and relationships are an important component of resilience, and religion facilitates this sense of connectedness through shared goals, values and meanings. A church or spiritual community can represent a strong network of people who can offer resources and support in times of need (Pargament, 1997). The final function pertains to the spiritual and sacred aspects of religion. As religion can provide a sense of common values, positive effect on emotions and a sense of community, individuals also seek religious ends themselves, such as a connection to God, a religious community or a commitment to a religious way of life (Pargament, 1997).

Outside of the context of institutional religion, spiritual intelligence has also been linked to being a component in psychological resilience. Spirituality is considered to help increase environmental adaptability. Spiritual intelligence is presented as the "third Q" or "SQ" along with rational intelligence (IQ) and emotional intelligence (EQ). Spiritual intelligence is composed of 15 different core components: compassion, critical existential thinking, divinity, egolessness, equanimity, flexibility, forgiveness, gratitude, meaning and purpose in life, openness to experience, self-acceptance, self-actualization, self-awareness, spiritual practise and transcendental awareness (Ajawani, 2017). As individuals are able to incorporate these components, their spiritual intelligence becomes more developed over time, which in turn builds upon the individual's resilience.

It seems religion and spirituality have a big role in one's ability to show resilience in the face of adversity. Although presented through different terms and concepts, the four functions of religion seem to incorporate the cognitive and social components of resilience; which brings to light the importance and relevance of this resource in further developing one's sense of resilience, and also its value in further exploring individual's spiritual beliefs in the context of therapy.

Building Resilience

Within the chronic illness experience, clients are faced with a lifelong battle against an unchangeable fate. Regardless of the type of chronic illness, clients will inevitably be confronted with difficult and trying challenges in their future. This section focuses on different resilience enhancing frameworks specifically oriented towards building upon the existing reserves of resilience within clients. Current research on resilience interventions and frameworks is still in its infancy. Inconsistencies within the research of resilience have made it difficult to assess the validity of resilience assessment tools; it is therefore appropriate to assume that this could also be the case for proposed interventions and frameworks. In an effort to stay consistent within the context of this chapter, the intervention frameworks presented below take into consideration an outcome and process-oriented conceptualization of resilience rather than a traits conceptualization. They also consider the different resilience components, namely cognitive, social ties and spirituality and the assessment tools that were presented above.

Depending on the type of adversity individuals are exposed to, the interventions or frameworks proposed to help increase resilience should be tailored to best suit the specific situation and needs of the clients. Chmitorz et al. (2017) proposed three different types of resilience intervention programmes. The first is provided before the stress exposure, such as training programmes within the military, and is designed to prepare participants for inevitable, intense or severe stressors. The second aims to provide training during the stressor, usually in the event of chronic stress, workplace stress or chronic illness. The third focuses on providing training after the stressor exposure, like after a natural disaster or a terrorist attack. Based on these three different types of intervention programmes, the programmes proposed in the context of chronically ill clients will be focused on providing interventions during the stress exposure.

Although many frameworks have been proposed and continue to be a topic of interest within the concept of resilience building, there is still limited research available that concentrates on the effectiveness of these interventions (Alvord, Rich & Berghorst, 2016). However, some frameworks focus on enhancing resilience components and research on these components has been extensive, therefore these frameworks may be more empirically valid and effective. A resilience intervention framework designed specifically for the chronic illness population has not been found within the available research, yet frameworks that focus mainly on resilience components can have a general applicability for several demographics and stressors including the chronic illness experience. An overview of three different intervention frameworks is presented below to provide a general insight on the different themes and concepts that are explored within a therapeutic context to help increase personal resilience.

The first intervention framework is the Interventions for those Recently Informed of their Seropositive Status (IRISS), which was designed specifically for people newly diagnosed with HIV (Moskowitz, 2010). This population can face similar challenges as chronically ill clients; they both require lifelong adjustments such as the need to navigate a complex health-care system, difficulty forming or maintaining social ties, and coming to grips with identifying oneself with a chronic illness or HIV (Hult, Maurer & Moskowitz, 2009; Moskowitz, Wurbel, Hult, Maurer & Stephens, 2007). This intervention framework focuses on providing five one-on-one sessions dedicated to teaching eight different skills: noting daily positive events; capitalizing on or savouring positive events; gratitude; mindfulness; positive reappraisal; focusing on personal strengths; goal setting and working towards attainable goals; and small acts of kindness. Moskowitz (2010) further emphasizes that these skills can help increase positive affect in daily life and can be applied within other contexts; they are not solely for people affected by HIV.

Stress Inoculation Training (SIT) is the second framework that could be applied within the chronic illness experience. It is based on the traditional model of stress and coping (Lazarus & Folkman, 1984). This model focuses on the individual's appraisal of stress; this appraisal can be guided by the complex development and interaction between one's biological, psychological, social and spiritual factors. When individuals believe that a stressful event surpasses their skills and resources, the appraisal can affect how they respond to the stressful event. The SIT approach was originally developed to treat anxiety (Meichenbaum, 1975, 1985; Meichenbaum & Jaremko, 1983) and was later adapted for other uses, such as PTSD (Southwick, Pietrzak & White, 2011). There are three overlapping phases within the SIT approach, with the first being the conceptual and educational phase. During this phase, a therapeutic relationship is established, and psychoeducation about the impacts of trauma and stress-related neurological and psychological symptoms are then discussed and normalized. The second phase emphasizes skills acquisition and rehearsal. Individuals are taught practical coping skills, such as: thought stopping, guided self-talk, identification and replacement of irrational and maladaptive thinking and problem solving. This phase also focuses on helping clients consolidate these skills, and introduces relaxation techniques. During the third stage, clients are encouraged to practise the various skills learned in the first two phases, which is done through modelling, role-playing and imagining stressful situations in which they could apply the new skills (Southwick et al., 2011).

Lastly, well-being therapy also provides a framework in which resilience can be enhanced within the chronic illness experience. The main goal is to generate positive outcomes rather than mitigating psychological distress. This model focuses on six different dimensions – autonomy, personal growth, environmental mastery, purpose of life, positive relationships and self-acceptance – and there are two distinct phases. The first concentrates on learning to notice personal experiences of well-being, identifying when these experiences occur and then rating the magnitude or intensity of each one, even when brief. Phase two focuses on recognizing and increasing awareness of the intrusive and negative thoughts that interrupt the experiences of well-being. Clients are then taught how to challenge these irrational and intrusive thoughts through traditional cognitive behaviour therapy techniques. During phase three, the six different dimensions are further explored and enhanced. For example, practising being more assertive and resistant to social pressure helps develop autonomy; recognizing one's improvements and achievements relates to personal growth (Southwick et al., 2011).

These frameworks focus on developing and enhancing the resilience components that have been explored in previous research. They provide a guideline for therapists that help to align the treatment plan towards developing skills that clients can use and integrate in order to increase their resilience. Furthermore, these frameworks allow therapists to include well-established interventions such as CBT thought behaviour pathway tools, thought reappraisal techniques, and ACT thought diffusion techniques, to help clients gain better awareness and control over their thoughts. Mindfulness also has a place in these frameworks to help incorporate more awareness and being in the present moment. Kabat-Zinn (1990) introduced intentional, non-judgemental awareness as a definition of mindfulness that is commonly used throughout literature. Mindfulness has also been incorporated in several different therapeutic approaches such as ACT, DBT and mindfulness-based cognitive therapy.

Conclusion

This literature review exposed the unexplored challenges and difficulties young adults face in the event of a sudden onset of chronic illness. Although the research for this population is limited, this review offers insights on some of the struggles and problematics these clients may want to discuss in therapy. Chronic illness can be a difficult and deteriorating experience; as therapists, there is little we can do when it comes to reducing physical pain, alleviating symptoms or finding alternative health-care practices that could help improve their health. Resilience enhancing therapy offers clients a different way to explore their resources and inner strength. Kralik et al. (2006) explained that developing "resilience in chronic illness involves the belief that personal worth transcends physical limitations" (Kralik et al., 2006, p. 194). This perfectly describes how resilience becomes a sense of spiritual growth. It is beyond physical and it represents an individual's emotional and mental strength in their ability to recover and live authentically. Therapists have the difficult but rewarding task of helping clients find their inner strength and tap into this resource that can help them pursue a meaningful life filled with purpose despite the difficulties of chronic illness.

Resilience research has evolved significantly since its initial conception. Its focus on positive outcomes rather than symptomatology offers clients an opportunity to explore their internal and external resources. Within the chronic illness experience, young adults may feel that they have no sense of control over what is happening to their body and health; however, with the help of resilience enhancing interventions, they can practise gaining a higher sense of control over their minds and thoughts. This review aimed to highlight the significance of resilience as a whole. It also aimed to educate therapists on how to implement resilience enhancing interventions in a way that is empirically supported and valid, while remaining open enough to allow therapists to use their own approach and style throughout the process.

References

Ajawani, J.C. (2017). Spiritual intelligence: A core ability behind psychosocial resilience. In U. Kumar (Ed.), *The Routledge international handbook of psychosocial resilience* (pp. 173–186). New York: Routledge.

Alvord, M.K., Rich, B.A., & Berghorst, L.H. (2016). Resilience interventions. In J.C. Norcross, G.R. VandenBos, D.K. Freedheim, & N. Pole (Eds.), *APA handbook of clinical psychology: Psychopathology and health* (pp. 502–519). Washington, DC: American Psychological Association.

Benight, C.C., & Cieslak, R. (2011). Cognitive factors and resilience: How self-efficacy contributes to coping with adversity. In M.S. Southwick, T.B. Litz, D. Charney, & J.M. Friedman (Eds.), *Resilience and mental health: Challenges across the lifespan* (pp. 45–55). New York: Cambridge University Press.

Bombardier, C.H., Ehde, D.M., Stoelb, B., & Molton, I.R. (2010). The relationship of age-related factors to psychological functioning among people with disabilities. *Physical Medicine and Rehabilitation Clinics of North America*, 21(2), 281–297.

Chmitorz, A., Kunzler, A., Helmreich, I., Tüscher, O., Kalish, R., Kibiak, T., … Lieb, K. (2017). Intervention studies to foster resilience: A systematic review and proposal for a resilience framework in future intervention studies. *Clinical Psychology Review*, 59, 78–100.

Deverts, D., & Cohen, S. (2011). Social ties and resilience in chronic disease. In S.M. Southwick, T.B. Litz, D. Charney, & J.M. Friedman (Eds.), *Resilience and mental health: Challenges across the lifespan* (pp. 45–55). New York: Cambridge University Press.

Feder, A., Nestler, E.J., Westphal, M., & Charney, D.S. (2010). Psychobiological mechanisms of resilience to stress. In J.W. Reich, A.J. Zautra, & J.S. Hall (Eds.), *Handbook of adult resilience* (pp. 35–54). New York: Guilford Press.

Ferro, M.A., Gorter, J.W., & Boyle, M.H. (2015). Trajectories of depressive symptoms during the transition to young adulthood: The role of chronic illness. *Journal of Affective Disorders*, 174, 594–601.

Fletcher, D., & Sarkar, M. (2013). Psychological resilience: A review and critique of definitions, concepts and theory. *European Psychologist*, 18(1), 12–23.

Friedman, M.J. (2000). What might the psychobiology of posttraumatic stress disorder teach us about future approaches to pharmacotherapy? *Journal of Clinical Psychiatry*, 61(7), 44–51.

Gao, T., Ding, X., Chai, J., Zhang, Z., Zhang, H., Kong, Y., & Mei, S. (2017). The influence of resilience on mental health: The role of general well-being. *International Journal of Nursing Practice*, 23, 1–7.

Gorter, J.W. (2009). Transition to adult-oriented health care: perspectives of youth and adults with complex physical disabilities. *Phys, Occup. Ther. Pediatr*, 29, 362–366.

Gorter, J.W., Stewart, D., & Woodbury-Smith, M. (2011). Youth in transition: Health care and development. *Child Care Health Dev.*, 37, 757–763.

Hariharan, M., & Rana, S. (2017). Conceptual complexity of resilience: Synergy approach to measurement. In U. Kumar (Ed.), *The Routledge international handbook of psychosocial resilience* (pp. 24–33). New York: Routledge.

Heaton, J., Räisänen, U., & Salinas, M. (2016). "Rule your condition, don't let it rule you": Young adults' sense of mastery in their accounts of growing up with a chronic illness. *Sociology of Health & Illness*, 38(1), 3–20.

Hult, J., Maurer, S., & Moskowitz, J.T. (2009). "I'm sorry, you're positive": A qualitative study of individual experiences of testing positive for HIV. *AIDS Care*, 21, 185–188.

Kabat-Zinn, J. (1990). *Full catastrophe living: Using the wisdom of your body and mind to face stress, pain and illness*. New York: Delacorte.

Kralik, D. (2002). The quest for ordinariness: Transition experienced by midlife women living with chronic illness. *Journal of Advanced Nursing*, 39(2), 146–154.

Kralik, D., van Loon, A., & Visentin, K. (2006). Resilience in the chronic illness experience. *Educational Action Research*, 14(2), 187–201.

Lennon, J.M., Psihogios, A.M., Murray, C.B., Holbein, C.E., & Holmbeck, G.N. (2016). Promoting resilience during the transition to adolescence in chronically ill children and their families. In C. DeMichelis, & M. Ferrari (Eds.), *Child and adolescent resilience within medical contexts, integrating research and practice* (pp. 51–75). Switzerland: Springer.

Manning, L.K., Carr, D.C., & Kail, B.L. (2014). Do higher levels of resilience buffer the deleterious impact of chronic illness on disability in later life? *Gerontologist*, 53(3), 514–524.

Meichenbaum, D. (1975). A self-instructional approach to stress management: A proposal for stress inoculation training. In C. Spielberger & I. Sarason (Eds.), *Stress and anxiety*, Vol. 2 (pp. 237–264). New York: Wiley.

Meichenbaum, D. (1985). *Psychology practitioner guidebooks: Stress inoculation training.* New York: Pergamon Press.

Meichenbaum, D., & Jaremko, M.E. (Eds.). (1983). *Stress reduction and prevention.* New York: Plenum Press.

Meyer, P.S., & Mueser, K.T. (2011). Resiliency in individuals with serious mental illness. In M.S. Southwick, T.B. Litz, D. Charney, & J.M. Friedman (Eds.), *Resilience and mental health: Challenges across the lifespan* (pp. 276–288). New York: Cambridge University Press.

Moskowitz, J.T. (2010). Positive affect at the onset of chronic illness. In J.W. Reich, A.J. Zautra, & J.S. Hall (Eds.), *Handbook of adult resilience* (pp. 465–483). New York: Guilford Press.

Moskowitz, J.T., Wurbel, J., Hult, J., Maurer, M.J., & Stehpens, E. (2007). Illness appraisals and coping in people newly diagnosed with HIV. *AIDS Care*, 21, 185–188.

Munford, R. (2016). Building strengths and resilience: Supporting families and disabled children. In C. DeMichelis, & M. Ferrari (Eds.), *Child and adolescent resilience within medical contexts, integrating research and practice* (pp. 51–75). Switzerland: Springer.

Murphy, L.B., & Moriarty, A.E. (1976). *Vulnerability, coping, and growth: From infancy to adolescence.* New Haven, CT: Yale University Press.
Pargament, K.I. (1997). *The psychology of religion and coping.* New York: Guilford Press.
Pargament, K.I., & Cummings J. (2010). Anchored by faith: Religion as a resilience factor. In J.W. Reich, A.J. Zautra, & J.S. Hall (Eds.), *Handbook of adult resilience* (pp. 193–212). New York: Guilford Press.
Pinquart, M., & Shen, Y. (2010). Depressive symptoms in children and adolescents with chronic physical illness: An updated meta-analysis. *Journal of Pediatric Psychology*, 36(4), 375–384.
Price-Embry, S. (2017). Community-level resiliency interventions in a post-disaster environment: The importance of information. In U. Kumar (Ed.), *The Routledge international handbook of psychosocial resilience* (pp. 248–259). New York: Routledge.
Rutter, M. (1987). Psychosocial resilience and protective mechanisms. *American Orthopsychiatric Association*, 57(3), 316–331.
Rybarczyk, B., Emery, E.E., Guequierre, L.L., Shamaskin, A., & Behel, J. (2012). The role of resilience in chronic illness and disability in older adults. *Annual Review of Gerontology and Geriatrics*, 32(1), 173–187.
Schulenberg, J.E., Bryant, A.L., & O'Malley, P.M. (2004). Taking hold of some kind of life: How developmental tasks related to trajectories of well-being during the transition of adulthood. *Development and Psychopathology*, 16, 1119–1140.
Schwartz, L.A., & Drotar, D. (2009). Health-related hindrances of personal goal pursuit and well-being of young adults with cystic fibrosis, pediatric cancer survivors, and peers without history of chronic illness. *Journal of Pediatric Psychology*, 34(9), 945–964.
Sinclair, R.R., & Britt, T.W. (2013). *Building psychological resilience in military personnel: Theory and practice.* Washington, DC: American Psychological Association.
Slezackova, A., & Sobotkova, I. (2017). Family resilience: Positive psychology approach to healthy family functioning. In U. Kumar (Ed.), *The Routledge international handbook of psychosocial resilience* (pp. 379–390). New York: Routledge.
Smith, B.J., & Bailey, W.A. (2017). Fostering resilience among older adults living with osteoporosis and osteoarthritis. In G.L. Welch & A.W. Harrist (Eds.), *Family resilience and chronic illness, emerging issues in family and individual resilience* (pp. 179–195). Switzerland: Springer.
Southwick, S.M., & Charney, D.S. (2012). *Resilience: The science of mastering life's greatest challenges.* New York: Cambridge University Press.
Southwick, S.M., Pietrzak, R.H., & White, G. (2011). Interventions to enhance resilience and resilience-related constructs in adults. In M.S. Southwick, T.B. Litz, D. Charney, & J.M. Friedman (Eds.), *Resilience and mental health: Challenges across the lifespan* (pp. 45–55). New York: Cambridge University Press.
Statistics Canada (2016, July 28). Research highlights on health and aging. Retrieved from: www.statcan.gc.ca/pub/11-631-x/11-631-x2016001-eng.htm.
Statistics Canada (2017, April 11). How healthy are Canadians? A trend analysis of the health of Canadians from a healthy living and chronic disease perspective. Retrieved from: www.canada.ca/en/public-health/services/publications/healthy-living/how-healthy-canadians.html#s2.

9 Acculturation Stress and Resilience Among Immigrant Families

Winnie Pak Wan Yeung and Christian R. Bellehumeur

Testimony of Carla: *Ten-year-old Carla, a Second-Generation Chinese Canadian, was shocked when she went to her friend Mary's house, a native English-speaking Canadian. She had never seen something like this in her own family before: Mary's father hugged and kissed his daughters when they entered the house. Mary told her father that she was upset that someone had stepped on her drawing by accident at school. Mary's father then consoled her and told her that her drawing was still good and colourful even though it had some dirt on it. Carla was curious about the affection that was expressed between father and daughter. A feeling of warmth surged within her and she reflected on her own experiences at home. "Dad is weird," she thought to herself. Her father seldom talked, and in fact, she hardly saw him. Carla's father was studying full-time and worked long hours at a grocery store ever since they moved to Canada. Carla knew that her parents loved her, trying to provide everything she and her brother needed. They gave them tutoring, piano lessons and all kinds of privileges, helping them to be competitive and achieve more than other children at school. Carla's parents had been working very hard to provide, but never had they done what Mary's father did on that day – openly express affection to his child. Carla admitted that she sometimes felt weird when telling her parents, "I love you!", though she loved them dearly. Carla wondered, "What is wrong? What makes my experience at home so different from Mary's?"*

Introduction

Migration has become a global phenomenon in this century. People move away from their place of birth to another city or continent due to violence, environmental and climate changes, economic advancement, or to secure a better opportunity for their children. According to the United Nations' International Organization for Migration (IOM) report (2017), the number of international worldwide migration reached 258 million in the same year. Overall, North America hosted 58 million international migrants in 2017. One in seven people in the world today are migrants (Denbok, 2018).

Migration leads to positive and negative outcomes. On a positive note, the world has become more connected, and intercultural contacts among people from different cultures have increased. Individuals are exposed to multiple cultures, and this can be perceived as being enriching for most people. On an individual level, the draw of migration includes various positive outcomes such as the possibility of paid work and a relatively decent quality of life, however, it often comes with considerable sacrifices. Those who leave their country of origin may face various losses and stressors (Nguyen, Bellehumeur & Malette, 2018). They must also cope with challenges of adjusting to new cultural values, norms, new ways of expression and languages in the host country. These challenges have often been examined under the notion of acculturation, a process of learning and adapting to a new culture (Berry, 2003).

Acculturation stress is a term coined by researchers (e.g. Berry, 1997), to describe immigrants' experience when they encounter conflictual values and behavioural repertoires, different from their culture of origin. Researchers claim that managing two cultures places a burden on the individual, which can lead to stress, isolation, and identity confusion (Rudmin, 2003; Vivero & Jenkins, 1999). In the context of acculturation, immigrants must develop resilience, which can be understood as a dynamic process which allows individuals to bounce back, overcome adversity, while continuing to enjoy a satisfying and meaningful life (Wong & Wong, 2012).

The topic of acculturation stress and resilience among immigrants is particularly relevant as the number of migrations worldwide continues to increase. Immigrants' success at adjusting to their adopted country will affect not only themselves, but their families, the prosperity of their chosen country and future generations. Immigrants' coping and integration into an adopted country has direct impact on their children's adjustment. Successful adjustment early in life is vital and contributes to future adaptation of their children (Masten, 2014). Success or failure of adaptation will influence other life domains, such as mental health and relationships. To illustrate this, Wyman's (2003) research showed that children who lived in high-adversity families had minimal engagement and emotional involvement with their primary caregivers and had low levels of affective response to other people's feelings. They were less competent as compared to those who lived in more favourable settings. Thus, early intervention to manage acculturation stress and minimize family adversity may lead to improved outcomes in immigrant children. Motti-Stefanidi (2018) asserted that positive resolution of earlier-stage developmental tasks may increase the probability of future successful adaptation. For that reason, studying resilience and helping immigrants manage acculturation stress will enhance and foster resilience and adaptation to an adopted country.

This chapter calls upon an anthropological perspective, taking into account the importance of culture viewed as a complex factor influencing the study and the understanding of resilience. More particularly, this chapter aims to examine the complex relationship between resilience and culture, in the context of immigration, focusing on acculturation stress. This latter notion is seen as a potential daily adversity in people having to constantly deal with dissonance between at least two different cultures.

This chapter, taking the form of a critical review of the literature, presents some relevant results of a recent phenomenological study of Second-Generation

Chinese Canadians (SGCC) of Yeung (2018), which will lead to the proposal of key factors for resilience, leading to a better adaption and well-being of SGCC. These individuals must deal with two different cultures daily: their heritage Chinese culture and the host mainstream Canadian culture. In order to reach the above goal, this chapter is divided into three main parts. The first part will define terms such as resilience, culture and acculturation. A brief introduction of the role of culture in resilience will follow. The second part will deepen our understanding of the influence of culture in resilience, focusing on the context of acculturation. Then, we will briefly refer to the Gilbert Durand's anthropological theory of imaginary,[1] which is considered culturally sensitive to both Western and Eastern worldviews (Wunenburger, 2013). The third part will present some key factors of resilience, fostering a better adaptation and well-being for immigrants, mostly SGCC, living in the context of acculturation.

Defining Terms: Resilience, Culture and Acculturation.

Defining resilience in the context of immigration and overcoming cultural adversity, Ungar and his colleagues (2008) considered how coping with stress varies across cultures. Thus, they proposed a framework to maintain well-being that is applicable to various cultural values and practices (Ungar et al., 2008). They believed that individuals who have been racially marginalized often have means of accessing their own resources to ensure their own development – means which may not be evident to mainstream societies. They broadened the definition of resilience to focus on the relationship between a person and their environment. According to Ungar and his colleagues (2008), resilience is "the capacity of individuals to navigate their way to health-enhancing resources and the capacity of an individual's physical and social ecologies to provide those resources in meaningful ways." (Ungar et al., 2008, p. 168). In their study of resilience, they noted a close relationship between supportive environments, resources and individuals' flexibility as they achieve a positive outcome. Thus, when studying the impact of culture on resilience, we must consider how mainstream and heritage cultures impact immigrant families and their needs, how well they are equipped with psychosocial and material resources, and how successful they are at balancing various needs to attain well-being. Consideration of these factors may provide better understanding of resilience among immigrant families, and allow culturally embedded research and interventions to contribute to families' successful adaptation.

Vanistendael and Lecomte (2000) and Lecomte (2004) present resilience as defined within a family construct. Vanistendael and Lecomte (2000) proposed three basic tenets in their model of resilience: the link (generated by the adult), the symbolic law (established by the adult) and the meaning (created by the youth). Figure 9.1 presents their relationships, which are relevant to the current study for various reasons. First, this model takes into account the complex relationship between the person and the environment. Second, it echoes the

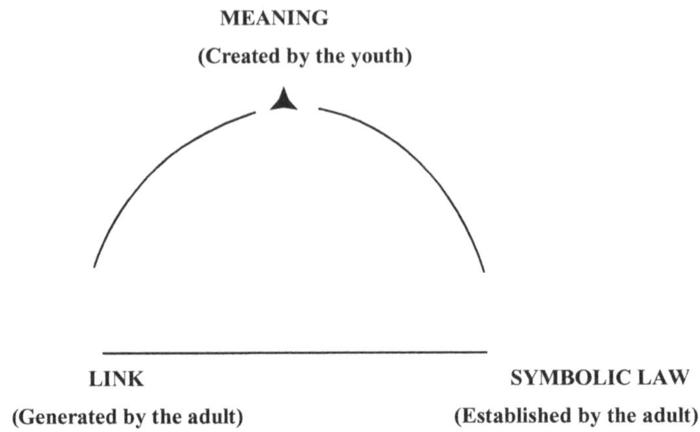

Figure 9.1 Three basic tenets of resilience (translated and adapted from Lecomte, 2010)

importance of culture and the symbolic capacity of individuals, which we will define shortly. Third, it highlights the crucial role of the parent–child relationship – a key factor for fostering youth's resilience, which will be discussed later in this chapter.

In this model, the link refers to the importance of creating bonds. This is because many studies have shown that warm human relationships are an essential source of resilience, regardless of the type of trauma (Vanistendael and Lecomte, 2000; Lecomte, 2004).

The second tenet, the symbolic law, refers to the parental rules, the structural framework, which is essential for the reconstruction of well-being for young people in distress. However, it only reflects an educational need for all children (Vanistendael and Lecomte, 2000; Lecomte, 2004). It takes on an assumption of an ideal scenario that a child is to grow up with loving parents who set rules and also enforce them.

Baumrind (1968) established a typology of educational styles, essentially from two attitudes: warmth and control, which led her to distinguish three parenting styles: authoritarian, permissive and authoritative (Vanistendael and Lecomte, 2000; Lecomte, 2004). In a nutshell, these three styles of parenting take into account the wishes of the child, but also explain why rules are necessary and sometimes sanctions must be taken. Children in these three categories of parenting tend to perceive the world differently. Children of authoritarian parents are anxious and withdrawn. They do well in school and follow social rules, but tend to view the adult world as a hostile and unfair place over which they have no control. Children of permissive parents learn early on that they will be rewarded, no matter what they do. They do not integrate the concepts of good and evil. They rebel when their desires are disputed and show little perseverance in difficult tasks. Children of authoritative parents generally exhibit a happy and lively mood. They have confidence in their ability to perform the tasks they undertake, and come to regard their actions as the cause of the good and bad things that have happened to them. They think independently and can make their own decisions.

The third tenet, creating meaning, refers to the fact that traumatic events frequently lead to existential crises that raise questions about the meaning of life, suffering and justice in the world (Vanistendael and Lecomte, 2000; Lecomte, 2004). According to Lecomte (2004), resilience occurs when the person moves from focusing on the past to looking forward. This process happens when the person seeks meaning and is eventually able to find satisfying meaning to her experience of adversity (Wong & Wong, 2012).

According to Lecomte (2010), people who have suffered from adversity with one or more traumas require these three essential elements, the link, the symbolic law and the meaning, to achieve psychological reconstruction. Individuals who suffer can also find support from those with whom they have a connection. For example, psychotherapists, or other professionals, such as social workers, can be "resilience tutors" and play a significant role in fostering resilience for clients. These supportive individuals have the capacity to generate a genuine link, establish the symbolic law, and provide a solid benchmark for clients and allow them to develop meaning in their own way and attain well-being (Lecomte, 2010). Vanistendael and Lecomte's (2000) model of resilience echoes the symbolic capacity of the individual and their imaginary, a notion that is related to culture and will be defined briefly later in this chapter.

Definition of Culture

Culture is considered as a social interactive process where members of the same community share cultural values, practices and meaning interpretation (Greenfield, Keller, Fuligni, & Maynard, 2003). It refers to the behaviours and beliefs of a particular group. Culture is a multidimensional construct which includes, languages, customs, history, philosophies and religions, etc. (Wong, 2016).

Furthermore, Ungar and his colleagues (2008) asserted that patterns of resilience are context-dependent. It is difficult to predict what common factors contribute to resilience among people who cope well across different continents and cultures. People survive adversity no matter where they are. There are many dimensions that contribute to resilience and some factors specific to Eastern collectivistic cultures, which have a large family focus, are still unknown to researchers from the West (Ungar et al., 2008). Thus, a single, invariant factor that promotes resilience is highly unlikely. What resilience looks like, and the factors that predict its outcome, vary among cultural groups. Thus, those who study resilience of bicultural individuals should consider how two different cultures impact them significantly and affect their adaptation (Berry & Sam, 2016).

Resilience is considered in the context of many domains – family, school, workplace, community, cultural values and activities, interpersonal relationships, language, religious experiences and other public domains. Any cultural practices that may adversely affect immigrant children's development must also be considered. For example, if immigrants perceive discrimination and injustice in the adopted country, their mental health would be compromised.

Furthermore, from a developmental perspective, Motti-Stefanidi (2018) offered an integrative framework for conceptualizing immigrant youth's resilience. In examining the adaptation of immigrants' children, she focused on proactive factors and positive outcomes such as assets and strengths, rather than on deficit-based factors such as risks, problems and vulnerabilities. The resilience developmental model emphasizes adaptation in three tasks: developmental tasks, acculturation tasks and psychological well-being, and under three different levels, the societal level, interactional level and individual levels (Motti-Stefanidi, 2018). In the societal level, cultural beliefs, ideology, social representation and social position, such as social class, immigrant statues and ethnicity, were examined. In the interactional level, relationships with family, neighbours, friends, teachers or school that influence individuals' development and acculturation were examined. At the individual level, individuals' personal characteristics, personality, cognition and motivation were examined. Motti-Stefanidi (2018) believed that influences at these levels affect individuals' adaptation, either putting them at risk or promoting positive adaptation.

Researchers must consider some of the key indicators of positive adaptation. Positive adaptation include:

> success in school, having close friends/being accepted (not rejected by peers), exhibiting positive conduct, civic engagement, or on internal adaptation, such as development of self-control, of a cohesive and integrated sense of identity, and an increasing individuation and independence from parents.
>
> (Motti-Stefanidi, 2018, p. 2)

Children's success at fulfilling developmental tasks indicates their level of function in the broader social world and the quality of their relationship with parents, teachers and peers (Sroufe, Egeland, Carlson, & Collins, 2005). To foster resilience, Masten (2014) cited two factors that promote resilience and prevent negative influences on adaptation and development – there are *promotive factors*, such as assets, resources, social or human capital that promote positive adaptation despite facing adversity in life, and there are *protective factors*, such as good attachment with parents, which play a special role for adaptation under high risk conditions.

Definition of Acculturation

Acculturation is the process of learning and adapting to a new culture (Berry, 2003). Traditionally, acculturation was measured unilinearly – where immigrants would reject their heritage culture and replace it with the dominant mainstream culture. However, acculturation can now be considered bilinearly, seen as a complex two-directional and multi-domain process (Nguyen & Benet-Martínez, 2013). Individuals may choose the extent to which they integrate mainstream and heritage cultures in their lives through language use, daily living habits, social affiliation, status, identity, culture knowledge, beliefs, values, etc. (Nguyen & Benet-Martínez, 2013; Zane & Mak, 2003). Individuals may choose to involve both, either or neither culture in their beliefs, practices, values and identity. There are four types of acculturation as described by Berry (1997, 2001):

Separation. Immigrants desire to only maintain their heritage culture. They are exclusively involved in their native ethnic community.
Assimilation. Immigrants desire to integrate into the mainstream culture. They are exclusively involved in the mainstream culture of the adopted country.
Marginalization. Immigrants reject both heritage culture and mainstream culture of the adopted country. Neither culture is important to them.
Integration. Immigrants desire to maintain their heritage culture and have a positive relationship with the adopted country. They have high levels of association in their heritage group and high levels of involvement in the mainstream group of the adopted country (Noels, Pon & Clement, 1996).

Culture and Previous Studies of Resilience

Motti-Stefanidi (2018) claimed that culture had largely been neglected in previous studies of resilience, focusing on the individual rather than how the environment impacts the individual's ability to cope. Furthermore, resilience was being understood as a psychological discourse from a Western perspective (Wyman, 2003). Ungar and his colleagues (2008) argued that many immigrants from the East may not reflect Western cultural values, traditions and thinking. Immigrants from the East may consider meeting the needs of their family as more important than their individual needs. Motti-Stefanidi (2018) claimed that culture plays an essential role in understanding individuals' differences in achieving well-being in the adopted country. She found that the greater the cultural gap between immigrant youth's ethnic and mainstream cultures, the poorer the adaptation of the youths (Motti-Stefanidi, 2018, p. 9). Very often, parents may want to retain their heritage culture when they come to an adopted country. Thus, parents' acculturation process may be slower than their children's, who had no exposure or less experience in their parents' heritage culture. Immigrants' children may be more oriented to mainstream culture. Researchers claim that a differing pace of acculturation between parents and children may widen the acculturation gap and generate intergenerational conflicts and family tension (Tasopoulos-Chan, Smetana & Yau, 2009; Giguère, Lalonde & Lou, 2010; Phinney, Kim-Jo, Osorio & Vilhjalmsdottir, 2005). Family tension hampers the resiliency of younger generations. Under the most unfavourable condition, it is considered one of the major factors which contribute to suicide among Asian American children (Costigan, Hua & Su, 2010).

Furthermore, Durand (1960) believed that culture shapes individuals' values and worldviews, and at the same time, individual attitudes, beliefs and ways of life also form culture. There is an "anthropological dialectic," a constant impact, ceaseless exchange and influence between individuals and their cultures within society (Durand, 1999, p. 41). Culture plays a role in influencing individuals' adjustment. Therefore, this implies that culture also plays a significant role in defining and understanding resilience.

In studying the resiliency of the youths of immigrant families, Motti-Stefanidi (2018) stated that culture, development of youths and their acculturation are intertwined. Culture plays an essential part in influencing their acculturation, their experience in the mainstream society of the adopted country, and their family, school and work environments (Motti-Stefanidi, 2018).

Culture, Imaginary and Resilience

Durand (1960) developed a theory of the imaginary in the study of symbols and images, the Anthropological Structures of Imaginary (ASI), which is considered culturally sensitive to both Western and Eastern worldviews (Wunenburger, 2013). Therefore, Durand's theory is applicable to all cultures because symbols and images are universal to all cultures. He classified and catalogued images and symbols by gathering images according to their similarities along the anthropological route, using analogical thinking from cultures. He divided cultural images and visual narratives into two large regimes – the "diurnal" and the "nocturnal" structures, which are in opposition. The diurnal regime includes the heroic category, and the nocturnal regime is subdivided further into the mystical category and synthetic category (Durand, 1999; Iranzo, 2001).

Durand asserted that individuals that are classified in the heroic category in the diurnal regime have characteristics of standing up and fighting against adversities in order to gain mastery over anxiety and struggles in life (Bellehumeur, Lavoie, Malette, Lapree & Guindon, 2013). These individuals perform, take action, achieve, distinguish and separate their identity from others in order to fulfil one's goal or achieve success. On the other hand, individuals that are sub-categorized into the mystical category in the nocturnal regime generally experience feelings of ease with intimacy, and may be enmeshed, peaceful, friendly, happy and gentle without experiencing disturbance or threat in life. These individuals feel warmth, unity and togetherness in their experience of relationships with others. In a group, emotions and identity may be united together without distinctiveness or individuality in the group dynamic (Laprée, 2013).

To ensure the continual existence and balance of the regimes, a third path, the synthetic category in the nocturnal regime exists. The synthetic category brings the diurnal and nocturnal regimes to co-exist harmoniously. Individuals in the synthetic category can tolerate conflict, discomfort and change. They resolve conflicts and demonstrate their resiliency by being flexible, taking control, observing, evaluating options and situations, and making changes constantly, trying to cope and harmonize differences. Laprée (2013) believed that regulation instead of fixation brings resilience, helping individuals to link, unite and balance opposing dynamic forces into a harmonious, objective way of living without falling into extreme polarization. Individuals in the synthetic category are able to deal with conflicts and communicate with others in functional ways without crumbling under stress.

Durand considered mental illness as the outcome of fixation in one of the structures of the imaginary (1960). Personality disorders, social unrest and military conflicts could result from fixation or imbalance of the heroic or mystical regimes (Bellehumeur et al., 2013; Laprée, 2000). Individuals who are under stress can have difficulty managing life and conflicts, and may be unable to function in a coherent way, such as people that are categorized in the unstructured category with less elaboration in their imagination (Bellehumeur et al., 2013). Durand (1980) asserted that heterogeneity and openness are important elements to foster well-being. Individuals should be open to accept diverse elements rather than only one option. Heterogeneity promotes optimal mental health and resiliency. Openness helps immigrants make connections with others and regulate themselves when encountering antitheses in two cultures. The ASI theory implies that individuals within the synthetic structure have better mental health than those who are polarized in the heroic or mystical structures or in the unstructured category.

Children of immigrants are often raised in a different cultural context than that of their parents. They live and grow between heritage cultures, represented by their family, and mainstream cultures, represented by their school or work. For example, many immigrants come from Eastern collectivistic societies which tend to place higher values on family connection, relationships, respect, obedience, orientation to a larger group and interdependence on one another. Well-being and identity are focused on the group rather than the individual, and individuals' needs are considered less important (Kağitçibaşi, 2012; Markus & Kitayama, 1991). When immigrants come to Western individualistic societies, priority is most likely placed on the individual. Thus, children of immigrants may be faced with opposing cultural values and experience cultural conflict. Various dimensions of dissonances are described below.

Conflicting Values in Relatedness and Separateness

As discussed, Eastern collectivistic cultures place emphasis on relationships, group and interdependence whereas in Western individualistic societies, the self is more clearly bounded and separated from others (Markus & Kitayama, 1991). The Western goal for development is to be autonomous, self-reliant and independent from others, reaching one's full potential (Greenfield et al.,

2003; Motti-Stefanidi, 2018). This may lead to discrepancy in the level of relatedness and separateness between cultures.

Withholding Affection vs. Expression of Emotions

In a phenomenological, qualitative study involving 34 adult SGCC, Yeung (2018) found that many Chinese parents did not openly express emotions to their children. Instead of experiencing love through gestures of affection like their Canadian peers, children of Chinese immigrants experienced love by witnessing their parents' acts of sacrifice. Although it was acceptable to openly express emotions in mainstream Canadian culture, it was not freely expressed in their heritage Chinese culture families. This left them feeling that their emotional needs were unfulfilled, despite their material needs being met.

Personal Choices vs. Obligation in Social Relationships

(Eastern) and (Western) cultures may disagree on the promotion and cultivation of autonomous, self-directed, assertive behaviours (Motti-Stefanidi, 2018). While Western teachers may expect children to explore one's own life goals and pursue personal interests, parents who were born from Eastern countries may want their children, living with them in the host (Western) country, to follow established pathways for financial security in their future occupation. Thus, these children may be pressured to conform to their parents' wishes, where individual freedom to achieve their own goals and interests may be limited.

Other Cultural Discrepancies

Yeung (2018) also found other sources of acculturation stress such as differences in: expectations between parents and children, explicit and implicit communication of needs, priority of work and play, meeting one's own vs. others' needs, working styles, level of openness to the mainstream community, religious beliefs and practices, and language in communication between parents and children. In this study of second-generation children of Chinese immigrants, 76 per cent of the participants' parents did not speak English, whereas 71 per cent described English as their primary language, and 59 per cent communicated in a different primary language than their parents (Yeung, 2018).

For children of immigrants who have remained separate from mainstream culture, inability to fluently express oneself in the heritage language can cause frustration. This may lead to misunderstanding by others, and affect the parent–child bond. Motti-Stefanidi (2018) raised the concern for positive adaptation in parenting in immigrant families. The authoritarian, controlling and punishing style of parenting is unacceptable in an individualistic culture. The lack of expression of affection from parents may make it difficult for offspring of immigrants to handle their own emotions or express their affections to parents or others verbally. Children of immigrants need to develop cultural competence in both heritage culture and mainstream culture (Oppedal & Toppelberg, 2016).

Key Factors for Resilience, Adaptation and Well-Being in the Context of Acculturation

There are many ways to examine resilience and adaptation of immigrant families. Motti-Stefanidi (2018) suggested examining resilience and adaptation from personal, interactional and societal levels.

Personal Level Factors for Resilience

Immigrants and their children must be active agents in coping with their adaptation. They are constantly in contact and navigating between two different cultures (heritage vs. mainstream). They receive two different sets of values and expectation from their colleagues, parents, teachers, peers and media. They must screen out differences, select, resist and manage competing messages, and actively contract their own working cultural model (Motti-Stefanidi, 2018). This process of negotiating two cultures involves various factors of resilience, such as the capacity for integrative complexity, which demands intellectual capacity, flexibility and creativity (Benet-Martínez, Lee & Leu, 2006). Panter-Brick (2015) asserted that hope is also a strong element in cultivating resilience and fostering positive adaptation, under adverse conditions and environments (Panter-Brick, 2015).

Spirituality, which can also be understood as a personal resource (Hill & Pargament, 2003), has a strong influence on the resilience of individuals. Individuals who stated that they had a relationship with the Higher Being reported its positive contribution to their well-being (Yeung, 2018). In the study of resilience among Vietnamese immigrants, Nguyen and her colleagues found that a positive perception of God was negatively correlated with somatization, anxiety and hostility, whereas negative perceptions of God was related to higher levels of emotional distress. Furthermore, based on use of the AT.9, a projective test to measure one's symbolic capacity or imaginary, those in the synthetic category have been associated with a positive perception of God, and negatively associated with somatization, intrusion and hypervigilance (Nguyen et al., 2018).

Integration in Acculturation

Berry and Sam (2016) claimed that the best developmental and mental outcome for immigrants were in those who had adopted *integration* as their acculturation strategy. These individuals maintain their own heritage culture and at the same time, take on characteristics of their adopted country. In Yeung's

(2018) research of SGCC, participants described their meaning of happiness as the integration of heritage and mainstream cultures. Rather than fulfilling individual pleasures and personal goals, participants maintained interpersonal harmony and promoted the welfare and prosperity of the family, fulfilling their role of filial piety, and the Confucian moral tradition (Lu, 2010). At the same time, they valued diversity, heterogeneity, multiple perspectives and freedom to explore life and pursue learning for personal growth and advance. They preferred to have both cultures instead of selecting one over the other (Yeung, 2018).

Bicultural Identity

Nguyen and Benet-Martínez (2013) asserted that culturally competent immigrants tend to be bicultural. Eighty-eight per cent of the participants of Yeung's (2018) research identified themselves as bicultural, Chinese Canadians. Bicultural individuals learn and maintain both heritage culture and mainstream culture. Researchers have considered biculturalism as the most ideal because it leads to adjustment and greater benefits to all areas of life (Berry, 1997; Phinney, Horenczyk, Liebkind & Vedder, 2001). Nguyen and Benet-Martínez (2013) found an overall positive association between biculturalism and adjustment. Bicultural individuals have higher self-esteem, lower anxiety, better academic achievement, better conduct, and strong and secure ethnic and national identities (Motti-Stefanidi, 2018). A link was found between biculturalism and positive psychological and sociocultural adjustment as compared to individuals with either heritage or mainstream cultural orientation alone (Nguyen & Benet-Martínez, 2013, p. 122).

Bicultural individuals do not comprise a homogeneous group (Nguyen & Benet-Martínez, 2013), they differ in how they negotiate and combine their two cultures. They may vary their cultural orientation based on a situational approach. They can choose to identify with their peers and colleagues by adopting mainstream values at school or work, but adopt practices and customs of the heritage culture at home. They may choose to alternate cultures, blend or fuse cultures (LaFromboise, Coleman & Gerton, 1993; Phinney & Devich-Navarro, 1997). Nguyen and Benet-Martínez (2013) stated that a positive relationship between bicultural status and adjustment may be due to multiple external and internal factors. As an example of external factor, it is worthwhile to mention that bicultural individuals can access social supports from both cultures (Mok, Morris, Benet-Martínez & Karakitapoglu-Aygun, 2007). Researchers consider bicultural individuals as most well-adjusted because they are competent in navigating both mainstream and heritage cultures (LaFromboise et al., 1993). In the process of learning and navigating two cultures, bicultural individuals acquire social skills, seen as internal factors, such as competencies, flexibility and expertly knowing how to adjust to various people and cultural situations (Nguyen & Benet-Martínez, 2013). Flexibility helps bicultural individuals to build social support networks in both cultures and prevent them from anxiety and loneliness, isolation and other maladjustment that occur in acculturation.

The anthropological findings of Yeung's (2018) research, based on the AT.9, indicated that 55 per cent of adult children in immigrant families were classified into the synthetic mythical category where individuals often have the ability to tolerate and balance oppositional forces without falling into extremes (Durand, 1988, 2005). These second-generation individuals in the synthetic category may be better equipped to tolerate conflict and cultural tensions in a coherent way. Nguyen and Benet-Martínez (2013) stated that biculturalism is more strongly related to adjustment (p. 133). Individuals in the synthetic category are likely to use resources from both cultures to prevent maladjustment; they may also participate in both cultures, and most likely become bicultural.

Kağitçibaşi (2012) asserted that individuals with an autonomous-related self, defined as those with the freedom to make their own choices and achieve their own goals and yet able to maintain intimate relationship with their loved ones, are considered as the most adaptive in the public and private domain. These individuals actively engage in challenges, asserting their personal agency and acting independently in the public domain. They navigate between conflicting values and developmental goals of heritage culture and mainstream cultures. Yet at the same time, they are able to maintain positive relations with parents, able to accommodate and negotiate with others, willing to uphold family values, yet demand autonomy.

Heterogeneity and Openness

Heterogeneity and openness were found to be important elements that fostered well-being (Yeung, 2018), a finding which is congruent with Durand's notion of optimal mental health. Heterogeneity is an important condition for mental health, as opposed to homogeneity (Laprée, 2000). To deal with cultural conflicts, a nurturing environment which supports heterogeneity is important in order to foster and cultivate a happy, healthy, mosaic, bicultural self. Furthermore, an openness to accept and integrate various cultures in a healthy manner to support positive acculturation is an important element to cultivate resiliency among immigrant families. The exposure and opportunity to learn different ideas and traditions from various cultural groups can widen one's worldview and perspective.

Navigation and Negotiation

Two processes are involved in resilience, navigation and negotiation (Ungar et al., 2008). Individuals must demonstrate personal agency to navigate their way to resources, such as experiences to improve self-esteem, obtain education, and participate in family and community endeavours. The family and the community must also be available and accessible as resources to immigrant families (Ungar et al., 2008). The process of negotiation is also required to ensure that the resources provided are meaningful to the individuals that require support.

Interactional Level Factors for Resilience

School

Motti-Stefanidi (2018) suggested the practice of inclusion, equality and value of cultures at school can foster resilience in students. In doing so, every student is respected and treated fairly with equal opportunity in terms of gender, race and religion. Students are encouraged to make contact and cooperate with other ethnic groups, and learn to work towards common goals to increase comfort with people of different ethnicity and cultural values.

Families

Parents have a significant influence on the adaptation of their children. They bring their beliefs, attitudes, values and child-rearing practices with them from their heritage culture. Motti-Stefanidi (2018) cited the importance of parental support. Parents' ability to support their children to adapt to their new culture, learn and maintain their ethnic culture, and deal with discrimination, is vital for adjustment (Motti-Stefanidi, 2018, p. 10). The effect of parenting on the child's development depends on how children perceive their parenting practices. Parenting can be a complex issue if parents remain strongly oriented to their heritage culture and practice an authoritarian parenting style where parents exert authority over their children, demand obedience and express lower levels of affection (Baumrind, 1971). As a result of an authoritarian style, children's autonomy would be undermined. In Yeung's (2018) research, adult children were found to obey their parents even as they reach adulthood in traditional Chinese culture, and high expectations from parents for academic performance and career goals led to unhealthy stress and anxiety, leading to alienation and resentment. Loneliness was found to be a common experience among second-generation immigrants, especially those that came from authoritarian families (Hing, 2013). Therefore, parents must consider which practices are most appropriate and adaptive for their children. Parenting style also reflects the level of parents' acculturation (Motti-Stefanidi, 2018). Parents may tend to use authoritarian parenting styles if they remain strongly oriented to a heritage culture with collectivistic values.

The acculturation gap between parent and child may affect the well-being of children. Costigan and Dokis (2006) found that immigrant children had adaptation difficulty if their parents were highly oriented towards the heritage culture, but the children were not. There should be a negotiation and dialogue between parents and their children with regard to having a balance and adopting values and beliefs of the mainstream culture and the heritage culture (Bornstein, 2017).

Workplace and Religious Institutions

The findings of Yeung (2018) indicated that the most frequent public settings of cultural tension were in the workplace (29 per cent) and in the church (26 per cent). Tension severity ranged from absent to moderate, with no participant citing tension in the upper moderate to severe range (Figure 9.2). Tensions from the workplace is not surprising as many participants were of working age, and it was expected that many would be exposed to demanding encounters with colleagues and customers of various cultures. However, it was a surprise that the church, a place generally regarded as a sacred, close-knit and supportive community, would be one of the leading sources of cultural tension. The Chinese ethnic church has likely adopted the same traditional, authoritarian attitude towards the SGCC. This second-generation is perceived as more Chinese than Canadian; they should submit to the leaders rather than their own will. Strong cultural influences can come from the heritage culture if individuals attend ethnic religious institutions.

Societal Level Factors for Resilience

Multicultural Societies

Motti-Stefanidi stated that "an accepting and welcoming society with multicultural ideology is a key resource for immigrant youth's positive adaptation" (Motti-Stefanidi, 2018, p. 9). Immigrants' children's acculturation is improved if the mainstream culture values cultural pluralism, respectfulness and

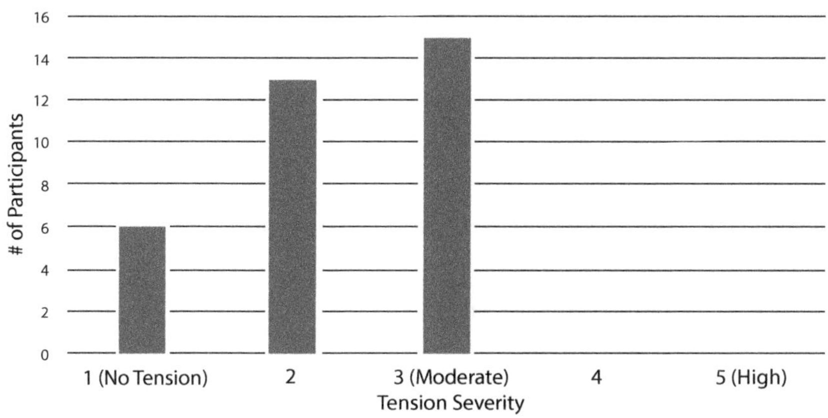

Figure 9.2 Severity of participants' experience of cultural tension

tolerance to ethnic diversity (Berry & Sabatier, 2010). Only within a culture where ethnic diversity is valued can there be respectful intercultural dialogue and exchange (Motti-Stefanidi, 2018). Nguyen and Benet-Martínez (2013) asserted that the dominant group's attitude towards immigrants is important. This includes multicultural policies in the adopted country, and the level at which mainstream culture is accepting and non-discriminating towards acculturating individuals. These societal measures foster biculturalism in immigrants and enhance higher levels of adjustment.

Conclusion

Studying immigrants' resilience and adaptation is a complex task. There is no one generalized model, universal principle or measurement design that can capture the diversity of their adaptation. We must understand resilience at various levels, from micro to macro levels, including personal, familial, cultural and societal levels.

Immigrant parents who support their children, grant them autonomy, and maintain close relational ties, will certainly help their children adapt. The ability to make one's own decisions and to maintain close relationship with loved ones is an asset to foster resilience and adaptation. A supportive multicultural environment with ample job and learning opportunities without racial discrimination will stimulate immigrants' exploration of learning, personal growth, well-being and productive contribution to their adopted country.

Last but not least, embracing heterogeneity and openness to cultural diversity can enrich individuals' lives. At the individual level, one's own symbolic capacity with the structure of the law, the social capacity to relate to others, and the ability to create meaning in the midst of affliction, are considered basic tenets of resilience (Lecomte, 2004); and at the societal level, these dimensions reflect the synthetic category, referring to highest level of collective imaginary (Durand, 1999).

Note

1 Chapter 6 in this volume presents more details of this theory.

References

Baumrind, D. (1968). Authoritarian vs. authoritative parental control. *Adolescence*, 3(11), 255–272.

Baumrind, D. (1971). Current patterns of parental authority. *Developmental Psychology*, 4(1, Pt.2), 1–103. doi:10.1037/h0030372.

Bellehumeur, C., Lavoie, L-C., Malette, J., Lapree, R., & Guindon, M. (2013). An empirical study of young French Quebecers' imaginary using the archetypal test with nine elements: Exploring the links between interpersonal styles and socio-economic status. *The International Journal of Interdisciplinary Cultural Studies*, 7(3), 11–25.

Benet-Martínez, V., Lee, F., & Leu, J. (2006). Biculturalism and cognitive complexity: Expertise in cultural representations. *Journal of Cross-Cultural Psychology*, 37, 386–407.

Berry, J.W. (1997). Immigration, acculturation and adaptation. *Applied Psychology*, 46(1), 5–68.

Berry, J.W. (2001). A psychology of immigration. *Journal of Social Issues*, 57(3), 615–631.

Berry, J.W. (2003). Conceptual approaches to acculturation. In K.M. Chun, P.B. Organista, & G. Marin (Eds.), *Acculturation: Advances in theory, measurement, and applied research* (pp. 17–37). Washington, DC: American Psychological Association.

Berry, J.W., & Sabatier, C. (2010). Acculturation, discrimination, and adaptation among second generation immigrant youth in Montreal and Paris. *International Journal of Intercultural Relations*, 34(3), 191–207.

Berry, J.W., & Sam, D.L. (2016). Theoretical perspectives. In D.L. Sam & J. Berry (Eds.), *Cambridge handbook of acculturation psychology*, 2nd edn (pp. 11–29). Cambridge: Cambridge University Press.

Bornstein, M.H. (2017). The specificity principle in acculturation science. *Perspectives on Psychological Science*, 12(1), 3–45.

Costigan, C.L., & Dokis, D.P. (2006). Relations between parent-child acculturation differences and adjustment within immigrant Chinese families. *Child Development*, 77 (5), 1252–1267.

Costigan, C.L., Hua, J.M., & Su, T.F. (2010). Living up to expectations: The strengths and challenges experienced by Chinese Canadian students. *Canadian Journal of School of Psychology*, 23(3), 223–245.

Durand, G. (1960). *Anthropological structures of the imaginary: Introduction to general archetypology*. Paris: PUF.

Durand, G. (1980). *L'Âme tigrée, les pluriels de Psyché*, Paris: Denoël.

Durand, G. (1999). *The anthropological structures of the imaginary*, 11th edn (translated by M. Sankey & J. Hatten). Brisbane: Boombana Publications. (Original work published 1992).

Durand, Y. (1988). *L'exploration de l'imaginaire: Introduction a' la modé lisation des univers mythiqés*. Paris: L'espace bleu.

Durand, Y. (2005). *Une technique d'étude de l'imaginaire: l'AT.9*. Paris: L'Harmattan.

Giguère, B., Lalonde, R., & Lou, E (2010). Living at crossroads of cultural worlds: The experience of normative conflicts by second generation immigrant youth. *Social and Personality Psychology Compass*, 4(1), 14–29.

Greenfield, P.M., Keller, H., Fuligni, A., & Maynard, A. (2003). Cultural pathways through universal development. *Annual Review of Psychology*, 54(1), 461–490.

Hill, P.C., & Pargament, K.I. (2003). Advances in the conceptualization and measurement of religion and spirituality: Implications for physical and mental health research. *American Psychologist*, 58(1), 64–74.

Hing, A.Y. (2013). Children and their fathers in Singapore: A generational perspective. In K. Chan (Ed.), *International handbook of Chinese families* (pp. 323–341). New York: Springer.

Iranzo, I.P. (2001). About the imaginary. *Formats: revista de comunicació audiovisual*, 3, Edició en anglès. Retrieved from: www.iua.upf.edu/formats/formats3/pin1_a.htm.

Kağitçibaşi, C. (2012). Autonomous-related self and competence: The potential of immigrant youth. In A.S. Masten, K. Liebkind, & D.J. Hernandez (Eds.), *Realizing the potential of immigrant youth* (pp. 281–306). New York: Cambridge University Press.

LaFromboise, T., Coleman, H.L.K., & Gerton, J. (1993). Psychological impact of biculturalism: Evidence and theory. *Psychological Bulletin*, 114, 395–412.

Laprée, R. (2000). *La psychagogie des valeurs. Symbolique et imaginaire en education.* Montréal: Logiques.

Laprée, R. (2013). La dynamique de groupe et les structures anthropologiques de l'imaginaire. In R. Laprée & C.R. Bellehumeur (Eds.), *L'imaginaire durandien. Enracinements et envols en Terre d'Amérique* (pp. 149–165). Québec: Presses de l'Université Laval.

Lecomte, J. (2004). *Guérir de son enfance.* Paris: Odile Jacob.

Lecomte, J. (2010). *La résilience: Se reconstruire après un traumatisme.* Paris: Éditions Rue d'Ulm. doi:10.3917/ulm.lecom.2010.01..

Lu, L. (2010). Chinese well-being. In M.H. Bond (Ed.), *The Oxford handbook of Chinese psychology* (pp. 327–342). New York: Oxford University Press.

Markus, H.R., & Kitayama, S. (1991). Culture and self: Implications for cognition, emotion and motivation. *Psychological Review*, 98, 224–253.

Masten, A.S. (2014). Ordinary magic: Resilience in development. In A.S. Masten (Ed.), *Ordinary magic: Resilience in development.* New York: Guilford Press.

Mok, A., Morris, M., Benet-Martínez, V., & Karakitapoglu-Aygun, Z. (2007). Embracing American culture: Structures of social identity and social networks among first-generation biculturals. *Journal of Cross-Cultural Psychology*, 38, 629–635.

Motti-Stefanidi, F. (2018). Resilience among immigrant youth: The role of culture, development and acculturation. *Developmental Review*, 62, 218–221.

Nguyen, A.-M.T., & Benet-Martínez, V. (2013). Biculturalism and adjustment: A meta- analysis. *Journal of Cross-Cultural Psychology*, 44(1), 122–159.

Nguyen, T.T., Bellehumeur, C., & Malette, J. (2018). Images of God and the imaginary in the face of loss: A quantitative research on Vietnamese immigrants living in Canada. *Mental Health, Religion & Culture.* doi:10.1080/13674676.2018.1499715.

Noels, K., Pon, G., & Clement, R. (1996). Language, identity, and adjustment: The role of linguistic self-confidence in the acculturation process. *Journal of Language and Social Psychology*, 15(3), 246–264.

Oppedal, B., & Toppelberg, C.O. (2016). Acculturation and development. In D.L. Sam & J. Berry (Eds.), *Cambridge handbook of acculturation psychology*, 2nd edn (pp. 71–92). New York: Cambridge University Press.

Panter-Brick, C. (2015). Culture and resilience: Next steps for theory and practice. In L. Theron, L. Liebenberg, & M. Ungar (Eds.), *Youth resilience and culture crosscultural advancements in positive psychology: Vol. 11* (pp. 223–244). Dordrecht: Springer.

Phinney, J.S., & Devich-Navarro, M. (1997). Variations in bicultural identification among African American and Mexican American adolescents. *Journal of Research on Adolescence*, 7, 3–32.

Phinney, J.S., Horenczyk, G., Liebkind, K., & Vedder, P. (2001). Ethnic identity, immigration, and wellbeing: An interactional perspective. *Journal of Social Issues*, 57, 493–510.

Phinney, J.S., Kim-Jo, T., Osorio, S., & Vilhjalmsdottir, P. (2005). Autonomy and relatedness in adolescent-parent disagreements: ethnic and developmental factors. *Journal of Adolescent Research*, 20, 8–39.

Rudmin, F.W. (2003). Critical history of the acculturation psychology of assimilation, separation, integration, and marginalization. *Review of General Psychology*, 7, 3–37.

SIM (2016). Serving where Christ is least known. *SIM Now.* Retrieved from: https://simnow.sim.ca/stories/welcome-to-our-2016-gift-guide.

Sroufe, L.A., Egeland, B., Carlson, E.A., & Collins, W.A. (2005). *The development of the person: The Minnesota study of risk and adaptation from birth to adulthood.* New York: Guilford.

Tasopoulos-Chan, M., Smetana, J.G., & Yau, J.P. (2009). How much do I tell thee? Strategies for managing information to parents among American adolescents from Chinese, Mexican, and European backgrounds. *Journal of Family Psychology*, 23(3), 364–374.

Ungar, M., Liebenberg, L., Boothroyd, R., Kwong, W.-M., Lee, T., Leblanc, J., Duque, L., & Makhnach, A. (2008). The study of youth resilience across cultures: Lessons from a pilot study of measurement development. *Research in Human Development*, 5, 166–180.

United Nations, Department of Economic and Social Affairs, Population Division (2017). *International Migration Report 2017: Highlights* (ST/ESA/SER.A/404). Retrieved from: www.un.org/en/development/desa/population/migration/publications/migrationreport/docs/MigrationReport2017_Highlights.pdf.

Vanistendael, S., & Lecomte, J. (2000). *Le bonheur est toujours possible, construire la resilience.* Paris: Bayard.

Vivero, V.N., & Jenkins, S.R. (1999). Existential hazards of the multicultural individual: Defining and understanding "cultural homelessness." *Cultural Diversity & Ethnic Minority Psychology*, 5, 6–26.

Wong, P.T.P. (2016). Chinese positive psychology revisited. *International Journal of Existential Psychology & Psychotherapy*, 6(1), 1–7. Retrieved from: http://journal.existentialpsychology.org/index.php/ExPsy/article/view/174/157.

Wong, P.T.P., & Wong, L.C.J. (2012). A meaning-centered approach to building youth resilience. In P.T.P. Wong (Ed.), *The human quest for meaning: Theories, research, and applications*, 2nd edn (pp. 585–617). New York: Routledge.

Wunenburger, J.-J. (2013). L'anthropologie de l'imaginaire selon Gilbert Durand: contextes, options, enjeux. In R. Laprée & C.R. Bellehumeur (Eds.), *L'imaginaire durandien, enracinements et envols* (pp. 3–17). Laval: Presses de l'Université Laval.

Wyman, P.A. (2003). Emerging perspectives on context specificity of children's adaptation and resilience: Evidence from a decade of research with urban children in adversity. In S.S. Luthar (Ed.), *Resilience and vulnerability: Adaptation in the context of childhood adversities* (pp. 293–317). Cambridge: Cambridge University Press.

Yeung, W.P.W. (2018). Imaginary, spirituality and subjective well-being of second-generation Chinese Canadians: Exploring the lived experience of well-being in a bicultural environment (Doctoral dissertation). Saint Paul University, Ottawa, Canada.

Zane, N., & Mak, W. (2003). Major approaches to the measurement of acculturation among ethnic minority populations: A content analysis and an alternative empirical strategy. In K.M. Chun, P.B. Organista, & G. Marin (Eds.), *Acculturation: Advances in theory, measurement, and applied research* (pp. 39–60). Washington, DC: American Psychological Association.

Part III

Nurturing Resilience Following Traumatic Events

10 Grieving and Resilience Factors for the Widow(er)

Role Transition

Ghislaine Benmoussa and Buuma Maisha

Resilience and Widowhood: An Introduction

The focus of this chapter is about resilience in widowhood; specifically, how resilient widow(er)s can overcome stressful events such as the death of a spouse. Identifying resilience based on the experience of individuals seems like a dichotomous observation associated within a context of a specific adversity (Jenkins, Paulson, Kelley, & Lewis, 2016). However, resilience can be better studied if it is considered as a continuous variable. Indeed, this continuous variable can teach us about the adaptability of the individual through several situations of adversity (Condly, 2006; Jenkins et al., 2016). That being said, even people who are considered resilient cannot maintain their level of resilience through all types of situations. Therefore, it may be useful to understand resilience as a continuous variable since this construct allows researchers to observe the various mechanisms of adaptation during different circumstances (Jenkins et al., 2016).

Resilience is defined as a consequence of a healthy adaptation to adversity (Zautra, Hall & Murray, 2010; Clements, 2014). Resilient people can quickly return to functioning normally while continuing to overcome adversity. According to Boerner, Wortman and Bonanno (2005) resilient individuals have a perspective on life which makes them less vulnerable to external stresses searching to avoid being the centre of attention or being the cause of others' worries. However, they are not always understood by others, especially when they end their mourning too quickly (Clements, 2014).

Zautra et al. (2010) report that adapting to resilience is not without emotional difficulties. Even though researchers commonly study the resilience response, there are resilience characteristics that make each experience unique to individuals; these are internal endurance, flexibility and the extent of the person's capacity. Other researchers have also defined resilience recovery as the ability to absorb disturbances before fundamental changes occur (Clements, 2014).

Resilient individuals have the ability to pursue their life goals and meaningful activities during the challenges of adversity. Even more, a resilient recovery focuses on the continuation and the healing of the personal, social and professional life domains. Skodol (2010) described resilience through individual differences that make it easier for people to adapt to their adversity challenges, thus making them more capable of dealing with stress in the future. The similarity in all definitions of resilience resides in the perception of resilience as a positive response to adversity (Skodol, 2010; Clements, 2014).

It should also be noted that there seems to be no consensus on the definition of adversity and its relation to the concept of resilience. Therefore, it is crucial to understand the adversity situation in order to identify the factors of resilience linked to it (Jenkins et al., 2016). Marital mourning is an excellent example of a stressful context involving enormous changes and requires high adaptability.

Moreover, Walsh (2006) explains that the bereavement of a spouse can also have enormous repercussions on the mental health of widow(er)s since it is one of the most stressful events of a lifetime (Holmes & Rahe, 1967; Alemayehu, 2014). As a result, survivors also experience grief because of issues with their physical and emotional well-being. Among documented mental health diagnosis related to bereavement are depression (Sasson & Umberson, 2014; Williams 2005; West, Dreeben & Busing, 2019) and anxiety (Onrust & Cuijpers, 2006; Williams, 2005; West, Dreeben & Busing, 2019). Widow(er)s are also a population with a higher mortality rate compared to non-widow(er)s and especially in the first year following the death of their spouse (Williams, 2005; West, Dreeben & Busing, 2019). Let us argue that resilience relates to identifying and understanding the experience of adversity. In the situation of marital mourning, coping behaviours to help overcome the stress related to loss are worthy examples of resilience.

Context of Marital Mourning

According to Papalia, Sterns, Feldman and Camp (2002), mourning is a process that an individual experiences when facing the loss of a loved one (Stretch, 2013). The internal experience of loss, also called grief involves a variety of cognitive and emotional distresses (Wheeler-Roy & Amyot, 2004; Stretch, 2013) leading to a set of behaviours exhibited by the bereaved who tries to adapt to the loss (Papalia et al., 2002; Stretch, 2013).

Grief is a troubling and challenging experience and when it is accompanied by emotional pain, even for a limited time, it may be referred to as acute grief. A minority of people experience prolonged and complicated grief characterized by symptoms different from that of normal grief, such as major depression. It is not always easy to identify complicated grief, because, in addition to the symptomology offered by the DSM, the experience of grief is strongly linked with several other factors such as those discussed in this chapter (Shear & Shair, 2005).

Researchers and clinicians such as Clayton, Desmarais and Winokur (1968) have focused on the grieving process in adults (Osterweis et al., 1984). In addition, scientific literature reveals a consensus among researchers with regard to emotional, cognitive, behavioral and somatic complaints during the grieving process. It is important to understand this process as non-linear, because it is fluid. Research shows there can be different reactions or changing phases representing the person's state of mind during the bereavement. Theorists often have their jargon to describe these phases, but the fact remains that most clinicians see them as predictable reactions, nonetheless. In sum, everyone reacts to grief differently and the process is not the same from one person to another (Osterweis et al., 1984).

Theories on the subject of bereavement are psycho-educational benchmarks that can help clients understand what they are experiencing (Bee, 2000; Stretch, 2013). Over the past 60 years, there have been contributions from several theoretical models regarding bereavement in psychology. There are now theories available to psychotherapists who offer the tools necessary to detect where their clients find themselves during their grieving process (Servaty-Seib, 2004; Stretch, 2013). For example, Kübler-Ross's theory (1969) is an informative framework which professionals can consult in order to best support the bereaved (Lapsley, 1970; Kübler-Ross, 1969; Servaty-Seib, 2004; Stretch, 2013).

In 1969, Kubler-Ross identified five stages of mourning as part of a theory to offer a description of the possible bereavement experiences and the adaptation that follows (Bee, 2000; Stretch, 2013). The stages are denial, anger, bargaining, depression and acceptance. It is interesting to note that each of the stages has a cognitive and emotional response, which represents how the person adapts to their loss (Kübler-Ross, 1969; Stretch, 2013). The denial is the response to the shock that the person experiences when he/she realizes the death of their loved one and do not accept this reality. This response allows the person to take the time necessary to find the right space to experience the loss (Kübler-Ross, 1969; Stretch, 2013). Anger is the phase associated with the emotional state in which the bereaved externalizes the suffering by blaming themselves or seeking to blame others for the death of the loved one. Kübler-Ross describes this experience as being a way of regaining a temporary sense of loss. The bargaining phase can help the widow(er) regain a sense of hope since it provides them with a way of attempting to modify the course of events by offering something in return (Kübler-Ross, 1969; Stretch, 2013). When the bereaved reaches the phase of depression, he or she must accept that they cannot change the course of past events, and end up succumbing to live the emotional impact of what happened (Kübler-Ross, 1969; Stretch, 2013). Finally, the last phase is acceptance; achieved when the bereaved accepts the reality, that is to say, realizes that their loved one has died and that they must move on (Kübler-Ross, 1969; Stretch, 2013). Maciejewski, Zhang, Block and Prigerson (2007) studied 233 mourners to find that all of them had gone through the five phases of mourning described by Kübler-Ross.

The descriptive phases of existing grief theories are potential therapeutic tools to help grieving individuals normalize their experience. However, health professionals, more specifically psychotherapists and psychologists, must beware of the pathologization of symptoms for clients.

Pathologization occurs when individuals are classified as having a mental disorder to explain their behaviours (McNally, 2011; Wasserman & Wasserman, 2016). In other words, pathologization can result in a feeling of abnormality by the person being helped and thus worsen their distress (Stretch, 2013). It is crucial to explore and take into consideration the possibility of aggravating or facilitating some of the factors in the grieving process. For example, in American society, there is a beginning, a middle and an end to the process of mourning, which depend on the rhythm of each bereaved (Granek, Bartels, Scheinemann, Labrecque & Barrera, 2015; Stretch, 2013). One of the main objectives of this chapter is to broaden our understanding beyond theoretical models. We believe it is essential to consider the possible challenges hindering an individual's experience and contributing to its uniqueness.

The Loss of a Spouse

It is essential to study resilience in the context of the loss of a spouse. This theme is related to the many losses associated with bereavement. For example, grieving can leave the survivor feeling overwhelmed by all the responsibilities left by their spouse after their death. Also, the survivor must regain the courage to filter their available resources and seize the opportunities to face difficult circumstances. The loss of the confidant and the source of stability within the relationship, but also the many facets of the survivor's life, is a great challenge (West, Dreeben & Busing, 2019).

Indeed, in the context of the loss of a spouse, there is a psychosocial transition that consists of an amalgamation of losses (Parkes, 1988; Vachon et al., 1976; Derman, 1999). This loss is not limited to a simple physical absence of the spouse, but rather it involves losses on several levels such as loss of a companion, loss of a friend, loss of a sexual partner, loss of protection, loss of support, loss of resources, loss of status, loss of planned future, loss of self-confidence and loss of a potential parent for children (Lopata, 1988; Parkes, 1988; Derman, 1999).

The loss of a partner in a marriage or committed relationship is an intense and disruptive emotional experience. The intensity and duration of the pain experienced are specific to an emotional bond and closeness within the relationship between the widow(er) and the deceased, varying from one marriage to another. When a marriage comes to an end because a spouse dies, the bonds of the relationship are always present. Even more, the feeling of abandonment heightens to the point that the survivor ends up maintaining a relationship despite the physical absence of the deceased (Derman, 1999).

Often, with the presence of children, widow(er)s feel an enormous burden of responsibility that they must overcome alone. Tasks within the family can no longer be divided, making the transition to the new life more difficult. In terms of resources, the survivor is often at risk of financial difficulties since family income is reduced (Derman, 1999).

The survivor must also change his or her identity as he takes on the role of widow(er) and it starts as soon as he or she goes into mourning. The widow(er) must reconfigure his or her social circle and abandon their former role of being married since the situation has now changed (Osterweis et al., 1984). In short, the death of a spouse generates changes in the sense of self and in the configurations of situations that no longer correspond to the changed life of the survivor (Osterweis et al., 1984).

Moreover, when they are young adults, survivors tend to suffer more intense grief and in prolonged ways, with a significant impact to their physical and psychological health. This vulnerable bereaved population often consult their physicians for physical or emotional problems: they resort to drugs, smoking and alcohol use after the loss of a loved one (Brent et al., 2009; Melhem et al., 2004; Parkes, 1987; Stroebe & Stroebe, 1987; Lichtenberg, 2017). The experience of loss at a young age raises many risks for maladaptive responses to bereavement stress (Mash, Fullerton, Shear & Ursano, 2014).

However, while individuals may feel overwhelmed during grief, others may respond to a loss with remarkable resilience. This could mean that resilient people are less affected by grief; they can lessen the negative impact of the loss (Boerner & Jopp, 2010). Researchers also demonstrated that these people have minimal grief symptoms in response to their loss. In 2010, Boerner and Jopp supported the idea that individuals who have had minimal grief symptoms have taken the trajectory of resilience. This trajectory is tinged by an adaptation to the distress of bereavement and in the form of a return to normal functioning. Research has shown that resilience in these people manifests itself through the expression of positive emotion during the commemoration of their deceased (Clements, 2014).

Balk (2008) debated that resilience should be understood as a return to normal functioning and through the positive results in the trajectory of recovery from healing. The term "trajectory" is defined by a possible path that can describe how individuals can go through a traumatic event or a loss. This finding also emerges from the literature on the topic of resilience. Since the mourning is also understood as a trajectory (Clements, 2014), let us take a close look at the risk and protective factors of resilience. Let us note that lifelong adversity experiences are a fundamental construct in the study of resilience (Luthar & Cushing, 1999; Pierorazio, Hawkins, Hutchison & Morin, 2009).

Loss of a Partner and Resilience Factors

It should be noted that research on bereavement reveals that the human response to the death of a loved one can be a complex and varying process. Indeed, culture, religion and interpersonal context can influence how people experience their grief (Bee, 2000; Papalia et al., 2002; Stretch, 2013). The contribution of the biopsychosocial factors is also apparent when the bereaved person demonstrates a reaction shaped by their temperament, their past and their present environment (Wheeler-Roy & Amyot, 2004, ; Stretch, 2013). Mourning is a varying process since it is regulated by one's unique personality and coping mechanisms (Bee, 2000,; Stretch, 2013). In addition, the factors facilitating the response of mourning also depend on access to social support, family dynamics, cognitive capacity and the gender of the individual (Lewis & Trzinski, 2006; Stretch, 2013). Moreover, Fry (2001) states that spirituality, religion and the creation of personal meaning can affect the way of mourning since they are factors favourable to the well-being of widow(er)s after the loss of their spouse (Osterweis et al., 1984). All these elements cited represent an amalgamation of risk and protective factors, which we will discuss in detail below, starting with the risk factors and ending with the presentation of the posttraumatic growth.

Risk Factor: The Environment

The environment can be a risk and/or a protective factor depending on the nature of its influence during a person's adjustment to their loss (Kumpfer, 1991; Alemayehu, 2014). However, studies often highlight the environment as one of the most predominant of the risk factors in terms of its influence on a person's adaptation to adversity. Risk factors are harmful and increase the chances of people developing a disease or health disorder (Pierorazio, 2009; Alemayehu, 2014).

Theorists have studied the influences and interactions of individuals with their environment to better understand the risk factors involved (Alemayehu, 2014). These factors are an aspect of personal behaviour or lifestyle, exposure to an environment, or an innate characteristic known to be associated with health-related conditions (Stroebe & Stroebe, 1987). They can be general factors or specific to grief. Risk factors specific to bereavement are situational aspects. These influence the impact that this challenging event (death) will have on widow(er)s and affect their rehabilitation. An example of this can be a sudden and unexpected loss, which may greatly jeopardize the health of the survivor (Stroebe & Stroebe, 1987). General risk factors are the personality or the social context's variables, which have an impact on the widow's health. They can be divided into categories that are not moderators of the effects of bereavement or factors having effects specific to bereavement. As such, socio-economic status is a good example since it is positively associated with the health of the mourners but does not moderate the effects of bereavement (Stroebe & Stroebe, 1987).

Risk Factors: Cause of Death and Age of Widow(er)

Ball (1977) studied the impact that age and cause of death have on a person's reaction to the death of their spouse. In this study, Ball targeted three different age groups; younger adults (18–46), middle-aged (47–59) and older adults (60–73) to compare individual symptoms according to their age group. The researcher found that younger widow(er)s had much higher burnout syndrome symptoms, compared to widow(er)s from other age groups. In addition, the study reported higher scores on a number of responses among younger widow(er)s, including the intensity of irritability and restlessness. Finally, the study concluded that age can be more of a critical factor than the cause of death in regard to the intensity of the responses to grief.

Ball's research shows that younger widows and widowers suffer from several levels of depression, suggesting that losing a spouse at a young age is associated with much more severe grief than older widows and widowers will face. This is due to the fact that death can often be sudden and unexpected for this population. For example, in this study, participants reported that the unpredicted nature of death worsened their pain (Guiaux, Van Tilburg & Broese, 2007; Ha, 2008; Jones, Oka, Dorsch & Seedall, 2016).

Notably, there is a big difference between sudden and expected death. When death is unexpected, it is traumatic for the survivors because the young person and their support network did not have time to prepare for it (Valentine, 2007; Jones et al., 2016). The loss becomes especially intense for survivors who do not have the opportunity to say goodbye and when they are unable to process the end of the relationship, which is the case for most younger widows and widowers (Valentine, 2007; Jones et al., 2016).

Another risk factor linked to young widowhood is the financial hardships that they face. Indeed, widow(er)s represent one of the most impoverished segments of the population (U.S. Census Bureau, 2012; Dunn et al., 2015) as just a quarter of them contribute to the workforce, and 80 per cent of them receive an income which lies below the poverty line (Elliott & Simmons, 2011; Dunn et al., 2015). For example, a widow might be at risk of suffering an important reduction in income, budget and time while she finds ways to acclimate. At the same time, losing a spouse includes experiencing mourning, but also learning to manage several new responsibilities (Gass-Sternas, 1994; Sevak, Weir & Willis, 2003; Dunn et al.,).

Protective and Resilience Factors

Despite the risk factors discussed above, there are protective factors that can reduce harmful responses by the person during adaptation (Kumpfer, 1991). Protective factors are resources in the form of individual characteristics, family factors and external support that promote resilience as a path of mourning (Blum, 1998; Garmezy, 1983; Pierorazio, 2009; Alemayehu, 2014). Thus, the positive factors are contributing variables to the resilience of the bereaved. These fall into three categories.

Individual Dispositions

The individual characteristics of resilient people are often essential in understanding the process of resilience since these have a particular impact on their adaptation to adversity (Alemayehu, 2014). Other studies have also valued interpersonal and shared similarities between the participants, also referring to those as the resilient individuals (Fergusson & Horwood, 2003; Black & Lobo, 2008; Laser & Nicotera, 2011; Alemayehu, 2014). Thus, it might be possible to distinguish resilient people from non-resilient people since they use key dispositions to succeed and overcome a difficult event (Alemayehu, 2014).

Individual characteristics are among the strengths more often cited in literature on the process of resilience; the characteristics significantly contribute to a favourable adjustment during bereavement and/or other trauma (Black & Lobo, 2008, Kumpfer, 1991, Fergusson & Horwood, 2003; Walsh, 2006; Alemayehu, 2014). Thus, personality, the feeling of competence, perseverance, talent, intelligence and sociability are all necessary assets so that the person can face this challenge positively (Alemayehu, 2014).

The strengths mentioned above help resilient people transform their environment or their context, in order to make it more protective. These transformative strengths include: selective perception, cognitive reframing, planning, identification and attachment to prosocial people, active modifications of their environment, and active adaptation (Kumpfer, 1991; Alemayehu, 2014).

When talking about individual dispositions, it is important to consider developmental skills, accessible and personal environments, followed by the person's cultural background. A widow(er) must have cognitive, social, physical, emotional and spiritual skills in order to be resilient enough to overcome grief (Alemayehu, 2014). Cognitive skills (i.e. response inhibition, self-awareness, etc.) related to resilience are more important than the learning processes or the academic skills of widow(er)s. Therefore, the ability to make effective decisions quickly is very relevant to resilient survivors in a stressful environment. Resilient people have rational reasoning and sound judgement in order to dodge risks when facing a challenge. For example, during mourning, survivors who have lost a dear spouse must organize themselves, plan and prioritize appropriately in the management and setting of objectives. When forming an action plan, they must keep an eye on the results of their actions and continue to make unforeseen adjustments to overcome obstacles (Alemayehu, 2014).

In addition, the life history of the bereaved is also an essential factor when predicting the adaptation of a widow(er), since a difficult past can shape the meaning and response of the survivor during and after the bereavement (Walsh, 2006; Alemayehu, 2014). The personal strengths of resilient individuals are conducive to a better success rate in difficult situations (Black & Lobo, 2008; Alemayehu, 2014).

Family and Social Support

Positive adjustment is more plausible with the presence of social support. When a person faces a difficult situation, their environmental context can shape the risks in the resilience process. Furthermore, the neighbourhood, the school, the communities and the family all have a significant impact on the adaptation process of resilience and its degree of success. All depending on the quality of the environment, there may be protective resources in the community of the individual coming from their educational background, the attention he or she receives from caregivers, as well as financial security and parental models of prosocial behaviour (Luthar, 2003; Alemayehu, 2014). When the stress is chronic or acute, the environmental context can accentuate or reduce the negative impact of stressors on the individual (Kumpfer, 1991; Alemayehu, 2014).

Resourceful environments can provide opportunities to the bereaved to engage in solution-making activities focused on reducing the effects of stress. Participation in a community structure promotes a sense of belonging and encourages the person to adapt to adversity in a socially acceptable manner (Heilbrun, Goldstein & Redding, 2005; Alemayehu, 2014). Thus, in the context of grief and/or trauma, the individuals must mobilize their social resources and community to rely on a practical and emotional support network (Walsh, 2006; Alemayehu, 2014).

Scientific literature focusing on family characteristics as assets to resilience shows that the presence of a suitable parental figure is crucial for the establishment of resilience among family members who have experienced stress or trauma. Also, relatives, extended or blood-related and married families may be another source to building resilience (Walsh, 2003; Alemayehu, 2014).

In 2011, Lowe and McClement found through an analysis of several studies that there was a significant presence of interpersonal relationships, and more particularly, of a support network conducive to resilient adaptation for individuals in a challenging situation (West, Dreeben & Busing, 2019). Due to the contribution of a favourable support network, the commitment to interpersonal relationships can allow widowed people to have an opportunity to adapt to their new identity; their status of survivors. Besides, the presence of positive relationships provides a sense of security (West, Dreeben & Busing, 2019; Maisha, Malette & Bellehumeur, 2019). For example, Bisconti, Bergeman and Boker (2006) found in their research that emotional support was often associated with resilience after the loss of a partner (West, Dreeben & Busing, 2019). Engagement and resilience are positively related (O'Rourke, 2004; West, Dreeben & Busing, 2019). Therefore, interpersonal relationships are significantly associated with survivors' engagement in their adjustment process (Mo & Singh, 2008; West, Dreeben & Busing, 2019).

Family members and social networks are predominant resources during times of widowhood difficulties. This is especially due to their help in psychosocial support. In the context of bereavement, it may be relevant for the loved ones of the bereaved to become mentors or models of resilience who can be trusted. Not to mention that their possible commitment to a religious community or any faith/spirituality may help these individuals strengthen their resilience. Widow(er)s who are well surrounded by family are at a lower risk of experiencing harmful symptoms to their physical health, and this seems to reduce the adverse effects of bereavement (Pierorazio, 2009; Alemayehu, 2014).

The constant resilience towards conditions brought on by bereavement can be explained by an amalgamation of interactions between protective factors and risk factors and through the process of adaptation, good or poor, and followed by the contribution of family impact, sociocultural influences and the widow(er)s themselves (Walsh, 2003; Alemayehu, 2014). In addition, research addresses other protective factors that promote resilience such as identity, well-being, attitude, meaning of life, spirituality and religion.

A New Identity

Adapting to a new identity associated with widowed status is a challenging life transition and has an important implication in the product of resilience after the death of the spouse (West, Dreeben & Busing, 2019). It is important to note that proper management of the new identity can be beneficial for survivors by promoting resilience among the bereaved population (Bennett, Gibbons & Mackenzie-Smith, 2010; Lowe & McClement, 2011; West, Dreeben & Busing, 2019) and the non-bereaved population (Clauss-Ehlers, Yang & Chen, 2006; Pearce & Morrison, 2011; West, Dreeben & Busing, 2019).

The resilient bereaved shows a strong sense of self (Bennett, Hughes & Smith, 2005; Bonanno, Papa & O'Neill, 2001; West, Dreeben & Busing, 2019). The question "Who am I now?" is an essential question during mourning since the widow(er) may have built his or her identity and the meaning of his/her existence through their marital relationship, which is a stressful experience to overcome after a loss (West, Dreeben & Busing, 2019).

A constant and robust feeling of individuality after the death of a spouse could be a protective factor shielding the survivor from identity instability (Friborg, Hjemdal, Rosenvinge & Martinussen, 2003; West, Dreeben & Busing, 2019). Having a stable self-image is an internal resource and is followed by appropriate thought management and or better emotional self-regulation during grief. Thus, it is by regulating positive emotions that an individual can demonstrate their resilience (Lund, Utz, Caserta & de Vries, 2009; West, Dreeben & Busing, 2019).

Psychological and Physical Well-Being

Emotional and physical well-being are factors that influence resilience (Cartwright, Wardle, Steggles, Simon, Croker & Jarvis, 2003; West, Dreeben & Busing, 2019). Resilience is an essential tool for the bereaved since the absence of it can render them mentally weak due to a lack of self-care. Depression is a common phenomenon in the absence of resilience and is often linked with an increased risk of cardiovascular disease (Williams, 2005;

West, Dreeben & Busing, 2019). According to statistics, the mortality rate in widow(er)s increases, especially after two years following the death of their partner. This is to say that the habit of self-care is important and is a key factor in the resilience of widow(er)s (Naef, Ward, Mahrer-Imhof & Grande, 2013; West, Dreeben & Busing, 2019).

It is documented that psychoeducation based interventions help with development of their resilience among this population; by focusing on learning behaviours and skills (Naef et al., 2013; West, Dreeben & Busing, 2019). Concerning the adaptation, professionals can help the bereaved become resilient; the work focuses on building a constant structure in their daily lives (Muller & Thompson, 2003; West, Dreeben & Busing, 2019). Naef et al. (2013) demonstrated that setting goals has a positive impact on the resilience of widow(er)s (Leary & DeRosier, 2012; West, Dreeben & Busing, 2019).

The Stress-Resistant Attitude

It appears that resilient people are perceived to have a constant stress-resistant attitude (Staudinger, Marsiske & Baltes, 1993; Watt, David, Ladd & Shamos, 1995; Werner, 1995; Jenkins et al., 2016). Condly (2006) describes this attitude as an optimistic way of believing that one can overcome a difficult situation. This attitude includes a feeling of competence in the person allowing him or her to mobilize their resources in order to succeed (Condly, 2006; Jenkins et al., 2016). The determination of resilient people is an attitude, also known as "stress-resistant attitude." Researchers have also defined resilience as synonymous with this attitude because it represents the process by which the individual evaluates his ability to adapt to the stressful situations (Connor & Davidson, 2003; Karreman & Vingerhoets, 2012; Jenkins et al., 2016).

Condly (2006) found in his study that resilient participants demonstrated a constant belief in their ability to overcome adverse circumstances because they have the inner strength to succeed. Past experiences can also be a source of assurance for these resilient individuals; they have become much less vulnerable to stress due to repeated exposure to stress (Fergusson & Horwood, 2003; Alemayehu, 2014). This phenomenon has been called the "steeling effect," also known for the ability to learn and grow confident from past experiences during repeated stressful experiences. However, this effect does not take into account the wide range of years and the various environments shared between resilient individuals (Elder, 1974; Jenkins et al., 2016).

Maddi (2005) debated that resilient people have a go-getter attitude since they can particularly and courageously face sources of stressors. They are not avoidant and do not use harmful adaptation mechanisms. Resilient people will seek support if they need it to endure the stressful event, and they avoid isolation. Beliefs, thoughts and aspirations are also aspects of our psychology necessary for resilience. Also known as "dispositional resilience," it refers to the idea that widow(er)s are convinced that they feel competent enough to lead to a positive adjustment during their bereavement (Resnick, Gwyther & Roberto, 2011; Alemayehu, 2014).

That said, widow(er)s who have overcome their grief positively have resorted to this "dispositional resilience." Resnick et al. (2011) revealed three personal characteristics that contribute to this form of resilience: feeling of control, commitment and confrontation with challenges. In other words, a resilient survivor has a sense of control over their situation in order to feel that they can overcome their grief. However, this positive perception of oneself is also manifested by a constant commitment of the bereaved. This commitment is demonstrated in the way the widow(er) maintains a connection with the loved one who used to be supportive of him or her. Finally, the individual in question is not afraid of challenges; he or she faces them and learns from their experiences. Resnick et al. (2011) reported that people with high levels of dispositional resilience perceive the source of stress differently from participants classified as being less resilient (Alemayehu, 2014).

In short, resilient widow(er)s use dispositional resilience, which can manifest itself in their pattern of attitudes and behaviour. This attitude incites them to transform a stressful situation in order to dodge a potential disaster and finally come out of it with success and a wealth of experience (Maddi, 2005; Rossi, Bisconti & Bergeman, 2007; West, Dreeben & Busing, 2019)

The Meaning-Making

Academics present meaning as an element at the heart of the mourning process (Davis & Nolen-Hoeksema, 2001; Neimeyer, 2000; Parkes, 1971; Schwartzberg & Janoff-Bulman, 1991; Bonanno et al., 2002). There is a significant percentage of mourners who try to find the meaning behind their loss, but still do not succeed (Davis & Nolen-Hoeksema, 2001; Lehman, Wortman & Williams, 1987; Bonanno et al., 2002). These individuals, therefore, have much more pronounced grief reactions than others (Davis, Wortman, Lehman & Silver, 2000; Bonanno et al., 2002). That said, it is important to distinguish healthy mourning from unhealthy and chronic mourning; a perception of loss often accompanies widowhood as being unjust and uncontrollable (Schwartzberg & Janoff-Bulman, 1991; Bonanno et al., 2002). Non-resilient widow(er)s are presented in social-cognitive models with negative thoughts prolonging their grief (Janoff-Bulman, 1992; Parkes, 1971, 1998 Bonanno et al., 2002).

However, the presence of positive beliefs ingrained in resilient individuals even before they have experienced trauma or loss can be beneficial to them. These people are distinguished by resilience because they can adapt quickly during their mourning. Resilient people hold positive beliefs about themselves and their world. Their life experiences, which once shaped their belief system, facilitate their acclimation to death, because their search for an explanation for the loss is not predominant. A good example of a resilient person following the death of their spouse is one who can better assimilate this loss compared to one who is less comfortable with or is afraid of death (Bonanno et al., 2002).

In short, people who are resilient during bereavement are generally individuals with a stable outlook on their world. They, therefore, live it with less distress than the others and end up accepting the death of their spouse. Individuals considered non-resilient generally experience distress in connection with their pessimistic beliefs of an unfair world which is confirmed by their loss (Davis et al., 2000; Bonanno et al., 2002).

Spirituality and Religion

Lowe and McClement (2011) noted the importance and dominance of the theme of spirituality in the grieving process among young widows and widowers. This theme is tainted by premonitions or experiences, contributing to a sense of mourning (Taylor & Robinson, 2016). That said, the meaning behind the experience calls for the use of spirituality as a coping mechanism. Nonetheless, most research lacks attention to the impact of religion and spirituality on young widow(er)s.

McFadden et al. (2015) describe the importance of spirituality and religion during mourning. The author describes that as people age, they go through threatening experiences, and this contributes to their experience (Lichtenberg, 2017). Events such as losses are a source of suffering, contributing to the meaning of life for widows and widowers (Lichtenberg, 2017). Religious beliefs can facilitate the quest for meaning as coping mechanisms during grief (Michael, Crowther, Schmid & Allen, 2003; Lichtenberg, 2017). In order to understand bereavement and coping with the loss, it is necessary to study the effects of spirituality and religion (Lichtenberg, 2017).

A study of widow(er)s attempted to determine whether participation in spiritual or religious activities would have an impact on the bereaved (Roff, Durkin, Sun & Klemmack, 2007). Evidence suggests that the presence of prayer and the use of religion as a coping mechanism is much more common in the widowed (Roff et al., 2007). The study of Miller and Thoresen (2003) had also proven this when they found a relationship between prayer and a sense of well-being (Roff et al., 2007). It seems that faith can be a helpful resource for older widow(er)s because several studies show a positive correlation between their religious rituals and their overall well-being (Roff et al., 2007).

Another study of the bereaved after the fire at the Sunshine mine in 1972 found that widows and widowers with religious beliefs accompanied by involvement in their church experienced a better quality of life five years after the loss of their spouse compared to groups of non-religious widow(er)s who were not involved in a church (Bahr & Harvey, 1979). Based on the data on the older bereaved, there is a clear link between religious affiliations, the practice of prayer and the meaning of life, however this does not seem well studied yet at the level of young widowhood.

Resilience Factors and Posttraumatic Growth for the Widow(er)

After presenting the risk and protective factors of resilience in the context of marital bereavement, let's address the posttraumatic growth model as it applies to the same context. Posttraumatic growth (PTG) refers to positive changes that occur as a result of going through a traumatic event (Li, Bai, Lou & Cao, 2019; Tedeschi & Calhoun, 2004). Both individual resilience and social support have been studied and presented as contributors to PTG (Li et al., 2019; Ekim & Ocakci, 2015; Tedeschi & Calhoun, 2004).

In fact, Walsh (2002) finds that social support is an important factor in nurturing resilience. In a grieving situation, individuals mobilize their social and community resources to receive support and overcome the negative effects of loss (Alemayehu, 2014; Walsh, 2006). In the same line of thought, resilience studies on family characteristics demonstrate that a parental figure is necessary for the development of resilience in widow(er)s; helping them lower the risks of poor physical health and other negative effects of bereavement (Alemayehu, 2014; Pierorazio, 2009). Therefore, family can provide an essential support in grieving, because it contains the primary attachment relationships. A secure attachment will allow positive coping when one faces adversity like the passing of a spouse (Li et al., 2019).

Secure attachment relationships and a high degree of intimacy among family members promotes family resilience and can predict PTG (Li et al., 2019). Family resilience is the ability of the family to be resilient during a traumatic event and demonstrate to be even stronger, more resourced and confident. Walsh (2007) points out that the belief system, the organizational pattern and the communication transmitted from the heart of the family to the individual help reduce the risk of vulnerability from adversity such as the passing of a loved one. As per Li et al. (2019), individual resilience holds a positive and predictive relationship to trauma and personal growth. Both individual resilience and family resilience constitute a strong base for posttraumatic growth.

Conclusion

In conclusion, this chapter has sought to discuss resilience as a process for widow(er)s. Resilience factors provide the ground for much needed coping strategies to survivors during the bereavement process (Beasley, Thompson & Davidson, 2003; Jenkins et al., 2016). This chapter presents the most salient factors around resilience in the process of marital mourning available in the current scientific literature. Considering that resilience is relevant to a successful adaptation at a particular time, keeping a balance between vulnerability and access to resilience factors is essential. It is dependent on the ability to navigate the context risk factors as well as protective factors (Scott et al., 2007). Resiliency can be a fluid concept and resilient individuals can also experience struggles and pain. The loss of a loved one is a life-changing adversity. This chapter has provided both clinical and self-help information on how resilient widow(er)s cope.

References

Alemayehu, T. (2014). Exploring the resilience of widows who lost their partners to HIV: A case study of 6 widows in Suki neighborhood in Addis Ababa [Masters' thesis, université Addis Ababa]. AAU. Retrieved from: http://etd.aau.edu.et/handle/123456789/2709.

Bahr, H., & Harvey, C. (1979). Correlates of loneliness among widows bereaved in a mining disaster. *Psychological Reports*, 44(2), 367–385. https://doi.org/10.2466/pr0.1979.44.2.367.

Balk, D.E. (2008). Grieving: 22 to 30 percent of all college students. *New Directions for Student Services*, 121, 5–14. doi:10.1002/ss.262.

Ball, J.F. (1977). Widow's grief: The impact of age and mode of death. *OMEGA: Journal of Death and Dying*, 7(4), 307–333. https://doi.org/10.2190/WEEF-N0HD-0CQ5-18TY.

Beasley, M., Thompson, T., & Davidson, J. (2003). Resilience in response to life stress: The effects of coping and cognitive hardiness. *Personality and Individual Differences*, 34(1), 77–95. https://doi.org/10.1016/S0191-8869(02)00027-00022.

Bee, H.L. (2000). *Journey of adulthood* (4th ed.). Upper Saddle River, NJ: Prentice Hall.

Bennett, K., Hughes, G., & Smith, P. (2005). Psychological response to later life widowhood: Coping and the effects of gender. *OMEGA: Journal of Death and Dying*, 51(1), 33–52. https://doi.org/10.2190/9JPJ-1FM1-37NX-2DEC.

Bennett, K., Gibbons, K., & Mackenzie-Smith, S. (2010). Loss and restoration in later life: An examination of dual process model of coping with bereavement. *OMEGA: Journal of Death and Dying*, 61(4), 315–332. https://doi.org/10.2190/OM.61.4.d.

Bisconti, T., Bergeman, C., & Boker, S. (2006). Social support as a predictor of variability: An examination of the adjustment trajectories of recent widows. *Psychology and Aging*, 21(3), 590–599. https://doi.org/10.1037/0882-7974.21.3.590.

Black, K., & Lobo, M. (2008). A conceptual review of family resilience factors. *Journal of Family Nursing*, 14(1), 33–55. https://doi.org/10.1177/1074840707312237.

Blum, R. (1998). Review of healthy youth development as a model for youth health promotion: A review. *Journal of Adolescent Health*, 22(5), 368–375. https://doi.org/10.1016/S1054-139X(97)00261–00269.

Boerner, K., & Jopp, D. (2010). Resilience in response to loss. In J.W. Reich, A.J. Zautra, & J.S. Hall (Eds.), *Handbook of adult resilience* (pp. 126–145). New York: The Guilford Press.

Boerner, K., Wortman, C., & Bonanno, G. (2005). Resilient or at risk? A 4-year study of older adults who initially showed high or low distress following conjugal loss. *The Journals of Gerontology. Series B, Psychological Sciences and Social Sciences*, 60(2), 67–73.

Bonanno, G., Papa, A., & O'Neill, K. (2001). Loss and human resilience. *Applied and Preventive Psychology*, 10(3), 193–206. https://doi.org/10.1016/S0962-1849(01)80014–80017.

Bonanno, G., Wortman, C., Lehman, D., Tweed, R., Haring, M., Sonnega, J., & Nesse, R. (2002). Resilience to loss and chronic grief: A prospective study from preloss to 18-months postloss. *Journal of Personality and Social Psychology*, 83(5), 1150–1164. https://doi.org/10.1037/0022-3514.83.5.1150.

Brent, D., Emslie, G., Clarke, G., Asarnow, J.R., Spirito, A., Ritz, L., Vitiello, B., Iyengar, S., Ryan, N., Zelazny, J., Onorato, M., Kennard, B., Mayes, T., DeBar, L., McCracken, J., Strober, M., Suddath, R., Leonard, H., Porta, G., & Keller, M. (2009). Predictors of spontaneous and systematically assessed suicidal adverse events in the treatment of SSRI-resistant depression in adolescents (TORDIA) study. *Am J Psychiatry*, 166(4), 418–426.

Cartwright, M., Wardle, J., Steggles, N., Simon, A., Croker, H., & Jarvis, M. (2003). Stress and dietary practices in adolescents. *Health Psychology*, 22(4), 362–369. https://doi.org/10.1037/0278-6133.22.4.362.

Clauss-Ehlers, C., Yang, Y., & Chen, W. (2006). Resilience from childhood stressors: The role of cultural resilience, ethnic identity, and gender identity. *Journal of Infant, Child, and Adolescent Psychotherapy*, 5(1), 124–138.

Clayton, P., Desmarais, L., & Winokur, G. (1968). A study of normal bereavement. *American Journal of Psychiatry*, 125(2), 168–178. https://doi.org/10.1176/ajp.125.2.168.

Clements, J. (2014). The relationship between resilience and grief symptomatology [Master's thesis, University of Georgia State]. Odum Library. https://vtext.valdosta.edu/xmlui/bitstream/handle/10428/1895/clements-jorden_thesis.pdf?sequence=1&isAllowed=y.

Condly, S. (2006). Resilience in children: A review of literature with implications for education. *Urban Education*, 41(3), 211–236. https://doi.org/10.1177/0042085906287902.

Connor, K., & Davidson, J. (2003). Development of a new resilience scale: The Connor-Davidson Resilience Scale (CD-RISC). *Depression and Anxiety*, 18(2), 76–82. https://doi.org/10.1002/da.10113.

Davis, C.G., & Nolen-Hoeksema, S. (2001). Loss and meaning: How do people make sense of loss? *American Behavioral Scientist*, 44, 718–735. doi:10.1177/00027640121956467.

Davis, C.G., Wortman, C.B., Lehman, D.R., & Silver, R.C. (2000). Searching for meaning in loss: Are clinical assumptions correct? *Death Studies*, 24, 497–540. doi:10.1080/07481180050121471.

Derman, S.D. (1999). Grief and attachment in young widowhood (publication n.9938660) [Doctoral thesis, Temple University]. ProQuest Dissertations and Theses Global. Retrieved from: http://search.proquest.com/docview/304526832

Dunn, C., Piercy, K., Norton, M., Bradford, K., Peak, T., & Robinson, D. (2015). Young widows' grief: A study of personal and contextual factors associated with conjugal loss (publication n. 3733815). [Doctoral thesis, Utah State University]. ProQuest Dissertations and Theses Global. Retrieved from: http://search.proquest.com/docview/1731940705

Ekim, A., & Ocakci, A.F. (2015). Relationship between posttraumatic growth and perceived social support for adolescents with cancer. *Journal of Hospice & Palliative Nursing*, 17(5), 450–455.

Elder, G. (1974). *Children of the great depression: Social change in life experience*. Chicago: University of Chicago Press.

Elliott, D.B., & Simmons, T. (2011). *Marital events of Americans: 2009*. Washington, DC: U.S. Department of Commerce, Economics and Statistics Administration, U.S. Census Bureau. Retrieved from: www.census.gov/library/publications/2011/acs/acs-13.html.

Fergusson, D., & Horwood, L. (2003). Resilience to childhood adversity: Results of a 21-year study. In S. Luthar (Ed.), *Resilience and vulnerability: Adaptation in the context of childhood adversities* (pp. 130–155). Cambridge: Cambridge University Press. https://doi.org/10.1017/CBO9780511615788.008.

Friborg, O., Hjemdal, O., Rosenvinge, J.H., & Martinussen, M. (2003). A new rating scale for adult resilience: What are the central protective resources behind healthy adjustment? *International Journal of Methods in Psychiatric Research*, 12(2), 65–76. https://doi.org/10.1002/mpr.143.

Fry, K. (2001). E-learning markets and providers: Some issues and prospects. *Education & Training*, 43(4/5), 233–239.

Garmezy, N. (1983). Stressors of childhood. In N. Garmezy & M. Rutter, *Stress, coping, and development in children* (pp. 43–84). Johns Hopkins University Press.

Gass-Sternas, K. (1994). Single parent widows: Stressors, appraisal, coping, resources, grieving responses and health. *Marriage & Family Review*, 20(3–4), 411–445. https://doi.org/10.1300/J002v20n03_06.

Granek, L., Bartels, U., Scheinemann, K., Labrecque, M., & Barrera, M. (2015). Grief reactions and impact of patient death on pediatric oncologists. *Pediatr Blood Cancer*, 62(1), 134–142.

Guiaux, M., Van Tilburg, T., & Broese, M. (2007). Changes in contact and support exchange in personal networks after widowhood. *Personal Relationships*, 14(3), 457–473. http://dx.doi.org/10.1111/j.1475-6811.2007.00165.x.

Ha, J. (2008). Changes in support from confidants, children, and friends following widowhood. *Journal of Marriage and Family*, 70(2), 306–318. https://doi.org/10.1111/j.1741-3737.2008.00483.x.

Heilbrun, K., Goldstein, N.E.S., & Redding, R.E. (Eds.). (2005). *Juvenile delinquency: Prevention, assessment, and intervention*. New York: Oxford University Press. https://doi.org/10.1093/med:psych/9780195160079.001.0001.

Holmes, T.H., & Rahe, R.H. (1967). The social readjustment rating scale. *Journal of Psychosomatic Research*, 11(2), 213–218.

Janoff-Bulman, R. (1992). *Shattered assumptions: Towards a new psychology of trauma*. New York: Free Press.

Jenkins, J., Paulson, J., Kelley, M., & Lewis, R. (2016). The relationship between resilience, attachment, and emotional coping styles (publication n.10162274) [Doctoral thesis, Georgia College & State University]. ProQuest Dissertations and Theses Global. Retrieved from: http://search.proquest.com/docview/1844067831.

Jones, E., Oka, M., Dorsch, T., & Seedall, R. (2016). Lived experience of young widowed individuals (publication n.10241800) [Master's thesis, Utah State University]. ProQuest Dissertations and Theses Global. Retrieved from: http://search.proquest.com/docview/1854133693/.

Karreman, A., & Vingerhoets, A. (2012). Attachment and well-being: The mediating role of emotion regulation and resilience. *Personality and Individual Differences*, 53(7), 821–826. https://doi.org/10.1016/j.paid.2012.06.014.

Kübler-Ross, E.(1969). *On death and dying*. New York: The Macmillan Company.

Kumpfer, K. (1991). Factors and processes contributing to resilience: The resilience framework. In M.D. Glantz & J.J. Johnson (Eds.), *Resilience and development: Positive life adaptations* (pp. 179–214). New York: Plenum Publishers.

Lapsley, J.N. (1970). On death and dying, by Elisabeth Kübler-Ross. New York, Macmillan, 1969. *Theology Today*, 27(1), 88–93. https://doi.org/10.1177/004057367002700112.

Laser, J., & Nicotera, N. (2011). *Working with adolescents: A guide for practitioners*, 1st edn. New York: Guilford Publications.

Leary, K.A., & DeRosier, M.E. (2012). Factors promoting positive adaptation and resilience during the transition to college. *Psychology*, 3(12), 1215–1222. https://doi.org/10.4236/psych.2012.312A180.

Lehman, D.R., Wortman, C.B., & Williams, A.F. (1987). Long-term effects of losing a spouse or child in a motor vehicle crash. *Journal of Personality and Social Psychology*, 52(1), 218–231.

Lewis, M.M., & Trzinski, A.L. (2006). Counseling older adults with dementia who are dealing with death: Innovative intervention for practitioners. *Death Studies*, 30(8), 777–787.

Li, Y., Bai, H., Lou, F., & Cao, F. (2019). A conceptual model of posttraumatic growth of nursing students with a disabled parent. *International Journal of Nursing Sciences*, 6(4), 406–413. https://doi.org/10.1016/j.ijnss.2019.09.002.

Lichtenberg, P. (2017). Grief and healing in young and middle age: A widower's journey. *The Gerontologist*, 57(1), 96–102. https://doi.org/10.1093/geront/gnw115.

Lopata, H.Z. (1988). Support systems of American urban widowhood. *Journal of Social Issues: The Society for the Psychological Study of Social Issues*, 44(3), 113–128.

Lowe, M.E., & McClement, S.E. (2011). Spousal bereavement: The lived experience of young Canadian widows. *OMEGA – Journal of Death and Dying*, 62(2), 127–148.

Lund, D., Utz, R., Caserta, M., & de Vries, B. (2009). Humor, laughter, and happiness in the daily lives of recently bereaved spouses. *OMEGA: Journal of Death and Dying*, 58(2), 87–105. https://doi.org/10.2190/OM.58.2.a.

Luthar, S.S. (Ed.). (2003). *Resilience and vulnerability: Adaptation in the context of childhood adversities*. New York: Cambridge University Press. https://doi.org/10.1017/CBO9780511615788.

Luthar, S.S., & Cushing, G. (1999). Measurement issues in the empirical study of resilience: An overview. In M.D. Glantz & J.L. Johnson (Eds.), *Longitudinal research in the social and behavioral sciences. Resilience and development: Positive life adaptations* (pp. 129–160). Norwell, MA: Kluwer Academic Publishers.

Maciejewski, P.K., Zhang, B., Block, S.D., & Prigerson, H.G. (2007). An empirical examination of the stage theory of grief. *The Journal of the American Medical Association*, 297(7), 716–723.

Maddi, S.R. (2005). On hardiness and other pathways to resilience. *American Psychologist*, 60(3), 261–262.

Maisha, M., Malette, J., & Bellehumeur, C. (2019). Les liens entre la souillure du viol et le pouvoir guérisseur du plaisir relationnel auprès des victimes congolaises en contexte de guerre. In C. Bellehumeur & J. Malette (Eds.), *Psychologie positive et spiritualité en psychothérapie: Fondements, recherches et applications*. Québec: Presses de l'Université Laval.

Mash, H.B.H., Fullerton, C.S., Shear, M.K., & Ursano, R.J. (2014). Complicated grief and depression in young adults: Personality and relationship quality. *The Journal of Nervous and Mental Disease*, 202(7), 539–543. https://doi.org/10.1097/NMD.0000000000000155.

Mcfadden, S., Lichtenberg, P., Mast, B., Carpenter, B., & Loebach Wetherell, J. (2015). Spirituality, religion, and aging: Clinical geropsychology and aging people's need for meaning. In *APA handbook of clinical geropsychology*, Vol. 1: *History and status of the field and perspectives on aging* (pp. 473–496). https://doi.org/10.1037/14458-020.

McNally, R. (2011). *What is mental illness?*Boston: Belknap.

Melhem, N.M., Shear, K., Reynolds, C.F., Day, N., Day, R., & Brent, D. (2004). Traumatic grief among adolescents exposed to a peer's suicide. *American Journal of Psychiatry*, 161(8), 1411–1416.

Michael, S.T., Crowther, M.R., Schmid, B., & Allen, R.S. (2003). Widowhood and spirituality: Coping responses to bereavement. *Journal of Women & Aging*, 15(2–3), 145–165. http://dx.doi.org/10.1300/J074v15n02_09.

Miller, W.R., & Thoresen, C.E. (2003). Spirituality, religion, and health: An emerging research field. *American Psychologist*, 58(1), 24–35.

Mo, Y., & Singh, K. (2008). Parents' relationships and involvement: Effects on students' school engagement and performance. *RMLE Online*, 31(10), 1–11. https://doi.org/10.1080/19404476.2008.11462053.

Muller, E., & Thompson, C. (2003). The experience of grief after bereavement: A phenomenological study with implications for mental health counseling. *Journal of Mental Health Counseling*, 25(3), 183–203. https://doi.org/10.17744/mehc.25.3.wu4n7dljyekuh4ef.

Naef, R., Ward, R., Mahrer-Imhof, R., & Grande, G. (2013). Characteristics of the bereavement experience of older persons after spousal loss: An integrative review. *International Journal of Nursing Studies*, 50(8), 1108–1121. https://doi.org/10.1016/j.ijnurstu.2012.11.026.

Neimeyer, R.A. (2000). Searching for the meaning of meaning: Grief therapy and the process of reconstruction. *Death Studies*, 24(6), 541–558. https://doi.org/10.1080/074811800501214 80.

Onrust, S.A., & Cuijpers, P. (2006). Mood and anxiety disorders in widowhood: A systematic review. *Aging & Mental Health*, 10(4), 327–334.

O'Rourke, N. (2004). Psychological resilience and the well-being of widowed women. *Ageing International*, 29(3), 267–280. https://doi.org/10.1007/s12126-996-1002-x.

Osterweis, M., Solomon, F., Green, M., Institute of Medicine (U.S.), & Committee for the Study of Health Consequences of the Stress of Bereavement (1984). *Bereavement: Reactions, consequences, and care.* Washington, DC: National Academy Press.

Papalia, D., Sterns, H., Feldman, R., & Camp, C. (2002). *Adult development and aging* (2nd ed.). Whitby, ON, Canada: McGraw-Hill Ryerson.

Parkes, C.M. (1971). *Bereavement: Studies of grief in adult life.* London: Tavistock.

Parkes, C.M. (1987). Models of bereavement care. *Death Studies*, 11(4), 257–261.

Parkes, C.M. (1988). Bereavement as a psychosocial transition: Processes of adaptation to change. *Journal of Social Issues*, 44(3), 53–65.

Parkes, C.M. (1998). Traditional models and theories of grief. *Bereavement Care*, 17(2), 21–23.

Pearce, J., & Morrison, C. (2011). Teacher identity and early career resilience: Exploring the links. *Australian Journal of Teacher Education*, 36(1), 48–59. http://dx.doi.org/10.14221/ajte.2011v36n1.4.

Pierorazio, D. (2009). A reframing of protective factors in the contexts of risk, adversity and competence in adolescents (publication no 3356280) [Doctoral thesis, College of Saint-mary]. ProQuest Dissertations and Theses Global. Retrieved from: http://search.proquest.com/docview/305091043/.

Resnick, B., Gwyther, L., & Roberto, K. (2011). *Resilience in aging concepts, research, and outcomes.* New York: Springer.

Roff, L., Durkin, D., Sun, F., & Klemmack, D. (2007). Widowhood, religiousness, and self-assessed well-being among older adults. *Journal of Religion, Spirituality & Aging*, 19(4), 43–59. https://doi.org/10.1300/J496v19n04_04.

Rossi, N., Bisconti, T., & Bergeman, C. (2007). The role of dispositional resilience in regaining life satisfaction after the loss of a spouse. *Death Studies*, 31(10), 863–883. https://doi.org/10.1080/07481180701603246.

Sasson, I., & Umberson, D.J. (2014). Widowhood and depression: New light on gender differences, selection, and psychological adjustment. *Journals of Gerontology, Series B: Psychological Sciences and Social Sciences*, 69(1), 135–145.

Schwartzberg, S.S., & Janoff-Bulman, R. (1991). Grief and the search for meaning: Exploring the assumptive worlds of bereaved college students. *Journal of Social and Clinical Psychology*, 10(3), 270–288. https://doi.org/10.1521/jscp.1991.10.3.270.

Scott, S., Bergeman, C., Verney, A., Longenbaker, S., Markey, M., Bisconti, T., & Scott, S. (2007). Social support in widowhood: A mixed methods study. *Journal of Mixed Methods Research*, 1(3), 242–266. https://doi.org/10.1177/1558689807302453.

Servaty-Seib, H. (2004). Connections between counseling theories and current theories of grief and mourning. *Journal of Mental Health Counseling*, 26(2), 125–145. https://doi.org/10.17744/mehc.26.2.p9aukha7v8fqkc9g.

Sevak, P., Weir, D., & Willis, R. (2003). The economic consequences of a husband's death: Evidence from the HRS and AHEAD. *Social Security Bulletin*, 65(3), 31–44.

Shear, K., & Shair, H. (2005). Attachment, loss, and complicated grief. *Developmental Psychobiology*, 47(3), 253–267. https://doi.org/10.1002/dev.20091.

Skodol, A.E. (2010). The resilient personality. In J.W. Reich, A.J. Zautra, & J.S. Hall (Eds.), *Handbook of adult resilience* (pp. 112–125). New York: Guilford Press.

Staudinger, U., Marsiske, M., & Baltes, P. (1993). Resilience and levels of reserve capacity in later adulthood: Perspectives from life-span theory. *Development and Psychopathology*, 5(4), 541–566. doi:10.1017/S0954579400006155.

Stretch, C. (2013). Counselling seniors through grief and loss: An eight-week group therapy program [Master's thesis, Trinity Western University]. University of Lethbridge Research Repository, OPUS. http://hdl.handle.net/10133/3317.

Stroebe, W., & Stroebe, M.S. (1987). *Bereavement and health: The psychological and physical consequences of partner loss*. New York: Cambridge University Press.

Taylor, N., & Robinson, W. (2016). The lived experience of young widows and widowers. *The American Journal of Family Therapy*, 44(2), 67–79. https://doi.org/10.1080/01926187.2016.1145081.

Tedeschi, R.G., & Calhoun, L. (2004). Posttraumatic growth: A new perspective on psychotraumatology. *Psychiatric Times*, 21(4), 58–60.

U.S. Census Bureau (2012). *America's families and living arrangements: 2010. Table 1A, marital status of people 15 years and older, by age, sex personal earnings, race, and Hispanic origin: 2010*. Washington, DC: U.S. Government Printing Office. Retrieved from: www.census.gov/population/www/socdemo/hh-fam/cps2010.html.

Vachon, M.L., et al. (1976). Stress reactions to bereavement. *Essence: Issues in the Study of Ageing, Dying, and Death*, 1(1), 23–33.

Valentine, C. (2007). The "moment of death". *Omega*, 55(3), 219–236. https://doi.org/10.2190/OM.55.3.d.

Walsh, F. (2002). A family resilience framework: Innovative practice applications. *Family Relations*, 51(2), 130–137.

Walsh, F. (2003). Family resilience: A framework for clinical practice. *Family Process*, 42(1), 1–18.

Walsh, F. (2006). Strengthening family resilience. *The American Journal of Family Therapy*, 36(3), 262–263. doi:10.1080/01926180701290867.

Walsh, F. (2007). Traumatic loss and major disasters: Strengthening family and community resilience. *Family Process*, 46(2), 207–227.

Wasserman, T., & Wasserman, L. (2016). *Depathologizing psychopathology: The neuroscience of mental illness and its treatment.* New York: Springer. https://doi.org/10.1007/978-3-319-30910-1.

Watt, N., David, J., Ladd, K., & Shamos, S. (1995). The life course of psychological resilience: A phenomenological perspective on deflecting life's slings and arrows. *Journal of Primary Prevention*, 15(3), 209–246. https://doi.org/10.1007/BF02197473.

Werner, E. (1995). Resilience in development. *Current Directions in Psychological Science*, 4(3), 81–84. https://doi.org/10.1111/1467-8721.ep10772327.

West, C.L., Dreeben, S.J., & Busing, K. (2019). The development of the widowhood resilience scale. *OMEGA: Journal of Death and Dying*, 1–18. https://doi.org/10.1177/0030222819873489.

Wheeler-Roy, S., & Amyot, B. (2004). Grief counseling resource guide: A field manual. New York: New York State Office of Mental Health.

Williams, R. (2005). Depression as a mediator between spousal bereavement and mortality from cardiovascular disease: Appreciating and managing the adverse health consequences of depression in an elderly surviving spouse. *Southern Medical Journal*, 98(1), 90–95. https://doi.org/10.1097/01.SMJ.0000140832.14297.61.

Zautra, A.J., Hall, J.S., & Murray, K.E. (2010). Resilience: A new definition of health for people and communities. In J.W. Reich, A.J. Zautra, & J.S. Hall (Eds.), *Handbook of adult resilience* (pp. 3–29). New York: Guilford Press.

11 Relationships as Resilience and Posttraumatic Growth Factors for War-Time Survivors with Interpretations of Rape as Sexual Taboo

Healing Embrace

Buuma Maisha

Relationships with oneself and others present enormous challenges for survivors of rape. The social and personal values guiding these relationships are challenged, making survivors view themselves as undeserving of happy relationships (Maisha, Malette & Demasure, 2017; Dossa, Hatem, Zunzunegui & Fraser, 2014; Kelly et al., 2012). In fact, for survivors in the context of sexual taboos, the experience of rape triggers intrapersonal and interpersonal conflicts with three fundamental relationships: motherhood, conjugality and family (Maisha, Malette & Bellehumeur, 2019). The three types of relationship stand out as fundamental values for the participants in our research. They are fundamental to the participants' identity as valuable members of their community.

The ability to relate and belong is crucial for human beings; a notion Saint-Arnaud has referred to as religiosity (Maisha et al., 2019; Saint-Arnaud, 2005). The author refers to the notion of "religiosity" of the person as fundamental identity based on the natural need of every person to relate with others or with the Divine. Thus, every person needs to be able to create and maintain healthy relationships. However, the need to belong is met with specific challenges when it comes to survivors of rape in the context where the tragedy is seen as a transgression of sexual taboos and therefore a source of defilement (Lévy-Bruhl, 1963; Douglas, 1967, 2001). In such context, there is a general belief that survivors are defiled and have contracted a contagious condition of misfortune; making them a risk to self and other and seriously affecting their ability to form and maintain relationships. This chapter presents an emerging theory from a qualitative, grounded theory based research programme that has explored challenges for effective therapeutic care of survivors in a cultural context where rape is interpreted as sexual taboo, hence a source of defilement and danger for self and other; and based on about 10 years of clinical work on trauma from sexual violence. The condition of defilement distorts survivors' social identity. It imposes social and relational isolation on them.

The emerging theory builds on a deeper understanding of the impact of the distorted identity on survivors' ability to create and maintain relationships; it provides a conceptual framework on which relationship-centred therapeutic assessment and interventions can rely. Based on a brief review of the current literature, it is suggested that the emerging theory will contribute to building resilience and achieving posttraumatic growth for rape survivors.

Sexual Taboo and Defilement

Ricoeur (1967) talks about an inseparable relationship between sexuality and defilement that has existed for thousands of years, leading societies to develop ways to deal with such danger-evoking relationship. Norms such as requiring mutual consent for a sexual act, rites such as marriage and rites of purification in case of transgression of sexual norms all aim to limit the believed danger from sex in its forms of taboo. Freud (1973) describes taboo as including a sacred or impure condition of an individual or object, prohibitions of such condition and the consequences of transgressing those prohibitions. In primitive and still some societies today, taboos form the founding guidelines for social and spiritual interactions; including those of sexual nature. Any sexual activity that transgresses established norms is an attack on the social order resulting in different reactions with the goal to ease the consequences of such an act or remove its danger (Maisha, Demasure & Malette, 2017). Because rape is a transgression of sexual norms, it creates the condition of taboo and renders those involved and those associating with them defiled. Due to the contagious nature of defilement, any contact, voluntary or involuntary, with a person or an object under such condition results in being defiled as well (Maisha, Demasure & Malette, 2017; Cazeneuve, 1971). Through history and across cultures, contamination exposes a person to social and sometimes morbid isolation; the victim becomes unsafe for contact with others, as has been illustrated by the COVID-19 pandemic and other examples we will discuss in the following pages.

Disruptive Impact of Defilement on Sense of Self and Sense of Belonging

In the era of COVID-19, humanity has experienced the sad reality of avoiding contact with infected family members, friends and acquaintances. Families have witnessed solitary deaths and recoveries of loved ones whose health status present a risk for others. Those who did not apply physical isolation of the sick have suffered in numbers, losing multiple members of the same family. COVID-19 is real, a virus that can be detected with medical tools and testing. Its effect among individuals is fear of contamination, suffering and even death. Once identified as carrying the virus, a person is no longer safe to socialize with others. Governments and other institutions around the world recommended social distancing as a preventive measure; a move to protect against the spread of the virus and minimize its impact among the population. Despite its effectiveness in limiting the number of cases of COVID-19, social distancing, that is the limited connection with others, imposes its own suffering regardless of one's health status. We can imagine how emotionally and mentally difficult it is to agonize or die in isolation, away from friends and family. The same can be said for friends and family who find themselves unable to be there for their sick or dying loved ones. Being unable to count on those around us or provide comfort to those we love when they need us the most is disturbing. I have personal experience of this. I have 10 siblings, all from both my parents' only marriage. In the evening of August 13, 2018, a tragedy struck my family and left a question that continues to have no clear answer: what was my mother thinking on her deathbed as the hospital staff refused to take care of her without assurance that her medical bill will be paid? Earlier that day, in Kampala, Uganda, a person driving without a valid licence hit and mortally wounded my 67-year-old mother, who had left home alone to buy fish, her favourite dish. Without being able to identify her, the police took my mother to one of the state-run hospitals without anyone in the family knowing her whereabouts. Four hours later, concerned, some family members went to look for her, as they knew the market where she went. Once at the accident site, my father and my brother identified our late mother's headscarf then went to the hospital following information from witnesses. "Your mother just died a few minutes ago, she bled to death as there was no guarantor for her medical treatment," revealed a nurse to my brother.

Whether we are talking about a person carrying and potentially contagious of COVID-19, a rape survivor deemed dangerous to be in contact with or a person in my late mother's situation, left on the sidelines of those who deserve medical care; somehow, the person believes that she has lost the ability to connect safely with others. Norms and policies about the condition create a morbid distance between the person and the same personal and professional contacts from which she once sought and received comforting closeness.

This condition can have many names: a virus, lack of medical coverage, a curse, a taboo, a defilement. Regardless of what it is, its consequences can have a long-lasting impact on the life of the person suffering and their loved ones. All three situations above indicate the vital role of healthy relationships; reasons why this chapter presents an emerging relationship-based therapeutic model focusing on the condition of defilement, which we have studied with survivors and their therapists.

In fact, in the case of rape survivors in the Democratic Republic of Congo (DRC), social norms around sexuality have led to survivors being treated as outcasts, because, per social beliefs, they are defiled: others can no longer connect safely with them. Ricoeur (1967) refers to defilement as extraordinary, terrifying, attractive and repulsive at the same time; an infinite phenomenon almost impossible to get rid of. For Douglas (1967, 2001), defilement evokes fear and has a protective function for the specific culture. Associating survivors with defilement antagonizes them against their cultural norms and values;

against their own social identity. Lévy-Bruhl (1963) describes the defilement resulting from a sexual transgression as being social, because the violation of a sexual prohibition is an "organizational offense on which collective life rests." This means that rape creates a conflict between the victim and their values, a contradiction between their need to be in relationship and their state of defilement, which creates feelings of (self) rejection, of worthlessness and of spirit injury.

One's perception of self or others based on their values and identity has a significant impact on their psychological well-being, as well as their interpersonal relationships. This is challenging for rape survivors perceived as defiled; hence in contradiction with their ideal self. The same challenge applies to the survivor's community and family unable to assist their member effectively. For rape survivors whose trust in the humankind has been betrayed, being in contact represents a great risk; it evokes great fear. Furthermore, under the reign of taboo, the relationship with the survivor represents a risk with serious consequences for those around (Maisha, Demasure & Malette, 2017). Yet, people need relationships where they are able to love and feel loved, where they enjoy living, where they feel proud to be authentic with themselves and with others. It has been observed that the opposite creates deep suffering among survivors of rape: "victims facing rejection feel condemned to die, to disappear" (Maisha, 2016). The participant's reported experience aligns with the literature on relational attachment as a natural need. We examine relational attachment quality from the early years of life; children learn to assess if they feel emotionally and physically safe with their caregivers and internalize lasting messages about themselves and others. Secure relationships provide reassurance, pleasure and have the potential to heal wounds from difficult former relationships, including those from our family of origin (Rovers, 2005). Survivors need a relationship where bonding creates security and pleasure, not fear or pain, a nourishing and healing relationship. This is reflected in the stories of survivors in the DRC. Accepting themselves and feeling accepted by others provide a healing power: the freedom to be oneself. Indeed, as a result of rebuilding meaningful relationships, survivors report feelings of freedom, security and pleasure as reports one participant in our research: "what helps me, we work together; I feel free. Going to the field together makes me free, it gives me peace … I also feel free in the church and in the neighborhood … [I] am starting to feel joy. My husband no longer insults me." (Maisha, 2016; Kelly et al., 2012).

A Relationship-Based Therapy for Survivors: R-STO

Many therapeutic theories recognize the health benefits of healthy relationships; particularly those on which one can rely in times of distress (Rovers, 2005; Uchino, Caccioppo & Kiecolt-Glaser, 1996). For example, like the theory we are proposing, theories focusing on the interactions between a person and their environment attribute a central role to close relationships through which individuals will form healthy or distorted worldviews (Bowlby, 2005; Ainsworth, Blehar, Waters & Wall, 1978). Among these theories, attachment-based theory is founded on the idea that the quality of early relationships, particularly the relationship to the infant's main caregiver, otherwise known as the attachment figure, creates potentially lifelong internalized messages of representation of self in relationship with others (Bowlby, 2005; Rovers, 2005; Ainsworth et al., 1978). Further research on attachment also suggest that other significant relationships may also have a positive or negative impact on a person's "internalized working model" of self and others (Guédeney & Guédeney, 2009); an idea also supported by several accounts of participants to our research (Maisha, 2016).

Results from our research with rape survivors, in a cultural context where rape is interpreted as sexual taboo and source of defilement, indicate that survivors, therapists, community leaders and even regular members of their community insist on the need to mend the broken relationship between survivors and the rest of the community; including divinity. We studied rites of purification as traditional ways to remedy the state of defilement and mend the broken relationship. We are also currently studying social values on which survivors base their new self that has estranged from the ideal self; creating ground for social discrimination and systemic revictimization. Preliminary results show that identity based on social roles such as motherhood, romantic partner and group membership are central to survivors' recovery process.

As mentioned in the introduction, readers are reminded that the current chapter reflects on our research observations and clinical experience, which suggest that supporting rape survivors requires special attention to the way they conceive and approach the relational universe; as well as the way members of their social and family environments perceive them. We published most of our completed research results in scientific journals (Maisha, 2020; Maisha, Malette & Demasure, 2017), a book (Maisha, Demasure & Malette, 2017) and a book chapter (Maisha, Malette,& Bellehumeur, 2019). Therefore, the chapter is about presenting the emerging theory to helping survivors of rape whose identities have changed based on their belief system about sexual taboos.

We have identified three categories of relationships upon which the therapeutic process is built:

1) relationship with self;
2) relationship with therapist or caregiver; and
3) relationship with others – understood here as any physical, imaginary or spiritual being considered as significant by the survivor.

R-STO (which stands for Relationship to Self, Therapist and Others) based therapy takes into account the quality of these three types of relationships. In practical terms, R-STO therapy will rest on three nonlinear phases: exploration of the intra-psychic process on the concept of self;

exploration of therapeutic alliance; and exploration of the abilities to create and maintain meaningful relationships based on the clients' paradigms of relationships. To survivors, rape changes their identity and breaks relationship ties.

First, for the intra-psychic process, therapy will take into account dysfunctional cognitive patterns of self, based on the client's belief system. For example, therapy will involve taking into consideration the impact of the notion of defilement on self-image and the quality of the relationship that the survivor has with this image; is it acceptance, disgust or self-rejection? The literature shows that survivors internalize feelings of being contaminated (Maisha, Malette & Bellehumeur, 2019; Maisha, Demasure & Malette, 2017); developing a belief that they are no longer worthy of loving relationships (Maisha, Malette & Demasure, 2017). Second, therapeutic alliance is an opportunity for the clients to reimagine themselves in a safe, accepting relationship. While therapeutic alliance is an essential part of therapy with any category of clients, it is more so for survivors whose belief system makes them interpret closeness as risky for others who attempt to come near them (Verelst, De Schryver, Broekaert & Derluyn, 2014; Dossa et al., 2014). Third and finally, still on the relational level, therapy will take into account the quality of client's attachment in significant relationships. Here, it is a question of taking into account the impact of the notion of defilement on the victim's perception of her ability to create and maintain meaningful relationships. This therapeutic approach will take into account the social outlook on the survivor and her social values suffering from being viewed as defiled. This means that therapists will work on the impact of the belief system that considers rape as a source of defilement on the social acceptance of the survivor: how does she think members of her community perceive her? Such therapy may include outreach interventions for community awareness, in particular on the suffering of the victim and the healing role of safe and nurturing relationships.

R-STO aims to help develop a modified vision of self in the survivor, leading to self-acceptance, and a modified vision of interpersonal relationships allowing the ability to create and maintain relationships with others. The process includes interventions leading to self-acceptance, building or regaining relational skills and connecting or reconnecting safely and meaningfully. Self-acceptance refers to overcoming the loss of the "ideal self," raising awareness of one's potential and embodying the renewed self. Relational skills refer to fostering safe interactions, building trust and reshaping a healthy worldview. As for connecting or reconnecting, it refers to identifying adapted relationships, supporting the clients through the re-engaging process with a goal to develop a secure sense of belonging. This depends a lot on engaging with the client's systems of relationships: couple, family; even the community at large. Figure 11.1 presents an illustration of the R-STO framework, followed by an illustration of its therapeutic assessment and intervention goals in Figure 11.2..

Survivors respond to traumatic events in many ways, based on accessible coping strategies and resources. While everyone in a traumatic situation endures

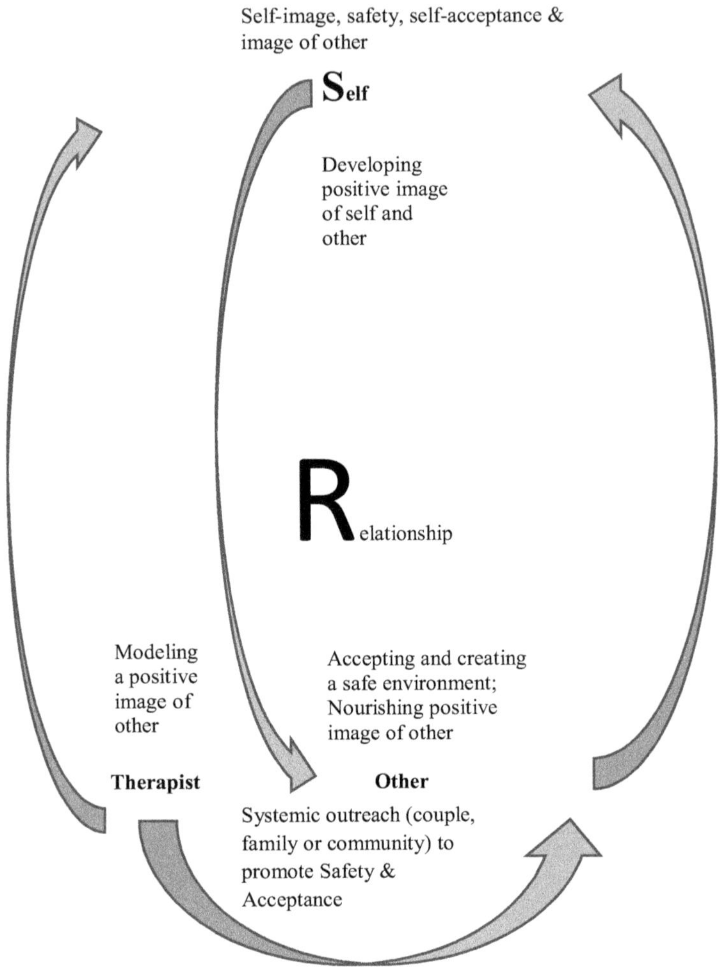

Figure 11.1 R-STO illustration

suffering, studies have shown that the long-term outcome varies between developing posttraumatic stress disorder (PTSD) and achieving posttraumatic growth (PTG) (Arikan, Stopa, Carnelley & Karl, 2016; Dekel, Mandl & Solomon, 2011; Tedeschi & Calhoun, 1996, 2004). PTSD is characterized by recurrent intrusive memories of the traumatic event, recurrent dreams about the event, dissociative reactions as if one were reliving the event, as well as strong psychological and physiological reactions to stimuli reminding of the event (American Psychiatric Association, 2013). PTG is "the experience of positive psychological changes that occur in the wake of a traumatic event as a result of the ensuing (psychological) struggle with what happened" (Dekel et al., 2011). PTG theorists suggest that individuals who experience trauma "may perceive at least some good emerging

R-STO therapeutic assessment and intervention goals

Goals for R-**S**:

Modify vision of self to achieve **self-acceptance** (overcoming the loss of 'ideal self', becoming aware of one's potentials and embodying the 'new self'); help the client view self as **safe** and worthy of **connection** with others

Goals for R-**T**:

Modify vision of other by building **safe alliance** as a **model** of trustworthiness through **validation of self-acceptance** and **need** as well as **worthiness** to **belong**

R

Goals for R-**O**:

Modify vision of other, **trust** and **connect** with others **safely,** and achieve a **sense of belonging**

Figure 11.2 R-STO and posttraumatic growth

from their struggle with such tragedies" as they gain information on self-reliance and develop a sense of competence (Tedeschi & Calhoun, 2004). Self-disclosure through discussions of the event, recognizing one's vulnerability and willingness to accept help from one's social support are among the factors that support the emerging of PTG (Tedeschi & Calhoun, 2004). Focusing on three dimensions of relationships (Self, Therapist and Other), the R-STO explores notions related to social support and self-evaluation (which may lead to self-acceptance, self-confidence or self-reliance), also associated with PTG (Arikan et al., 2016; Sippel, Pietrzak, Charney, Mayes & Southwick, 2015; Tedeschi & Calhoun, 2004). Moreover, R-STO supports existing literature about the contribution of social support to a positive mental health outcome after a traumatic event (Dossa et al., 2014; Ozbay et al., 2007; Criss, Pettit, Bates, Dodge & Lapp, 2002). Therefore, R-STO will foster clients' PTG through an in-depth work on the quality of relationships in the client's support system; including social relations, therapeutic alliance and relationship to a spiritual figure such as God. In our research upon which R-STO is founded, participants confirmed available scientific findings about social support as an important factor for maintaining good mental health following a traumatic event. For example, staying in a marriage relationship, being included in community activities and joining church services were associated with the feeling of freedom to be oneself. This fosters self-acceptance and trust in one's ability to build and maintain connections with others. In a literature review on the issue, Shaw, Joseph and Linley (2005) found that religion and spirituality contributed to PTG; this aligns with the healing role of relationship with religious community and the divine reported by participants to our research. By emphasizing the role of meaningful, safe and nurturing relationships to self, the therapist and other; R-STO taps into an important PTG factor: developing positive views of self and other as these are crucial in developing self-acceptance and self-confidence as well as seeking and accepting help from one's social support.

R-STO and Resilience

As a therapeutic model, R-STO focuses on the client's own sense of being able to build and maintain connection with others founded on their beliefs about relationships. Let us stress the fact that R-STO stems from research on traumatic situations such as sexual violence; making it a therapeutic model interested in factors contributing to clients' resilience. Ozbay et al. (2007) define resilience as "a process of adapting well in the face of adversity." As such, resilience also means being able to make adjustments based on the conditions created by the traumatic situation. It takes an awareness of and access to available means to make an adjustment. In other words, resilience relies on calling upon available known means or factors to do so; including one's support system, good relationships and good self-image. One crucial type of support system is social support, which "can enhance resilience to stress, help protect against developing trauma-related psychopathology, decrease the functional consequences of trauma-induced disorders, such as posttraumatic stress disorder (PTSD), and reduce medical morbidity and mortality" (Ozbay et al., 2007). The authors have described social support as one that is accessible to an individual (in this case, a trauma survivor). However, as we started this chapter, we discussed challenges facing rape survivors with social interpretation of rape as a taboo, therefore a source of defilement that deems survivors dangerous and worthy of social rejection (Dossa et al., 2014; Verelst et al., 2014). In this context, accessing social support becomes even more challenging; an imperative therapeutic goal for those in a helping relationship with the survivors. This is why R-STO focuses on the notion of relationship. By restoring the ability to relate safely for the client, R-STO guided therapy taps into a core factor of resilience, which, as described above, depends on the clients' ability to access available social support. R-STO works mainly on restoring that ability. Besides resilience theories, other approaches to improving mental health following a traumatic event have recognized the crucial role of healthy relationships. These include relationship and attachment driven theorists (Braithwaite & Holt-Lunstad, 2017; Braithwaite, Delevi & Fincham, 2010; Doucet & Rovers, 2010; Mikulincer, Shaver & Horesh, 2006; Rovers, 2005; Salo, Qouta & Punamaki, 2005; Levendosky, Huth-Bocks & Semel, 2002; Criss et al., 2002), and emotion focused theorists (MacIntosh & John, 2008; Johnson & Williams-Keeler, 1998).

Conclusion

By seeking to promote healing relationships for survivors as the path to their mental health recovery, R-STO reaffirms the vital health benefits of relationships. Through this model, it is argued that by helping change dysfunctional beliefs about self and other resulting from the interpretation of rape as sexual taboo and consequently deeming survivors as dangerous for contact, therapy will promote self-acceptance, which also will allow the clients to see themselves as worthy of connection with others. This empowers the clients to seek close and fulfilling relationships leading to an increased sense of belonging. Many trauma-informed theories stress the role of meaningful relationships as key factor for resilience and PTG; the emerging theory presented in this chapter supports that.

References

Ainsworth, M., Blehar, M.C., Waters, E., & Wall, S. (1978). *Patterns of attachment: A psychological study of the strange situation.* Hillsdale, NJ: Erlbaum.

American Psychiatric Association (2013). *Diagnostic and statistical manual of mental disorders*, 5th edn. https://doi.org/10.1176/appi.books.9780890425596.

Arikan, G., Stopa, L., Carnelley, K.B., & Karl, A. (2016). The associations between adult attachment, posttraumatic symptoms, and posttraumatic growth. *Anxiety, Stress, & Coping*, 29(1), 1–20.

Bowlby, J. (2005). *A secure base.* New York: Routledge.

Braithwaite, S., & Holt-Lunstad, J. (2017). Romantic relationships and mental health. *Current Opinion in Psychology*, 13, 120–125.

Braithwaite, S.R., Delevi, R., & Fincham, F.D. (2010). Romantic relationships and the physical and mental health of college students. *Personal Relationships*, 17, 1–12.

Cazeneuve, J. (1971). *Sociologie du rite (Tabou, magie, sacré).* Paris: Presses Universitaires de France.

Criss, M.M., Pettit, G.S., Bates, J.E., Dodge, K.A., & Lapp, A.L. (2002). Family adversity, positive peer relationships, and children's externalizing behavior: A longitudinal perspective on risk and resilience. *Child Development*, 73(4), 1220–1237.

Dekel, S., Mandl, C., & Solomon, Z. (2011). Shared and unique predictors of post-traumatic growth and distress. *Journal of Clinical Psychology*, 67(3), 241–252.

Dossa, N.I., Hatem, M., Zunzunegui, M.V., & Fraser, W. (2014). Social consequences of conflict-related rape: The case of survivors in the Eastern Democratic Republic of Congo. *Peace and Conflict: Journal of Peace Psychology*, 20(3), 241–255.

Doucet, M., & Rovers, M. (2010). Generational trauma, attachment, and spiritual/religious interventions. *Journal of Loss and Trauma*, 15, 93–105.

Douglas, M. (1967). *Purity and danger.* New York: Routledge.

Douglas, M. (2001). *De la souillure: Essai sur les notions de pollutions et de tabou.* Paris: Éditions de la découverte.

Freud, S. (1973). *Totem et Tabou: Interprétation par la psychanalyse de la vie sociale des peuples primitifs.* Paris: Petite Bibliothèque Payot.

Guédeney, N., & Guédeney, A. (2009). *L'attachement: Approche théorique. Du bébé à la personne âgée.* Cedex: Elsevier Masson SAS.

Johnson, S., & Williams-Keeler, L. (1998). Creating healing relationships for couples dealing with trauma: The use of emotionally focused marital therapy. *Journal of Marital and Family Therapy*, 24(1), 25–40.

Kelly, J., Kabanga, J., Cragin, W., Alcayna-Stevens, L., Haider, S., & Vanrooyen, M.J. (2012). "If your husband doesn't humiliate you, other people won't": Gendered attitudes, towards sexual violence in eastern Democratic Republic of Congo. *Global Public Health*, 7(3), 285–288.
Levendosky, A.A., Huth-Bocks, A., & Semel, M.A. (2002). Adolescent peer relationships and mental health functioning in families with domestic violence. *Journal of Clinical Child and Adolescent Psychology*, 31(2), 206–218.
Lévy-Bruhl, L. (1963). *Le surnaturel et la nature dans la mentalité primitive, nouvelle Édition.* Paris: Presses Universitaires de Franc.
MacIntosh, H., & John, S. (2008). Emotionally focused therapy for couples and childhood sexual abuse survivors. *Journal of Marital and Family Therapy*, 34(3), 298–315.
Maisha, B. (2016). Image de soi et de l'autre souillées: La problématique des tabous sexuels en thérapie et l'apport du rite de purification dans la reconstruction du "soi" chez la femme survivante de viol à l'Est de la R.D. Congo, Doctoral thesis, Saint Paul, University, Ottawa, ON.
Maisha, B. (2020). Contextualising therapeutic care for child survivors of sexual violence in situations of war: A reflection on theory, context and practice. *Intervention*, 18(1), 45–51.
Maisha, B., Demasure, K., & Malette, J. (2017). *Les tabous sexuels transgressés: Viol en temps de guerre.* Paris: L'Harmattan.
Maisha, B., Malette, J., & Bellehumeur, C. (2019). Les liens entre la souillure du viol et le pouvoir guérisseur du plaisir relationnel auprès des victimes congolaises en contexte de guerre. In C. Bellehumeur & J. Malette (Eds.), *Psychologie positive et spiritualité en psychothérapie* (pp. 185–206). Québec: Presses de l'Université Laval.
Maisha, B., Malette, J., & Demasure, K. (2017). Survivors' sociocultural status in Mwenga: A comparison of the issue before and after rape. *Social Sciences*, 6(64). doi:10.3390/socsci6020064.
Mikulincer, M., Shaver, P.R., & Horesh, N. (2006). Attachment bases of emotion regulation and posttraumatic adjustment. In D.K. Snyder, J.A. Simpson, & J.N. Hughes (Eds.), *Emotion regulation in families: Pathways to dysfunction and health* (pp. 77–99). Washington, DC: American Psychological Association.
Ozbay, F., Johnson, D.C., Dimoulas, E., Morgan III, C.A., Charney, D., & Southwick, S. (2007). Social support and resilience to stress: From neurobiology to clinical practice. *Psychiatry*, 4(5), 35–40.
Ricoeur, P. (1967). *The symbolism of evil.* Boston: Beacon Press.
Rovers, M. (2005). *Healing the wounds in couple relationship.* Ottawa: Novalis.
Saint-Arnaud, Y. (2005). *La guérison par le Plaisir.* Ottawa: Novalis.
Salo, J.A., Qouta, S., & Punamaki, R.L. (2005). Adult attachment, posttraumatic growth and negative emotions among former political prisoners. *Anxiety, Stress and Coping*, 18, 361–378.
Shaw, A., Joseph, S., & Linley, P.A. (2005). Religion, spirituality, and posttraumatic growth: A systematic review. *Mental Health, Religion & Culture*, 8(1), 1–11.
Sippel, L.M., Pietrzak, R.H., Charney, D.S., Mayes, L.C., & Southwick, S.M. (2015). How does social support enhance resilience in the trauma-exposed individual? *Ecology and Society*, 20(4), 10. http://dx.doi.org/10.5751/ES-07832-200410.
Tedeschi, R.G., & Calhoun, L.G. (1996). The posttraumatic growth inventory: Measuring the positive legacy of trauma. *Journal of Traumatic Stress*, 9(3), 455–471.
Tedeschi, R.G., & Calhoun, L.G. (2004). Posttraumatic growth: Conceptual foundations and empirical evidence. *Psychological Inquiry*, 15(1), 1–18.

Uchino, B.N., Cacioppo, J.T., & Kiecolt-Glaser, J.K. (1996). The relationship between social support and physiological processes: A review with emphasis on underlying mechanisms and implications for health. *Psychol Bull*, 119(3), 488–531.

Verelst, A., DeSchryver, M., Broekaert, E., & Derluyn, I. (2014). Mental health of victims of sexual violence in eastern Congo: Associations with daily stressors, stigma, and labelling. *BMC Women's Health*, 14. doi:10.1186/1472-6874-14-106.

12 The Narrative of Resilience Through Social Media in the Black Community

#Overcome

Shanna Ossé and Stephanie Massicotte

In the summer of 2020, the denouncement of racism began to make headlines across the world as protests and riots flooded the streets denouncing police brutality against the Black community in the United States. This movement brought systematic racism to the forefront of many formal discourses. While some people believed racial injustice to be a thing of the past, the uproar brought a fresh awareness to an age-old conflict still plaguing the modern world. The depth and insidiousness of racism still persists to this day and is dumbfounding for many, exhausting for others, and deeply disheartening for us all.

With a long and heavy history of discrimination and violence, from slavery to racial segregation and the fight for Civil Rights, the North American Black community has persevered through centuries of racism. Yet, in spite of so much hardship and a challenging history, the landscape for the Black community in the twenty-first century is not exclusively filled with doom and gloom. From deep oppression, in order to survive, the Black community has made itself resilient. However, is resilience the only way to survive as a Black person in North America? What if the friction is engrained and long-standing in everyday lives? In this context, what if survival is not only circumstantial, but generational? Therefore, in a quest to better understand the Black community's ability in overcoming so much adversity, this chapter will explore how resilience has been stitched into the fabric of the Black community.

Since overcoming adversity can be a complex journey and many various factors can contribute to this goal, this chapter will specifically explore how one tool in particular has most recently fostered resilience: social media. Because social media has given the power to change narratives to its users, it can be seen as a tool for collective resilience enabling a community to have a voice, to change and reappropriate its own narrative as well as build up a positive sense of connectivity and collective identity.

A Word on the History of Adversity and Trauma to Overcome

Although racism and discrimination exist against many various ethnic, racial and religious groups across the world and throughout history, the struggle in the Black community has its own unique history of generational oppression in North America. It is worth examining in order to better understand the Black community as it stands today.

Of course, studying resilience in such a large group with deep historical roots is no small feat. Therefore, this chapter will focus on key benefits this community has gained from the use of social media as a tool for resilience. Before digging into these ideas, this section of the chapter will briefly summarize the complex history of adversity and trauma this community has experienced. This will allow for better understanding of the ways in which resilience was birthed and has grown.

In today's modern era, the horrors of slavery are still being explored and uncovered. But it is of high interest to remember that "Black oppression through the system of slavery had survived the Declaration of Independence and American Revolution and would … become an integral part of American constitutional law" (Berry, 1995). In other words, the principles upholding systematic slavery and all its horrors permeated throughout the formal foundations upon which the United States was built, arguably the entirety of North America. Although slavery was introduced in the late 1600s in the United States, the effects of this painful legacy are deceitfully deep and long lasting (Berry, 1995).

One of many examples of the long lasting effects of this legacy and the slow progress made towards equality can be found in the legal status of Black people who, from the 1600s to 1865, were typically slaves without any civil or human rights whatsoever, and after emancipation from slavery in 1865 they were considered "as second-class citizens thereafter" (Berry, 1995). In fact, between 1877 and 1957, Black people did not have access to the help of federal troops or marshals "when state officials refused them protection" when crimes such as "pre-advertised lynching or other kinds of violence directed against African-Americans" took place (Berry, 1995). In spite of abolishing slavery in 1865, there was a great reluctance to punish crimes targeting Black people, including murder and assault, until as late as 1965, a hundred years after emancipation (Berry, 1995).

Unfortunately, the painstaking progression towards equality has been extremely challenging and far from simple. In 1964, President Johnson signed into law the Civil Rights Act to desegregate public places and outlaw employment discrimination (ourdocuments.gov). However:

> the passage of civil rights bills would not eliminate racial friction … Civil rights legislation had absolutely no meaning to [Black people] who were fed up with police brutality, de facto segregation, unemployment and underemployment, inferior education, political tokenism, and Jim Crow justice.
>
> (Berry, 1995)

In spite of the attempts towards equality, the everyday reality was clearly a stark contrast to the legal declarations for civil rights. In fact, well-seasoned journalist Ted Koppel released a documentary in 2008 called *The Last Lynching*, which examined the last acknowledged lynching of a Black person taking place in Alabama in 1981. In the twentieth century, thousands of Black people were victims of lynching in public displays, which Koppel labels as "acts of terrorism" (NPR, 2008). This shockingly recent torture and murder of an innocent young man perpetrated by the Ku Klux Klan does illustrate the gap between the insidious realities of racism and the fight for equality.

Without any doubt, this kind of painful adversity leaves psychological scars. In fact, Dr Joy Degruy coined the term "post traumatic slave syndrome" to explain how the trauma of generational slavery does not disappear in its descendants overnight (2005). Degruy suggests that there remains coping mechanisms, beliefs and heavy trauma that have been passed down through generations and have been learned indirectly by their descendants (Degruy, 2005). Therefore, according to Degruy, the psychological distress of trauma still lingers today and requires attention like any other form of PTSD. After centuries of oppression and trauma, it is only natural that the pain that remains will take time, consideration and patience in order to heal.

A Word on Resilience and Posttraumatic Growth

This chapter aspires to examine how resilience plays a role in the North American Black community's ability to persevere throughout history and cope in today's complex reality. Surprisingly, the scientific community has published precious few studies on the topic of resilience and the Black community. However, in the hope that this important topic will grow in prevalence over time, this chapter will content itself to be an exploratory search for the exhibition of resilience in this group. Of course, endeavouring to understand resilience in a large group facing adversity for centuries is no easy feat. Therefore, for the purposes of this chapter, the focus will be on some of the ways in which social media has been used as a tool to foster collective resilience within this community.

As this book has already established, resilience goes beyond simply surviving and is, in fact, the ability to thrive in spite of harsh conditions. However, one of the challenges in exploring resilience in such a large group is the natural diversity that can be found in any given group and finding the balance between individual and collective resilience as well as the link between the two. The complexity of collective resilience "is still not fully comprehended nor easily defined" in spite of various attempts to study it (Sousa, Haj-Yahia, Feldman & Lee, 2013). However, resilience in this context will generally refer to a positive adaptation to adversity "through the use of individual or community characteristics, resources, strategies, and processes" (Sousa et al., 2013). By exploring examples of how the Black community has adapted through time, it enables us as researchers to pinpoint the protective factors and resources which enabled them, both as individuals and as a group, to overcome adversity. Those protective factors can be numerous and vary according to the context and need, but they have a general common purpose to "lessen risk and/or promote well-being" while facing psychological stressors (Sousa et al., 2013).

Another phenomenon within the field of positive psychology is the concept of "posttraumatic growth," which, as the name indicates, refers to new growth taking place as a direct consequence of trauma. The Posttraumatic Growth Inventory (PTGI) is the scale typically used to measure this new growth and change in perspective by examining positive progress in five areas: new possibilities, relationships with others, personal strength, appreciation of life and spiritual change (Tedeschi & Calhoun, 1996). These measurements are conceptualized for individuals rather than groups, but on a speculative level, it might be suggested that all five of those criteria of posttraumatic growth are present in the Black community. Of course, the challenge here is that there is virtually no way of obtaining a "baseline" of how the Black community functioned as a whole before adversity came their way. Therefore, it becomes impossible to compare and see if there has been posttraumatic growth that did not exist before the trauma occurred. But these criteria will be explored nonetheless in this chapter, specifically by examining how the tool of media has facilitated growth, relationships/community and new possibilities among other benefits.

Mainstream Media as a Tool of Oppression

Taking into account the years of systemic discrimination and oppression that the Black community has faced, and continues to face today, it is of no surprise that these systems permeate every aspect of society. Unfortunately, media is no exception. It has the power to shape public opinion and provide new perspectives regarding various narratives. Media stands as the Fourth Estate, alongside the Judicial, Executive and Legislative divisions of power. Its mission to provide information to the public holds the power to shape the information that we receive. Mainstream media (television, movies, radio, journalism, etc.), being the primary source of information, news and entertainment for the general public, has had a hand in the negative representations of Black people, as its racist past cannot escape itself.

Media has been so pejorative to Black subjects that it has, in and of itself, created subgenres to represent black subjects in a negative light (i.e. Blaxploitation, minstrel shows, Blackface, etc.). As a form of expression, it has influenced public opinion and has been shaped by popular ideologies, such as racism. For example, the origin of the name "Jim Crow," of the Jim Crow Laws, came from a popularized minstrel fictional character played by a White actor, Thomas D. Rice, in blackface (Vann Woodard, 1955). In the early 1830s, this persona caricatured Black people, representing them as dim-witted and clumsy slaves. The popularity of this character not only skyrocketed Rice's career, but it became coined as a pejorative term for Black people (Andrews, 2014). The fact that this name was used to embody a series of segregational laws in the United States is of no coincidence. Media shapes our ideologies and our public opinion, and that is demonstrated through theories such as agenda-setting (McCombs & Shaw, 1972) and gatekeeping which is the conscious and biased process of cutting down information to fit a specific narrative in line with their beliefs (Shoemaker & Voss, 2009).

Since the modern structures of mainstream media primarily operate under a system of gatekeeping, the opinions of these gatekeepers control what information is released to the public. With the creation of mass media, such as television and radio, the population working in these fields have been predominantly White. In other words, because media productions were historically created by White people, for White people, there is a suppression of other narratives, including those of Black people. "The people targeted in the mass media were white … Men and women of color were treated by the media as fringe audiences, not large enough in number to influence the content directed to the mass audience" (Wilson, Gutierrez & Chao, 2012).

Because of the effects of gatekeeping and those traditionally in positions of leadership in media corporations, the White patriarchal perspective became the norm while shutting out Black narratives and Black stories. Consequently, Black people do not have their perspectives and opinions heard in mass media, seeing that they are neither the main producers of this content, nor seen as an important audience to reach. This status quo allows for the same insidious racist systems to go unchallenged, while being mixed in with media representations and information distribution. As illustrated in the following: "It is my contention that television representations of Blackness operates squarely within the boundaries of middle-class patriarchal discourse about 'whiteness' as well as the historic racialization of the social order" (Gray, 1995). There are many factors that influence this inequality but in order to analyze resilience, we will focus on gatekeeping and the influence of mass audiences.

Social Media as a Tool of Resilience

With the arrival of social media, the concept of gatekeepers has been turned on its head. Users become the creators and distributors of their own information and their own stories. They have the capacity to fact-check, create new narratives and express themselves creatively. We compare mainstream media to social media because we want to show what happens when status quo structures are questioned or removed completely. Platforms such as YouTube, Twitter and Instagram become spaces of Black expression, information-sharing, resources and even joy. With resilience comes changing up the dominant narrative to reshape the message and change it to one that puts oneself in a positive light. This is outlined in Nikita Carney's research on the evolving role of social media and the Black Lives Matter movement:

> Contrary to mass media, which plays a crucial role in shaping perceptions of race for a largely passive audience, social media allows users to actively

> engage and shape the discussions, offering [people] of color an opportunity to contest dominant ideologies.
>
> (Carney, 2016)

This comparison between mainstream media and their controlling structures, against the backdrop of new media platforms that allow users to change narratives which had previously been spoon-fed to them, engages them into new conversations and hearing perspectives of audiences that are, as previously stated, not the majority. For the Black community, this means negative narratives, racist stereotypes and problematic ideologies can be reshaped into positive and uplifting ones. This means that Black people are allocated freedom with these tools, and that this freedom is power over discourse and their opinions and viewpoints can be broadcasted the way they should (Carney, 2016).

In the world of resilient psychology, reframing hardships into different opportunities is one of the "effective ways to reduce the risk of psychological harm" (Brown, 2015). The ability to reframe or reinterpret circumstances in a more favourable light enables an individual, or in this case a group of individuals, to move beyond the defeat or despair that a given circumstance might normally impose (Southwick, Pietrzak & White, 2011). This concept is clear in the Black community and their use of social media. The ability to reframe is dependent on the mindset known as the "internal locus of control" initially suggested by Rotter in 1966 (Smith, Trrompenaars & Dugan, 1995). The internal locus of control and its opposite, the external locus of control, refers to a person's sense of agency and belief in regard to personal ability to impact one's circumstances. The internal locus of control is driven by the belief that the power, resources and ability to change and/or influence circumstances lies within oneself, contrary to an external locus of control where the belief is that the power, resources and ability to bring change lies outside one's control, usually at the mercy of luck or fate. The internal locus of control equips an individual with the belief that something can be done, no matter how big or how small, whereas an individual with an external locus of control believes nothing can be done and that defeat is unavoidable. By finding ways to reappropriate their own narrative in spite of obstacles, the Black community has undoubtedly exhibited resilience.

With that, another way that social media is used as a tool of resilience for the Black community is in the promotion of positive culture and awareness, which shifts the power dynamics from the oppressor (in mainstream media) to those that are oppressed. For example, Black users on Twitter have reshaped the use of the platform in ways to facilitate sharing and the participation in positive discourse about the black experience across North America. Often known as Black Twitter, black users use different features of the platform to foster joy and uplift one other. From hashtags such as #BlackBoyJoy, #BlackGirlMagic or #BlackExcellence, even creating Black spaces in popular discourse where they can create a safe place for their narrative (for example,

#GamesOfThrones to #DemThrones) black users promote black positivity by sharing images and narratives that are for them and by them:

> Black communities often craft hashtags that require pre-existing knowledge of African American history and culture for full participation. For example, #demthrones was used by Black fans of the popular show Game of Thrones to create a separate avenue of discourse for users often marginalized from fandom communities.
>
> (Lu & Steele, 2019)

Many others have described Black expressions of joy as tools of resistance. As Britanny Packett poses, "Joy is resistance. Oppression doesn't have room for your happiness. You resist it when you find joy anyhow" (Lu & Steele, 2019). Lu and Steele argue that written and oral cultures used as forms of resistance and expression during slavery, Jim Crow and the beginning of the Civil Rights era, have been recycled and used on social media (Lu & Steele, 2019). Black people embedded practices of song, storytelling and signifying in their everyday lives, and this is reflected in their uses of these platforms. Not to mention that these same ways are expressed online and offline, extending Black online cultures to the outside world. According to Monk-Payton, Black humour transforms Twitter into a place where "joy emanates from what can be communally imagined, where meaning can be made in or even beyond signification" (Monk-Payton, 2017).

Going against the main narrative of the depictions of Black people, Black positive discourse gives way to a new form of resistance, one full of laughter and of joy. It levels the playing field between the victims and their oppressors, giving a safe space to those that continue to be brought down, whether explicitly or implicitly by mainstream media.

> The joyful posts shared via these hashtags celebrate Black life in ways that challenge mainstream media's attempts to fix Black people and Black life into a position of death and despair; assert Black people as fully human, capable of experiencing and expressing a full, dynamic range of emotion; and capture, share, and circulate expressions of Black life without concern for the white gaze.
>
> (Lu & Steele, 2019)

These are the depictions of Black life that go against the dominant narrative, that depicts blackness as the antithesis of life and disassociated from joy (Chapman, 2017).

Finally, social media is used as a space of activism, fostering resilience and resistance by creating connections between members of the Black community and social justice initiatives happening across the globe. Mainstream media continues to harbour racial bias against Black people in cases of police brutality, for example (Kulaszewicz, 2015). Due to features, such as hashtags, social media has become an effective tool to foster conversations and spark a movement. A prominent example of this is #BlackLivesMatter. This hashtag shifted from a conversation regarding the lack of accountability from law enforcement and their unlawful acts of violence towards unarmed Black people, and became an activist group and global phenomenon. #BlackLivesMatter enabled Black people to take hold of their own narrative and expose a discriminatory system which favours a racist narrative. As Cullors-Brignac, cofounder of the Black Lives Matter movement says:

> Because of social media we reach people in the smallest corners of America. We are plucking at a cord that has not been plucked forever. There is a network and a hashtag to gather around. It is powerful to be in alignment with our own people.
>
> (De Choudhury, Jhaver, Sugar & Weber, 2016)

Social media gives the Black community a way to speak out, unite and resist these oppressive systems. In the history of the Black community, social media, as a tool, has completely revolutionized the way to seek justice because it is "fundamentally different than anything that's existed before in the black struggle" (De Choudhury et al., 2016). Therefore, social media is the new frontier and the latest tool for resilience in the Black community.

Conclusion

Although the challenge of racism may feel overwhelming and disheartening, it is important to remind ourselves of the small glimmers of hope. Every victory, every obstacle overcome, every time light is being shed on this matter in order to bring awareness adds to the progression towards equality and justice. In spite of the lack of studies done on this topic thus far, there is little doubt of the depth of resilience found within the fabric of the Black community. In the same way that the street protests against racism during the summer of 2020 gave way to the "scholar strike" across universities in the United States and Canada in the fall of 2020, the struggle for equality and the hope of a better tomorrow remains. As discussed in this chapter, social media has been an effective tool to promote a more resilient narrative and empower the Black community to represent and speak for itself.

References

Andrews, E. (January 29, 2014). Was Jim Crow a real person? Retrieved September 20, 2020 from www.history.com/news/was-jim-crow-a-real-person.

Berry, M.F. (1995). *Black resistance/white law: A history of constitutional racism in America.* Penguin Books: New York.

Brown, Ralph (2015). Building children and young people's resilience: Lessons from psychology. *International Journal of Disaster Risk Reduction*, 14, 115–124.

Carney, N. (2016). All lives matter, but so does race: Black Lives Matter and the evolving role of social media. *Humanity & Society*, 40(2), 180–199. https://doi.org/10.1177/0160597616643868.

Chapman, M. (2017). *Anti-black racism in early modern English drama: The other "other"*. Routledge: New York. https://doi.org/10.4324/9781315559544.

De Choudhury, M., Jhaver, S., Sugar, B., & Weber, I. (2016). Social media participation in an activist movement for racial equality. *Proceedings of the International AAAI Conference on Weblogs and Social Media. International AAAI Conference on Weblogs and Social Media, 2016*, 92–101.

Degruy, Joy (2005). *Post traumatic slave syndrome: America's legacy of enduring injury and healing*. Oregon: Uptone Press.

Gray, H. (1995). *Watching race: Television and the struggle for "Blackness"*. Minneapolis: University of Minnesota Press.

Kulaszewicz, K.E. (2015). Racism and the media: A textual analysis. Retrieved from Sophia, the St. Catherine University repository website: https://sophia.stkate.edu/msw_papers/477.

Lu, J., & Steele, C. (2019). "Joy is resistance": Cross-platform resilience and (re)invention of Black oral culture online. *Information, Communication & Society*, 22(6), 823–837. https://doi.org/10.1080/1369118x.2019.1575449.

McCombs, M., & Shaw, D. (1972). The agenda-setting function of mass media. *Public Opinion Quarterly*, 36(2), 176–187. https://doi.org/10.1086/267990.

Monk-Payton, B. (2017). #Laughingwhileblack: Gender and the comedy of social media blackness. *Feminist Media Histories*, 3(2), 15–35.

NPR (October 13, 2008). The "last lynching": How far have we come? Interview heard on "Talk of the Nation," NPR. www.npr.org/templates/story/story.php?storyId=95672737.

Shoemaker, P., & Vos, T. (2009). *Gatekeeping theory*. New York: Routledge. https://doi-org.proxy.bib.uottawa.ca/10.4324/9780203931653.

Smith, P.B., Trompenaars, F., & Dugan, S. (1995). The rotter locus of control scale in 43 countries: A test of cultural relativity. *International Journal of Psychology*, 30(3), 377–400.

Sousa, C.A., Haj-Yahia, M.M., Feldman, G., & Lee, J. (2013). Individual and collective dimensions of resilience within political violence. *Trauma, Violence, & Abuse*, 14(3), 235–254. doi:10.1177/1524838013493520.

Southwick, S.M., Pietrzak, R.H., & White, G. (2011). Interventions to enhance resilience and resilience-related constructs in adults. In S.M. Southwick, B.T. Litz, D. Charney, & M.J. Friedman (Eds.), *Resilience and mental health: Challenges across the lifespan* (pp. 289–306). United Kingdom: Cambridge University Press.

Tedeschi, R.G., & Calhoun, L.G. (1996). The posttraumatic growth inventory: Measuring the positive legacy of trauma. *Journal of Traumatic Stress*, 9(3), 455–471. doi:10.1007/BF02103658.

Vann Woodard, C. (1955). *The strange career of Jim Crow*. New York: Oxford University Press.

Wilson, C., Gutierrez, F., & Chao, L. (2012). Racism, sexism, and the media: Multicultural issues into the new communications age. In *Racism, sexism, and the media*. Los Angeles: SAGE Publications.

13 Conclusion

The Lessons We Learned on Resilience and Adversity

Buuma Maisha

As illustrated throughout this book, adversity can afflict anyone and strike at any time, but fortunately, resilience knows no borders. In its most common use, the concept of resilience calls upon the different kinds of internal and external resources helpful in the effort to alleviate the suffering caused by all kinds of adversities which individuals, or a group of individuals, have faced, or are facing. This book has shed light on other reasons to study resilience. For instance, authors have argued that learning skills associated with resilience can act as a buffer protecting one's mental health in the face of inevitable life challenges since they are essential supportive and transformative tools towards recovery and growth following such challenges (Masten & Obradovic, 2008; Henriksen, 2018). This means that our interest in understanding resilience precedes and goes beyond the moment we face challenges; such has been the theory supported by the different chapters in this collection. In addition to expanding the temporal dimension for the conceptualization of resilience, the book also documents a global conversation on the topic by looking at contextual and societal factors that hinder, or support, the efforts to build, access and improve resilience skills. Also, beyond studying resilience prior to, during and following a traumatic event, the authors discuss a body of literature on adversity and its characteristics, including the fact that it can be experienced at any age and anywhere; it can be sudden too. On a more positive note, the authors also argue that anybody, regardless of age and circumstances, can benefit from contextually accessible resources fostering resilience.

First, the book reports that noticing signs or risks of mental health issues among children can allow their support system of caregivers and professionals to respond adequately and equip the children with skills fostering resilience. Readers have learned practical tools on how to enhance resilience among children under their care, while taking care of their own personal well-being.

Second, despite the preconceived notion that young adults are a relatively healthier age group, this population also faces challenges that shake their faith in their abilities to continue the journey of life happily. Examples of traumatic events such as the sudden onset of illness, social discrimination or other forms of crimes such as victimization by sex trafficking and exploitation have been discussed. The book also documents an extensive discussion on challenges as well as potential for expressions of resilience specific to this population; including self-help and professionally encouraged strategies. Identity takes up an important place in the young adult's life: acquisition of new social identities and roles such as being in a relationship, graduating from school, starting and building a career. Adversity can therefore interfere with the high hopes many of the individuals in this population have as they also face significant social expectations. This is especially challenging in the era of social media where individuals are constantly presented with elements of their ideal self, which they now need to redefine in the light of their challenging condition for the emersion of their "new and healthy image of self" (LaCorte, 2019).

Third, as the saying goes, "the higher the tree is, the stronger the wind is": living longer comes with its own share of risks of facing or having faced a number of traumatic situations. Older adults have more likely to have experienced deaths of loved ones and may be ill or physically weak to the point of losing their autonomy (Resnick, 2014). While many of them may deal with complex trauma from repeated and long-lasting adversities, due to their long life experience, they are also more likely better equipped with strategies for resilience than the younger generations (O'Hara et al., 2012).

Authors in this book have argued that skills and resources for cultivating resilience can be a buffer against developing serious mental health issues such as posttraumatic stress disorder. Resilience provides a beacon of hope and allows for positive feelings such as gratitude and happiness in dark times, while helping to acknowledge and normalize the negative feelings as part of the present reality one needs to pay attention to and seek to improve. It is also the awesome legacy individuals and communities take away from the darkness of tragedies as they look back or become aware of their own transformation and growth resulting from the adversities they faced. It is resilience that allows Hélène Campbell, whose testimony was shared at the beginning of this book, to change her question from "why me" to "why not me" as a starting point towards acceptance of her new reality. "Softening the blow was my belief that suffering was a normal part of our lives as humans … Choosing to accept my condition and make the best out of it is what made all the difference," she writes. As illustrated in Hélène's quote, this book argues that individuals showing resilience do not just accept their condition; they seek to make the best out of it. First, they pace themselves and adapt. Then, they work with the available help towards turning the adversity into an opportunity for growth.

The journey to achieve growth is not linear; setbacks are not rare. As Hélène has shared, it is important to know that the suffering is not permanent either. Victor Frankl, probably the most regarded for having exemplified resilience, advises upon finding a meaning in the suffering (Frankl,

1984). Giving it your meaning, not the one intended by the aggressor in the case of a human-imposed traumatic event, gives you the power to steer your way through the waves of setbacks. Assigning meaning to the suffering can be incredibly powerful as it propels you towards continued growth.

Our hope is that this book has allowed you to reflect on what your suffering means to you today and what resilience looks like for you. Many definitions of resilience have been provided based on reports from the scientific literature and personal and professional experiences of the authors. With the help of these definitions, we hope that you can come up with your own, which best describes what resilience really looks like to you; based on your own experience and journey towards recovery. The authors have presented and discussed multiple cases and quotes from around the world. Individuals and communities assign different meanings to their suffering and use available and accessible resources to help build and nurture resilience; even to achieve personal and collective growth following traumatic events. With the help of mental health professionals, resilience-based therapy and learning opportunities, such as conferences, can help acquire healthier ways of coping with the suffering, rebuild and improve one's health. The book enlists a number of approaches and tools to support therapists and their clients, as well as other professionals learning how to help individuals and groups of individuals under their care to enhance resilience. While we share what seems to be a consensus in the literature, which is that resilience can be defined in many ways, we strongly argue that resilience is not simply for people currently facing adversity, it is a concept of interest for everyone. Resilience also develops from childhood experiences, adult relationships as well as relationships with other forms of attachment, such as figures of spiritual authority. This means that resilience is not a merely clinical concept; it is also a social concept that builds from and influences social non-traumatic experiences. In the time of global pandemic (COVID-19) and collective rejection of systemic racism and social discrimination of others, we are reminded of the necessity to prepare well to face life's challenges rather than waiting passively for the challenges to strike. We are also reminded that the challenges become an opportunity to change whatever is not working at any societal level; or for personal well-being. It is helpful to do a self-assessment and be aware of one's resilience-enhancing skills and resources, to fill potential gaps with the support available or new resilience learning programmes. Such learning can be an individual initiative, but also a societal responsibility to carry out through policies promoting safety and mental health wellness for all; especially for survivors of traumatic events.

References

Frankl, V.E. (1984). *Man's search for meaning.* Boston: Beacon Press.

Henriksen, K. (2018). Dare to prepare for reality: Helping national orienteering team athletes handle adversity. *Case Studies in Sport and Exercise*, 1(2), 30–35.

LaCorte, S. (2019). Shaping professional identity & influence on social media. *HemOnc Times*, 41(17). doi:10.1097/01.COT.0000581740.07319.a7.

Masten, A.S., & Obradovic, J. (2008). Disaster preparation and recovery: Lessons from research on resilience in human development. *Ecology and Society*, 13(1). doi:10.5751/ES-02282-130109.

O'Hara, R., Marcus, P., Thompson, W.K., Flournoy, J., Vahia, I., Lin, X., Hallmayer, J., Depp, C., & Jeste, D.V. (2012). 5-HTTLPR short allele, resilience, and successful aging in older adults. *Am J Geriatr Psychiatry*, 20(5), 452–456.

Resnick, B. (2014). Resilience in older adults. *Topics in Geriatric Rehabilitation*, 30(3), 155–163.

Index

Page numbers in **bold** indicate tables; *italics* indicate figures.

For Product Safety Concerns and Information please contact our EU
representative GPSR@taylorandfrancis.com
Taylor & Francis Verlag GmbH, Kaufingerstraße 24, 80331 München, Germany

www.ingramcontent.com/pod-product-compliance
Ingram Content Group UK Ltd.
Pitfield, Milton Keynes, MK11 3LW, UK
UKHW022353190926
475702UK00015B/2271
* 9 7 8 0 3 6 7 7 1 4 3 4 5 *